THE GUN DEBATE

WHAT EVERYONE NEEDS TO KNOW®

THE GUN DEBATE

WHAT EVERYONE NEEDS TO KNOW®

2nd Edition

PHILIP J. COOK AND KRISTIN A. GOSS

OXFORD
UNIVERSITY PRESS

OXFORD
UNIVERSITY PRESS

Oxford University Press is a department of the University of Oxford. It furthers
the University's objective of excellence in research, scholarship, and education
by publishing worldwide. Oxford is a registered trade mark of Oxford University
Press in the UK and certain other countries.

"What Everyone Needs to Know" is a registered trademark of
Oxford University Press

Published in the United States of America by Oxford University Press
198 Madison Avenue, New York, NY 10016, United States of America.

CIP data is on file at the Library of Congress
Names: Cook, Philip J., 1946– author. | Goss, Kristin A., 1965–
Title: The gun debate : what everyone needs to know /
Philip J. Cook, Kristin A. Goss.
Description: 2nd edition. | New York : Oxford University Press, 2020. |
Series: What everyone needs to know® |
Revised edition of the authors' The gun debate, [2014] |
Includes bibliographical references and index.
Identifiers: LCCN 2019035359 (print) | LCCN 2019035360 (ebook) |
ISBN 9780190073466 (hardback) | ISBN 9780190073459 (paperback) |
ISBN 9780190073473 (updf) | ISBN 9780190073480 (epub)
Subjects: LCSH: Gun control—United States. | Firearms ownership—
United States. | Firearms—Law and legislation—United States.
Classification: LCC HV7436 .C657 2020 (print) | LCC HV7436 (ebook) |
DDC 363.330973—dc23
LC record available at https://lccn.loc.gov/2019035359
LC ebook record available at https://lccn.loc.gov/2019035360

CONTENTS

ACKNOWLEDGMENTS

We are indebted to a number of experts whose research and advice we sought in writing and rewriting this book. Despite our combined 75 years of experience studying gun violence and gun policy, we needed and greatly appreciated the help. We are also deeply grateful for the extraordinary research assistance provided by Julia Quinn for the first edition of the book, as well as Olivia Levine, Akanksha Ray, and Curtis Scarpignato for the second edition.

THE GUN DEBATE

WHAT EVERYONE NEEDS TO KNOW®

1

AMERICA AND ITS GUNS

What Is a Gun?

A more precise term for the subject of this book is firearm, which is a portable weapon that shoots projectiles from a metal tube, propelled at high speed by expanding gas that is generated by the explosion of gunpowder in a confined space. So, we will not be discussing water pistols or BB guns or pricing guns, or for that matter cannons or catapults or rocket launchers. The focus is on the weapons owned by households for hunting, target shooting, and self-defense and by police and private security officers as tools of their trade. There are many types of firearms, the most common of which can be categorized as rifles, shotguns, pistols, or revolvers.

What Is the Problem with Guns?

Like so many commodities, firearms serve a variety of useful purposes but are also subject to misuse. The misuse, whether accidental or intentional, accounts for 40,000 deaths per year in the United States[1] and more than 250,000 deaths worldwide.[2]

Probably the greatest concern is in conjunction with interpersonal violence—homicide, assault, and robbery. When the perpetrator uses a gun rather than a knife or club or bare fists, the likelihood that the victim will die is greatly increased. The same point applies to suicide attempts—there are more than 500,000 every year in the United States, mostly resulting in injury but not death. But when a gun is used, the fatality rate soars—to 85%.[3] In sum, guns *intensify* violence. They take a bad situation and make it deadly.[4] And because guns can be used to kill quickly, with little effort and from a distance, they give individuals who are so inclined the capacity to terrorize neighborhoods, assassinate even well-guarded public officials, and perpetrate one-man rampages in schools, workplaces, houses of worship, and other public places.

Although firearms can cause great harm, they also have value in recreation (hunting, target shooting, collecting) and as tools for self-defense and police work. Guns are similar to other consumer products and services in having both positive and negative uses. Motor vehicles are involved in crashes that kill about the same number of Americans each year as guns. Prescription painkillers are associated with 17,000 overdose deaths a year in the United States alone.[5] Infections contracted via hospitalization or medical procedures contribute to about 72,000 deaths in the United States each year.[6]

For vehicles, drugs, medical care, and many other products, including firearms, it is reasonable to ask, "How can we reduce the problems of misuse while preserving the benefit of normal prudent use?" For inspiration, we note that the highway-safety "problem" has been greatly reduced over the decades while preserving the value of highway travel. Thanks to better roads, safer vehicles, seatbelt requirements, and anti-drunk-driving enforcement (among other things), the highway fatality rate has been cut in half since 1950 (even though vehicle miles per capita have increased by a factor of three).[7] For firearms, too, we can aspire to reduce misuse while preserving value.

How Many Americans Own How Many Firearms?

Among the wealthy nations of the world, the United States has the highest prevalence of private gun ownership. Even in the

United States, however, gun ownership has dropped significantly in recent decades. In 2018, 35% of respondents to the highly respected General Social Survey indicated there was a gun in their home, down from near 54% in 1977.[8]

While the prevalence of households with guns is of interest, it is important to remember that guns usually are personal possessions, not household appliances with shared ownership. National surveys differ somewhat on the percentage of adults who own guns. Three reputable surveys conducted in 2014, 2015, and 2017 produced estimates for adult ownership of 24%,[9] 22%,[10] and 30%.[11] In many other respects, such as types of guns owned and reasons for gun ownership, these surveys are more consistent.

How many guns are in private hands altogether? Since guns are not registered in most jurisdictions, we have to rely on estimates rather than counts. If we take 25% as the best estimate of individual ownership for 2018, there were about 63 million adult owners in the United States. If we knew the average number of guns per owner or household, we'd be able to estimate the total household firearms inventory. But it is hard to elicit that information in a survey, and few surveys have attempted to do so. One exception is the 2015 National Firearms Survey, which asked respondents not just whether they had a gun in the home, but how many. Extrapolating from the results leads to an estimate of about 265 million firearms in private hands.[12] Sales data make clear that tens of millions of guns have been added since then. For 2018, we estimate that there are about 300 million guns in private hands, or almost 5 per individual owner.

Besides surveys, another approach to estimating the total is to use federal records on firearms commerce. It is possible to add up all the firearms that have been manufactured in the United States, add the imports, and subtract the exports. Applying this approach to data from 1899 to 2016 (and excluding sales to the military), the estimated total would be 344 million firearms as of 2016.[13] But of course not all of these firearms still exist today. If we assume that just 1% of the stock has been scrapped each year since 1945, and apply this assumption to the federal records, then the current total would be reduced to 259 million guns in 2016.

One problem with this estimate (besides the fact that the true rate of gun discarding is unknown and may be higher or lower than 1%) is that the official federal records of imports and exports miss off-the-books transactions. Smuggling guns from the United States to Mexico, Canada, and the Caribbean has a long tradition. Millions of weapons may have flowed to Mexican gangs in recent years; none of these guns is counted in official export statistics. On the other side of the ledger, some firearms are smuggled into the United States, including military weapons brought home by servicemen; these guns are not recorded in import statistics.

The bottom line is that no one knows how many firearms are in private hands in the United States. It does appear that the number has been increasing in recent years, with new additions to the gun stock greatly exceeding replacement. In 2016 there were 16 million firearms manufactured and imported (net of exports), and while retail sales of new guns may have declined somewhat since then, 300 million guns in private hands in 2018 appears to be a reasonable ballpark estimate.

Who Owns the Guns?

Gun owners are not a representative sample of the American public. Not surprisingly, most guns are owned by men. They are almost three times as likely as women to have a firearm. Race and ethnicity also matter. Whites are far more likely than African Americans or Latinos to own a gun. Finally, guns are more than twice as common in rural areas as in cities, as would be expected given that open spaces are the natural domain of gun sports.

Several other correlates of gun ownership are worth noting. Adults who came of age with a firearm in the home are far

more likely—by a ratio of three to one—to own one now compared to people who grew up without guns. This finding is
not surprising if you consider that children who grow up with
guns may learn to enjoy shooting sports and to feel comfortable having firearms around. Firearms ownership also is related to education. People with some college are more likely
to own a gun than are college graduates or those who stopped
with high school. And third, gun ownership is correlated with
people's political identification. Republicans are more than
twice as likely to own as are Democrats, with political independents in between.[14]

There are large regional disparities in gun ownership. To
paint a very rough picture, the New England, Mid-Atlantic,
and Pacific states tend to have relatively low rates (with certain exceptions, such as Alaska and Vermont). The Southern,
Midwestern, and old frontier states of the West have considerably higher rates. This pattern has changed very little in recent decades, although the prevalence of gun ownership has
undergone a broad decline. The rural tradition is reflected in
the geographic patterns: We can accurately predict the prevalence of gun ownership in a state today by simply knowing
what fraction of the state population was living in rural areas
in 1950.[15]

How do we know the relative levels of gun ownership by
state? Survey data might provide a rough clue. But we prefer
a more reliable proxy measure, the percentage of a state's suicides committed with a gun. By this measure, here are the
five states where people are most likely to have a gun in the
home: Alabama, Mississippi, West Virginia, Louisiana, and
Kentucky.[16] And here are the five states where people are least
likely to keep a gun: Hawaii, Massachusetts, Rhode Island,
New Jersey, and New York (as well as the District of Columbia).
An idea of the vast geographic differences in household gun
ownership is provided by this proxy measure: In Alabama in
2017, 69% of suicides were committed with a gun, while in
Hawaii the figure was just 13%.[17]

While urban areas generally have lower rates of gun ownership, there are some cities where gun ownership is the norm.
The greatest concentration of urban guns is in the large cities
of Texas and Arizona, as well as Tampa–St. Petersburg. At the
other end of the spectrum are New York City and Boston. The
differences are remarkable. In Phoenix and Dallas–Fort Worth,
more than half of suicides are by gun, whereas in New York
City, the rate is just 12%.

Why Do People Choose to Own Guns—or Not?

In a sharp departure from the past, defense against crime is the
leading reason why gun owners have their firearm. In a 2013
Pew poll, protection was cited by 48% of respondents, nearly
twice the fraction who cited protection in 1999. Protection
dominates other principal reasons to own a gun, including
hunting (32%) and sport shooting (7%).[18] You might suppose
that the increased concern about personal defense reflects a
spike in crime rates, but just the opposite is true—crime has
been heading down for decades, and most places are far safer
from predatory crime today than in 1999. So what explains the
dramatic increase in self-protection as the stated reason for
owning a gun?

We have a theory. Half of current gun owners grew up
with guns in their parents' home and likely had some experience with hunting or target shooting. Now they typically
have several guns, and more than one purpose—handguns
for self-protection, long guns for target shooting or hunting.
In short, these individuals like guns and have several uses for
them. The tendency to cite self-protection as a major reason for
owning may have to do in part with the public rhetoric over
guns, which the Supreme Court dignified as being at the heart
of a constitutional right under the Second Amendment.

There is some survey information on why most individuals choose not to own a gun. In the 1994 National Survey of
Private Ownership of Firearms, 33% of nonowners said that

guns were too expensive, while most others mentioned that guns are dangerous, or (relatedly) that they had children at home, or that they were opposed to guns for moral and other reasons.[19]

How Many Guns Do Gun Owners Own?

Most gun owners have more than one firearm, and some owners have scores of them. A 2017 Pew survey found that one-third of gun owners had just one (usually a handgun), while almost that many had five firearms or more.[20] Most of the guns in private hands are owned by those who own at least five. The tendency for ownership to be concentrated among few people is by no means limited to guns. One of the great lessons of marketing science is the Law of the Heavy Half (also known as the 20/80 Law or the Pareto Law). This principle holds that 20% of consumers account for 80% of sales. Whether gun ownership *literally* obeys that law is difficult to tell, given that very-high-end owners are likely to be reluctant to talk to survey interviewers.

Is Gun Ownership Rising or Falling?

The answer may be "both."

First, here is the evidence that it is falling. The trend in the household prevalence of firearms ownership is indeed downward over the last generation. In 1977, the widely respected General Social Survey found that 54% of all households had at least one gun. By 2010 (and also in 2018), this figure had dropped to about 35%, a remarkable change.[21] The percentage of individuals who own a gun also declined during that period, but not as much. The two trends do not line up perfectly because households are smaller now than they were decades ago and in particular are less likely to include an adult male. Remember that it is the men who own most of the guns.

So in what sense is gun ownership rising? The federal data on domestic manufactures, imports, and exports show a dynamic upward trend in recent years. Domestic shipments of new firearms between 2003 and 2016 increased from 4.6 million to a record level of 16.3 million.[22] This volume of new guns is driving an increase in the total private inventory—over and above population growth. The surge in gun sales is probably being absorbed primarily (though not entirely) by individuals who already own guns. In short, the average number of guns per gun owner has been increasing. One widely reported explanation is that some owners want to stock up on guns before Congress adopts stricter gun regulations, despite the fact that with minor exceptions, the only firearms legislation that Congress has enacted over the last generation has had the effect of *loosening* regulations. The election of President Donald Trump in 2016 on a pro-gun platform may have excited gun owners but also slowed firearm sales.

What Role Do Shooting Sports Play in American Life?

Hunting and other shooting sports have been an important feature of life for centuries. Echoing beliefs of the day, Thomas Jefferson, an avid hunter, advised his teenaged nephew that gun-related pursuits give both "a moderate exercise to the body" and "boldness, enterprise, and independence to the mind. Games played with the ball, and others of that nature, are too violent for the body, and stamp no character on the mind." He advised: "Let your gun, therefore, be the constant companion of your walks."[23]

The shooting sports began to take off in the early nineteenth century, when members of an emerging middle class had both the means to purchase a firearm and aspirations to upward mobility, which meant copying the leisure-time pursuits of the British nobility. In the 1820s and 1830s, sporting magazines appeared, devoting pages to cultivating a culture of gentlemanly bonding. Around the same time, immigrants created target-shooting clubs that became wildly popular among the middle classes, and shooting galleries popped up in many cities. As one historian wrote of the German clubs, "Members wore uniforms, marched in military style with firearms, practiced marksmanship as recreation, ate heartily, drank beer, and caroused with women."[24]

Although rural Americans in the seventeenth through the nineteenth centuries relied heavily on hunting for food and profit, hunting also became a sport—a means of demonstrating skill and manliness. Competitive squirrel hunting was popular in the East, buffalo hunting in the West. Indeed, buffalo were nearly wiped out; some hunters, including Buffalo Bill Cody, vied to see who could shoot the greatest number of bison in the shortest period of time.

Throughout the centuries, hunting in particular has been a family affair, to the point where specialty "youth rifles" began to be actively marketed in the late nineteenth century.[25] Modern studies show that one of the best predictors of whether someone hunts as an adult is whether his father (usually) introduced him to the sport as a child.[26] In some rural areas so many kids hunt with their families that schools traditionally have observed the first day of deer hunting season as an unofficial holiday.

Today, around 12 million adults hunt in any given year, less than 6% of the population age 16 and older.[27] Hunters are mostly white males from rural areas and small towns, and hunting is considerably more popular in the middle of the country than on the coasts.

Has Participation in Gun Sports Declined?

Broadly speaking, yes. Take hunting, the quintessential American shooting sport. Over the last generation, the fraction of adults who killed animals for food or sport has declined from 7.4% to 5.6%. The fraction of gun owners who mention hunting as their main reason for having a firearm has dropped to 32%, from 49% in 1999.[28] And the number of hunting licenses declined slightly from the early 1980s through 2018, even though the US population increased considerably.[29]

These trends are the result of a combination of factors, including urbanization, expanding leisure-time options, and shifting public attitudes. The decline of America's rural sporting culture is evident in the aging of the hunter population. In 2016, 37% of hunters were 55 or older, up from 14% in 1991.[30] The decline may be self-perpetuating, as hunting often is passed down from father to son. Hunting remains an overwhelmingly white, male sport.

In response to these trends, pro-gun organizations have lobbied for laws permitting children to obtain "apprentice" licenses, allowing them to "give hunting a try" without a hunter education course as long as a licensed adult accompanies them. Similar policies have created short-term licenses for "novice" adults.

What Are the Common Types of Modern Firearms?

Every firearm, whether rifle, shotgun, or pistol, has in common that it is designed to shoot projectiles out of a barrel at a high rate of speed, driven by the sudden expansion of gas caused by an explosion. The explosion is contained within the gun's chamber, which surrounds the cartridge case or shell.

Ammunition for rifles and pistols is made up of a cartridge case (typically brass, nickel, aluminum, or steel), primer, gunpowder, and bullet. When the primer, seated in the base of the cartridge case, is struck by the firing pin, it ignites the gunpowder, and the resulting expanding gas drives the bullet (usually made of lead) forward down the barrel. Shotgun shells are somewhat different. They are plastic or cardboard tubes with a brass base, containing a wad on top of the primer and powder. The wad typically consists of a plastic "shot cup" holding a number of pellets, which leave the barrel and spread

in a "pattern." Shotguns may also be used to fire solid projectiles called "slugs."

Firearms are classified as either handguns or long guns. The
former are relatively small and can be held in one hand when
fired. Long guns, including rifles and shotguns, have barrels
that are up to 30 inches in length and are designed to be fired
from the shoulder using two hands.[31]

Firearms are further differentiated by the mechanism for
loading cartridges into firing position, the rapidity with which
multiple shots can be fired, and the size of the ammunition.
Single-shot weapons require that a cartridge be loaded by
hand after each shot. Early shotguns required hand loading
after every shot or two depending on the number of barrels.
Modern shotguns are available in a variety of configurations
and can be equipped with various types of magazines. "Drum"
style magazines hold as many as 25 rounds.

Modern rifles and handguns are generally repeaters. For
handguns, the original repeater was the revolver invented by
Samuel Colt in the 1830s. In modern double-action versions
of a revolver, a built-in cylinder is loaded with a number of
rounds (usually six). With each pull of the trigger the cylinder
rotates to bring a cartridge into firing position, and the hammer
cocks back and then snaps forward. For semiautomatic pistols
and long guns, several rounds of ammunition are stored in a
magazine, which in most cases is detachable. When inserted,
the magazine feeds cartridges into firing position as the trigger
is pulled. Magazines differ widely in capacity, typically from 3
to 30 rounds but sometimes reaching 100.

The firearm's action dictates how fast the rounds in the
weapon can be fired. In between each shot a series of steps
prepares the gun for the next shot—remove the shell casing,
chamber a new round in preparation for firing, and cock the
hammer. In a single-shot, bolt-action or lever-action rifle, this
work is done manually by manipulating a bolt handle or lever
that ejects the old casing and allows a new cartridge to pop
into place from the magazine (or be inserted manually). In a

semiautomatic rifle or pistol this sequence is automated, so that the shooter can fire as fast as he can pull the trigger—one round per trigger pull—until the magazine is emptied, at which point it can be removed and replaced with a fresh magazine. Finally, a fully automatic firearm fires continuously with a single pull of the trigger. Weapons of this sort are widely used by armies and rebel militias around the world. Interestingly, some standard infantry rifles of the US armed forces in the M16 family have a selective-fire option including a burst of three rounds for each trigger pull. That setting is designed to save ammunition in comparison with fully automatic fire and makes the weapon easier to control when used.

Finally, the diameter of the barrel is an important characteristic of firearms, since it determines the size of the cartridge—which in turn affects the damage done to the target. (The velocity and design of the bullet are also relevant to determining damage.) For rifles and handguns, the diameter of the barrel is denoted as the "caliber." The caliber is measured either in fractions of an inch (.22, .38, .45) or with the metric system in millimeters. Among the most popular sizes are the .38-caliber revolver and 9mm pistol, which are close to identical in diameter and ballistic performance.

Once again shotguns are a bit different. The diameter of a shotgun barrel is denoted by its "gauge" rather than caliber. The most common gauge is 12, which is equivalent to .729 caliber. Confusingly, a smaller diameter shotgun has a larger gauge: A 20-gauge shotgun is just .615 caliber, and a 410-gauge shotgun equates to .458 caliber. The basic physics of action and reaction explains why larger barrels and the larger ammunition that fits them cause a greater recoil when the gun is fired. A .22-caliber pistol or 20-gauge shotgun is easier to control than its larger counterpart because of less felt recoil.

Why Do Gun Owners Usually Have Several Guns?

By and large people say that the main reason they have hand-guns is for self-defense, while their long guns are primarily for hunting or target shooting. Those who are knowledgeable about guns and enjoy them may be motivated to keep a variety on hand. For self-defense they may want to keep handguns in several locations, with a relatively small pistol to carry con-cealed when they go out and larger, more powerful models to keep in the bedside table or next to the front door. For shooting woodchucks and other varmints on the farm, a .22 rifle is suf-ficient (and uses cheap ammunition), but for deer hunting a larger caliber weapon is needed. For bird hunting and skeet shooting, people keep one or more shotguns, which may also be deemed good weapons for self-defense. Different circum-stances and purposes call for weapons of differing power, weight, accuracy, rapidity of fire, and so forth. And for some gun collectors, the utilitarian purposes are less important than the sheer fascination of these intricate machines.

As rural traditions have faded and self-defense uses become more prominent, the mix of guns sold in the United States has changed. Handguns have gained market share, from only 21% of all new guns in the 1950s to 36% in the 1970s to 42% in the 2000s. Since 2008, more than half of new gun shipments have been handguns.[32]

Handguns are also the weapon of choice for criminal use. About 75% of murders with firearms are committed with handguns, about the same as the percentage of suicides involving handguns.[33] During Prohibition both gangsters and law-enforcement officers used Thompson submachine guns (so-called Tommy guns), the "gun that made the 1920s roar."[34] Congress imposed strict regulations on such guns in 1934 with the National Firearms Act, so that criminal use of fully auto-matic weapons is uncommon in the United States.

What Is an Assault Weapon?

An assault weapon is most commonly defined as a semiautomatic firearm with some of the features of a military firearm. (An important difference is that a true military assault rifle, such as the US Army's M4, can fire continuously or in bursts with a single pull of the trigger.) An assault weapon has a detachable magazine and other common features of military weapons, such as a pistol grip, a folding stock, a bayonet mount, or a flash suppressor. Most assault weapons are rifles, although some pistols and shotguns qualify under some definitions. The TEC 9 pistol and the Street Sweeper shotgun are prominent examples. One of the most popular assault weapons is the AR-15, the civilian (semiautomatic) version of the US military's M16. The National Shooting Sports Foundation has campaigned to rebrand AR-15–style weapons as "modern sporting rifles."

In 1994 Congress adopted a ban on new assault weapons. The operational definition for this somewhat vague term was written into the law and included specific models but also any models with specified characteristics that were deemed problematic. Congress allowed the law to expire in 2004, but several states have adopted bans on assault weapons—each employing its own definition.

A closely related concern for lawmakers has been large-capacity magazines, since they are thought to facilitate rampage shootings. The 1994 federal law (which expired in 2004) limited new magazines to 10 rounds.

What Devices Are Available to Prevent Misuse?

Even in the hands of a well-intentioned adult, a firearm is a dangerous weapon. There are more than 20,000 accidental shootings each year, including about 500 fatalities.[35] People who have no experience or training with guns may be ignorant of safe practice when it comes to storage, carrying, loading and unloading, cleaning, and lining up a target. (No state requires that a rifle or shotgun buyer have any training or pass a test on gun safety.)

There are a variety of devices designed to prevent guns from being fired accidentally. For example, most rifles and some handguns have an external "safety" that when set prevents discharge. These safeties are usually just manual switches, although some handguns are designed with integral safeties that must be released with a key or combination. (Revolvers and some pistols, including the popular Glock brand, lack a manual safety of this sort.) Most modern firearms, including the Glock, are designed so that they are unlikely to discharge if dropped and in fact will not fire unless the trigger is pulled.

The owner's greatest concern may well be that his or her firearms end up in the wrong hands—a thief, a teenage son, a toddler, an inebriated spouse. In the interests of preventing such unauthorized transfers, owners may invest in a gun safe where some or all of the weapons can be locked up. A trigger lock may be fastened on a gun when it is not in use, although detachable locks of this sort are far from failsafe and interfere with the quick deployment of a gun for self-defense.

In 2005, Congress enacted a federal requirement that any handgun sold by a dealer come equipped with safety device such as a trigger lock. The law did not require that the owner use this device. Some states have imposed safe-storage requirements on owners, but Massachusetts is the only state that requires all firearms to be stored with a locking device in place.

What Are Smart Guns, and Do They Exist?

In the near future we expect to see the development of a satisfactory "personalized" or "smart" or "user-authorized" firearm that can be fired only by the rightful owner. Engineers have pursued a number of approaches. The possibilities include fingerprint and other biometric recognition devices, as well as an RFID mechanism, by which the lock is released through a radiofrequency signal from a "key" of some sort—essentially the same technology that is built into modern locks on vehicles. As of 2019, there were no user-authorized firearms available in the United States, although a German firm (Armatix GmbH) was selling its RFID Smart System pistol in Europe and Asia.

If guns were designed so that they could be fired only by the rightful owner, the hundreds of thousands of guns that are stolen each year could be rendered harmless (depending on the difficulty of overcoming the locking mechanism). The possibility of gun accidents within the household would be reduced, and suicidal teenagers could no longer appropriate their parents' guns. Interestingly, much of the R&D effort has been motivated by the goal of finding a way to protect law-enforcement officers from having their own weapons taken away and used against them. The main resistance to buying such guns (aside from the extra cost) by both law-enforcement agencies and the public appears to be a concern with reliability—the possibility that the gun might malfunction at a critical moment. But recent surveys indicate that a majority of adults would consider buying a smart gun.[36]

Several gun dealers have attempted to introduce the Armatix smart pistol for sale in the United States but reversed course in the face of death threats and boycotts. The pushback was inspired in part by New Jersey's Childproof Handgun Law, enacted in 2002. The law requires that when a smart handgun becomes available in the US market, New Jersey gun dealers cannot sell handguns that lack this technology. Pro-gun groups do not necessarily oppose the development and sale of such guns but do oppose restrictions on what dealers can sell.

Gun violence prevention advocates also have some concerns about smart guns. One worry is that these firearms could induce people who otherwise would not have bought a gun to acquire one. Another concern is that the "smart" technology could lull gun owners into being less careful about firearm storage. (Imagine, for example, a teenager who is an authorized user and decides on impulse to misuse the firearm because it's handy.) This sort of "risk compensation" behavior is surely a possibility, but there is no consensus on how common it would be.

We have become accustomed to using high-tech locking mechanisms on motor vehicles, phones, computers, and other products. Guns are the exception, so far.

2

THE VALUE OF GUNS FOR PERSONAL AND COLLECTIVE DEFENSE

Why Is Self-Defense Central to the Debate over Gun Control?

Personal safety is a vital matter, and self-protection is a more compelling rationale for owning guns than recreation. We can all conjure up the nightmare scenario of being defenseless in a violent confrontation with a burglar, mugger, carjacker, or rapist. For some people, the ready availability of a firearm brings peace of mind. Indeed, the predominant motivation for owning a gun is protection against other people.

Self-defense also has a privileged status in law over other uses of firearms. In 2008 the US Supreme Court for the first time recognized a personal right to "keep and bear arms." In *District of Columbia v. Heller*, the Court ruled that the Second Amendment provided a right to self-defense, and particularly defense of the home. More recently a federal appeals court interpreted the *Heller* decision to confer a right to have a gun for self-defense in public places, thereby overturning Illinois's ban on the carrying of concealed weapons. Every state now permits concealed carry in public places, and millions of private citizens regularly carry a loaded gun in their vehicle, in a purse, or in a holster. A 2017 poll found that the majority of Americans, 56%, believed that gun owners should be able to carry their firearms in most or nearly all public places.[1]

Is a Gun an Effective Means of Self-Protection?

The answer is a qualified yes. Someone who is able to effectively deploy a firearm when attacked or seriously threatened may emerge from the encounter in better shape than if he or she had been unarmed. Of course, it is also true that introducing a firearm into the confrontation may escalate the level of violence and ultimately result in greater harm to the victim than would have been caused by alternative strategies—such as fleeing, reasoning with the assailant, or summoning help. And there is always the possibility that the "victim" will misunderstand the other person's intentions, in which case the gun can be the mechanism for a tragic mistake.

While it is surely possible to imagine instances in which having ready access to a firearm would be a lifesaver, it is also possible that it would make a bad situation worse. The data on violent encounters provide some guidance on this matter. One study, by Jongyeon Tark and Gary Kleck, used National Crime Victimization Survey (NCVS) data for the decade 1992–2001.[2] More than 27,000 crimes with personal contact were included—assaults, robberies, rapes, and home invasions. In fewer than 1% of these cases (0.9%) did the victim use a gun in self-defense. About twice as many used another type of weapon, while most victims attempted to protect themselves through some other means—they screamed, ran away, reasoned with the assailant, struggled, and so forth. One measure of success for these various self-protective methods is the likelihood of forestalling further injury. Here are the rates of victim injury following self-protective action:

Self-protective action	Likelihood of subsequent injury
Used gun	2.4%
Used other weapon	1.7%
Attack or threaten without weapon	3.6%
Any self-protection action	2.8%

There is little difference among these injury rates, and surely no obvious advantage to using a gun. This finding was reproduced by Harvard researchers David Hemenway and Sara Solnick, using more recent data from the same survey.[3] One shortcoming of this approach is that fatal injuries to the victim are not included in these tabulations, as homicide victims cannot respond to surveys.

The other available evidence on consequences of self-defense with a gun includes anecdotes and common sense. Anecdotes of heroic self-defense cases are published in *The American Rifleman*'s weekly blog, "The Armed Citizen." (The organization does not publish cases where attempted self-defense with a gun backfired.) Common sense suggests that using a gun in response to a perceived threat could make things better or worse but tends to up the ante in the confrontation.

How Often Are Guns Used in Self-Defense?

This seemingly simple question has been the subject of intense debate. The answer is important but elusive. Police records are incomplete, since many defensive gun uses (DGUs) are never reported. Surveys seem to have the potential for providing a comprehensive estimate, but it turns out that survey results are hypersensitive to the exact method used to elicit this information. Thus, the answer is unknown, and in a sense unknowable, although there is no lack of statistics on the subject.

The NCVS is generally considered the most reliable source of information on predatory crime. The survey began in 1973 and incorporates the best thinking of survey methodologists. From this source it appears that the victim uses a gun in about 1 out of every 100 violent crimes, including robbery, assault, and rape. In the particular case of home invasion, about 3% of NCVS respondents who reported a break-in while they were home said that they used a gun to threaten or shoot the intruder. From NCVS data we learn that there were about 50,000

DGUs in cases of violent crime annually (2007–2011) and 20,000 annually in cases of property crimes.[4]

In contrast, the results of several smaller one-time telephone surveys suggest that there are millions of DGUs per year. The most widely circulated estimate, from criminologists Gary Kleck and Marc Gertz, is 2.5 million, although they and others have provided a range of estimates using this type of survey.[5] Why do these one-time surveys produce estimates that exceed the NCVS estimate by a factor of 25 or more?[6] One explanation is that the NCVS asks questions about defensive actions only to those who report that they were the victim of an assault or other crime with personal contact, while the phone surveys ask such questions of every respondent. As a logical matter it seems that it should make little difference—if the respondent was not the victim of a criminal threat or attack or break-in, how can she say she legitimately used a gun in self-defense? Still, in practice it is quite possible that some NCVS respondents do not have a chance to report a DGU because they do not report the criminal threat that initiated it. In that case the NCVS will include "false negatives" in its estimate of DGUs. On the other hand, one-shot surveys that ask an open-ended question about self-defense expand the scope for false positives—people who report that they defended themselves in the last year, say, who actually did so more than a year ago, or people who misremembered an event that occurred when they were drunk, or people who are simply trying to impress the interviewer with their heroics.

Another source of error is the fundamental fact that what constitutes a legitimate DGU may be a matter of definition. Someone who picks a fight at a bar and then flashes a gun may consider that he has defended himself with a gun, but it is not clear that the public interest has been served. In other cases, people with guns may be responding to vague threats. For example, in one survey of gun use, a respondent reported an incident involving an alarm that was sounding at his business. When he arrived to turn it off, he saw two men outside the building and shot at the ground near them.[7] In a study by David Hemenway and his colleagues, a panel of courtroom judges was asked to review this case and others like it where individuals reported DGUs. The jurists ruled a majority of these "self-defense" actions to be illegal.[8] The well-known case of the Trayvon Martin shooting illustrates the point that the distinction between self-defense and assault can be a matter of interpretation. Martin, an unarmed African American youth, was walking home from a store in Sanford, Florida, when George Zimmerman, a member of the community watch, saw him, guessed he was up to no good, followed him, and then confronted him, shooting him dead during the ensuing scuffle. In an intensely controversial outcome, a jury acquitted Zimmerman of second-degree murder.

The most compelling challenge to the survey-based claim that there are millions of DGUs per year derives from a comparison with what we know about crime rates. The oft-cited 2.5 million DGU estimate is more than twice the total number of gun crimes estimated at that time in the NCVS, which in turn is far more than the number of gun crimes known to the police. Likewise, the number of shootings reported by those who claimed to be defending themselves vastly exceeds the total number of gunshot cases treated in emergency rooms. The fact is that the estimated number of DGUs from surveys is highly sensitive to the sequence of questions and to whether the respondent is given some help in placing events in time (so that when asked about the previous 12 months the respondent does not bring in events that happened before that period). When the same respondents in the same sort of one-time survey are asked about both DGUs and about victimization by guns, they report many more victimizations than DGUs.[9]

What Are the Risks and Benefits of Keeping a Firearm in the Home?

The risks of keeping a firearm at home include accidental shootings, suicide, and the escalation of domestic violence. In a particularly telling analysis, Matthew Miller and colleagues at the Harvard School of Public Health compared the 16 states with the highest rates of gun ownership to the 6 states with the lowest rates.[10] The two groups of states each had a total of about 31 million adults in 2009, but the group with high gun-ownership rates had more than four times as many gun suicides as the states with low gun ownership. (The non-gun suicide rate was virtually identical in the two groups, and there was no correlation between the prevalence of gun ownership and the prevalence of people with suicidal thoughts.)

Keeping a firearm at home also has benefits. Most gun owners believe that a gun provides an effective means of fending off intruders, thereby reducing the chance of injury to a household member. In about 3% of such incidents, the occupant used a gun, which means about 31,000 times per year.[11] Hence the annual probability of a gun-owning household's using a gun against a home intruder is less than 1 in 3,500. In other words, in a given year, there is one DGU against an intruder for every 3,500 homes that keep guns.

Keeping a gun at home has other benefits, including ready access for recreational hunting, target shooting, and collecting, as well as for practical uses such as shooting pesky critters on the farm. All of these uses are compatible with safe storage practices that reduce the chance of accidental misuse. In the end, the benefits of keeping a firearm in the home must be weighed against the risks. Those who keep a loaded handgun accessible to fend off intruders buy their sense of security at a price of an increased chance of misuse by household members, especially if there are children at home, or violence-prone adults, or anyone who abuses drugs or is suicidal.

Do Burglars Avoid Neighborhoods Where Residents Are Well Armed?

The strongest claim in support of the public virtue of widespread gun possession (and against laws to curtail it) is that guns in private hands generate a general deterrent effect on crime. Early arguments along these lines speculated about the effect on residential burglary and especially burglaries of occupied homes (known as "hot" burglaries). Philip Cook and Jens Ludwig conducted the first systematic analysis of this issue, demonstrating that the likelihood of residential burglary or hot burglary is not reduced by living in a county with high gun prevalence.[12] In fact, they found that greater gun prevalence was associated with an *increase* in the residential burglary rate. One reason may be that more prevalent gun ownership increases the profitability of burglary, because stolen guns are readily fenced for good prices. In any event, the fraction of burglaries that are "hot" is not affected by the prevalence of gun ownership.

How Many People Are Licensed to Carry a Gun?

Pro-gun advocates have mounted a successful effort to deregulate gun carrying in recent years. But as of 2019, more than two-thirds of states still required a special permit or license to legally carry a concealed handgun. More than 17 million people currently have obtained a permit of this sort, which works out to about one of every four gun owners.[13]

Some states publish the demographic statistics of permit holders. What we learn from these statistics is that the characteristics of permit holders are a lot like those of gun owners. In Florida, which has the highest prevalence of permits in the nation, most are held by men (73%) and people over 50 years old (56%).[14] Similar patterns are found in other states for which there are data. Permits go disproportionately to those from small towns and rural areas, despite the fact that those areas tend to have lower crime rates than big cities.

What Is It Like to Carry a Concealed Gun?

Polls typically ask why people own guns, not why they carry. But ethnographic studies suggest that the main motivation is the same: protection. In a recent study, a small group of Michigan gun carriers was interviewed on the subject.[15] One theme that emerged from these interviews was that they had decided to go armed because public systems of protection—911, the police—were ineffective or absent. Gun carriers viewed gun toting as an act of good citizenship in which they serve as defenders not only of themselves but also of loved ones and broader society. In most cases, gun carriers—especially white men—viewed themselves as providing a service to supplement the police. As one journalistic account put it, "Shooters see their guns as emblems of a whole spectrum of virtuous lifestyle choices—rural over urban, self-reliance over dependence on the collective, vigorous outdoorsiness over pallid intellectualism, patriotism over internationalism, action over inaction."[16]

Shaping this belief system is the training sanctioned by the National Rifle Association (NRA) that many gun owners undergo to obtain their concealed-carry permit. Instructors reinforce the notion that gun carriers are good citizens and that taking a life in defense of self or others can be a moral act.[17] Instructors refer to concealed gun carriers as "sheepdogs" quietly guarding the flock, while people who refuse to arm themselves are sometimes derided as "sheep."[18] Concealed-carry courses often spend more time preparing people to kill than training them to shoot straight. A gun-owning journalist who took the courses concluded that "it was hard to discern the line between preparing for something awful to happen and praying for something awful to happen." When he asked his instructor if gun carrying didn't "bespeak a needlessly dark view of mankind," the instructor replied, "I'm an optimist, but we live in a world of assholes."[19]

Interestingly, the Michigan study found that African Americans differed from whites in their reasons for carrying, and women differed from men. For many African American permit holders, carrying was not so much an act of supplementing the police as an act of defiance against a law-enforcement community that they viewed as racist harassers. For many women, who represent a small fraction of permit holders, guns were tools of psychological empowerment and reassurance that liberated them to go places, including travel to their jobs, that they might have otherwise avoided. Of course, we must be cautious about drawing sweeping conclusions from a relatively small sample of people in one state; these findings are merely suggestive.

What is it like to carry a gun? Gun carriers report feeling the weight, both physical and moral, of their firearm, and they say that burden imbues them with a sense of civic responsibility. Having a gun puts carriers just one misstep away from breaking the law—for example, by packing heat in a gun-free zone or brandishing the firearm without legitimate cause. As a result, they walk away from unarmed hotheads and avoid driving infractions that might catch a police officer's eye.[20]

Here is a journalist's colorful account of what it's like to carry:[21]

Moving through a cocktail party with a gun holstered snug against my ribs makes me feel like James Bond— *I know something you don't know!*—but it's socially and physically unpleasant. I have to remember to keep adjusting the drape of my jacket so as not to expose myself, and make sure to get the arms-inside position when hugging a friend so that the hard lump on my hip or under my arm doesn't give itself away. In some settings my gun feels as big as a toaster oven, and I find myself tense with the expectation of being discovered. What's more, if there's a truly comfortable way to carry a gun, I haven't found it. The revolver's weight and pressure keep me constantly aware of how quickly and utterly my world could change. Gun carriers tell me that's exactly the point: at any moment, violence could change

anybody's world. Those who carry guns are the ones prepared to make the change come out in their favor.

Carriers also maintain a heightened state of vigilance, which
they call "condition yellow." They might choose a table in the
corner of the restaurant, for example, to maximize their view
of incoming threats, and they frequently concoct and replay in
their minds attack scenarios and the optimal response. "I run
sequences in my head," a gun carrier says. "If a guy jumps me
with a knife, should I throw money to the ground and run?
Take two steps back and draw? How about if he has a gun?
How will I distract him so I can get the drop? It can be fun. But
it can also be exhausting."[22]

Does Society Benefit If More Civilians Carry Concealed Weapons?

Once again, the strongest claim in support of the public virtue
of widespread gun possession is that guns in private hands
generate a general deterrent effect on crime. By far the most
prominent research findings on the general deterrence issue
were based on an evaluation of changes in state laws governing concealed carrying of handguns. In the 1980s and
1990s, a number of states eased restrictions on concealed carry,
adopting a regulation that required local authorities to issue
permits to all applicants who met minimum conditions. These
"shall issue" laws replaced "may issue" laws (which gave the
authorities discretion) or outright bans. Economists John Lott
and David Mustard published the first evaluation of these
shall-issue laws, finding that states that adopted them experienced a reduction in homicide and some other types of crime.[23]
Lott went on to publish *More Guns, Less Crime*, in which he
reported these results and several variations on them.[24] He
reached differing conclusions about the effect of shall-issue
laws on property crime depending on how he did the analysis,

but in every version of his statistical model he found that ending restrictive gun-carrying laws reduced homicide rates.

In the finest scientific tradition, a number of analysts have sought to replicate Lott's findings to confirm or disconfirm them. The importance of this academic debate was deemed sufficiently important for the National Academy of Sciences to convene an expert panel of 18 scholars to review the conflicting research.[25] Most of the panelists were chosen because they were experts on the relevant methods and had not been directly involved in research related to gun control. Among other things, this panel reanalyzed Lott's data, and, with just one dissent, judged his findings to be unreliable. Stanford Law professor John Donohue has continued this line of research, taking advantage of additional decades of data. He has found no evidence that liberalized concealed-carry laws deter homicide or other types of crime; indeed, his findings indicate that deregulating concealed carry tends to increase the rates of assault.[26]

Lott's remarkable findings received enormous attention because they provided academic support for pro-gun advocates. He has good credentials and utilized standard social science methods. The ensuing controversy can be viewed as a normal part of the scientific process when it is working well; his findings provoked other highly qualified researchers to investigate. At this point it is fair to say that the best science does not provide much guidance for policymakers, but little guidance is better than recommendations based on faulty evidence.

Do Americans Believe that Guns Make People Safer?

Not surprisingly, the answer depends on whom you ask and what scenario they are asked to consider. Certain subgroups—whites, conservatives, men, and gun owners—are more likely than others to see the protective value of firearms. But even many people who don't own a firearm are blasé about the role of guns in everyday life.

To understand Americans' beliefs about guns and safety, let's start on a personal level. The number-one reason for owning a firearm is personal security. A majority of gun owners say that protection is a major motivation, up from only a quarter two decades ago. Among gun owners, 4 in 10 keep their firearm loaded and accessible, and roughly one-quarter regularly carry their firearm in public.[27] Not surprisingly, having a gun in the home makes the vast majority of gun owners feel safer. However, even a good share of nonowners (40% in one recent survey) would be fine having a gun in the home—though women, older people, Democrats, and people of color were considerably less inclined to feel this way.[28]

The public's ease with firearms extends outside the home. In a recent poll, two-thirds of Americans said allowing gun owners to carry weapons in public either makes those spaces safer or has no impact.[29] However, support for guns in public has its limits. A narrow majority of Americans would oppose expanding the places where guns are allowed and would oppose allowing teachers and other personnel to carry guns in K-12 schools. A commanding majority—more than 8 in 10 adults—opposes dropping licensing requirements to carry concealed weapons. Most of these people feel *strongly* that so-called permitless carry is a bad idea, even as more and more states adopt the policy.[30]

Perceptions of whether guns make "us" safer depend to some extent on whether the person asked, or someone else, has the weapon. Consider a fun survey experiment conducted in the mid-1990s. The first of two surveys asked whether "ordinary Americans" after "proper training" should be able to carry a gun on their person. In response, 65% of respondents said no. The second survey personalized the scenario by asking whether "average Americans, such as yourself" should be allowed to get a concealed-carry license "for self-protection." Here the result flipped: 60% now were in support.[31]

Do Americans Believe that Guns Make Democracy Stronger?

Gun rights advocates argue that civilian gun ownership constitutes a bulwark against tyranny. More guns mean more freedom. However, as far as we can tell, no publicly available poll has ever asked Americans about whether they agree with these assertions. Nor have pollsters thought to ask whether stricter firearms laws, however defined, would harm or inevitably lead to the downfall of America's democratic system of government. However, several questions have come at the guns–democracy question sideways, and from these questions we know that Americans do equate private firearms ownership with core American values such as liberty, distrust of government, and individual self-reliance.

The NRA and other gun rights advocates long have tapped into such values to build a case for unfettered civilian ownership of firearms. The foundation of the NRA's narrative is the so-called slippery-slope argument, that even a mild step in the direction of gun control will put the country on a fast path to the confiscation of guns and the end of constitutional liberties.

The argument has sunk in. By 1993, half of Americans believed that gun control would inevitably lead to "stricter laws which will take guns away from all citizens." By 2013, roughly the same number agreed, but the fear had become especially acute among Republicans (63%) and independents (50%). Nearly half of people who didn't even have a gun in the home thought that there could be truth to the slippery-slope argument.[32]

In recent years, the seeds of the slippery-slope narrative have landed on fertile ground. Gallup polls show that more than half of Americans believe that the federal government has too much power.[33] As of 2015, roughly half believed that "the federal government poses an immediate threat to the rights and freedoms of ordinary citizens."[34] These numbers were up significantly from the early 2000s, with most of the shift occurring during the Bush administration. A 2017 poll found that three-quarters of gun owners see firearms as "essential" to their freedom.[35]

For many Americans, gun laws speak to these fears. In 2013, 57% of the public believed that gun laws "give too much power to government over average citizens," a figure considerably higher among Republicans and independents than among Democrats.[36] Likewise, more than 4 in 10 Americans believe that "laws limiting gun ownership" infringe on the right to bear arms—a position that not even the Supreme Court's recent pro-gun rulings have embraced.[37]

While the bulk of the evidence points to a fairly widespread concern among Americans about government power, especially when it might threaten gun rights. But there is one anomalous finding that suggests there is growing skepticism toward the slippery-slope argument. In 2013, 36% of Americans "strongly disagreed" that gun control would eventually lead to laws taking guns away from all citizens, up significantly from the 22% who strongly questioned the slippery-slope argument in 1993.[38]

Do Guns Protect Against Tyranny or Genocide?

A core tenet of gun rights ideology is that "the people" must deny government a monopoly on the use of force. A well-armed citizenry is necessary to counterbalance the state and if liberty so requires, to topple the government. A corollary to this tenet is that banning private ownership of guns, or even simply regulating them, makes tyranny—even genocide—more likely. Mass armament safeguards democracy by leaving to the people a right of insurrection if they judge that their government has gone astray. As Daniel Polsby and Don B. Kates Jr. have argued, "An armed population is simply more difficult to exterminate than one that is defenseless."[39]

Pro-gun advocates draw on historical examples. American democracy is indebted to citizens who deployed their muskets to throw off the British Crown. Surely, then, the founders intended for future patriots to maintain this right of revolt and thus enshrined it in state and federal constitutions. A Supreme Court majority embraced this view in 2008, when it agreed that a citizens' militia served as a "safeguard against tyranny."[40] Ardent gun rights proponents go further, citing Thomas Jefferson's admonition that "the tree of liberty must be refreshed from time to time with the blood of patriots and tyrants." Indeed, a 2013 poll found that 44% of Republicans (but only 18% of Democrats and 27% of independents) believed that to preserve liberty, America may need an armed revolution in the next few years.[41]

To these gun advocates, the horrors of the twentieth century only strengthen the argument that an armed people are a free people. Hitler, Stalin, and Pol Pot are invoked as evidence for what can happen when the people have no means of mustering private force against madmen. As pro-gun legal scholars have argued, "If every family on this planet owned a good-quality rifle, genocide would be on the path to extinction."[42] To the argument that "it can't happen here" in the United States or any other advanced industrial democracy, gun rights theorists say this is just blind conceit. Genocides have happened "among civilized, educated, cultured people."[43] Even the United States has its own shameful record of massacring Native Americans, lynching blacks, and interning Japanese Americans.

Advocates of gun violence prevention see these lessons differently. To them, the best guarantee against tyranny is a strong system of laws and ingrained traditions of tolerance and equality. States tend not to oppress their citizens if they have institutional arrangements that disperse power, safeguard individual rights and political representation, and provide mechanisms for peacefully resolving disputes and transferring power. The longer such traditions are locked in, the harder they are to dislodge. The founders vested their faith in a system of ordered liberty—not private-citizen gun owners—to frustrate would-be tyrants.

To supporters of this institutional view of democracy, the mass ownership of firearms only increases mayhem. Gun violence is higher in societies with more guns and less regulation thereof, so there is a present-day cost of stockpiling weapons. What's more, all those citizen gun owners can easily be mobilized to suppress freedom and threaten democracy—think the Ku Klux Klan in the American South or Hitler's brownshirts. Advocates of gun violence prevention note that history is littered with examples of revolutionaries who took up arms to throw off tyranny but ended up establishing very undemocratic regimes—China, Russia, and Cuba for starters.

So is it true, as pro-gun advocates argue, that "a connection exists between the restrictiveness of a country's civilian weapons policy and its liability to commit genocide against its people"—or even just to impose tyranny upon them?[44] The simplest and perhaps least satisfying answer is that we don't have enough data to judge. To feel comfortable asserting that guns preserve freedom, we would need to be able to point to well-armed democracies that have maintained their liberty and poorly armed (but otherwise similar) democracies that have backslid into tyranny. The problem is that there aren't a lot of countries in either category, certainly not enough to justify sweeping conclusions. Even if we resort to anecdotes, the case isn't all that persuasive. Heavily armed America is a longstanding beacon of democracy, but so is the United Kingdom, even though few in Britain own guns. And, as we discuss later, Germany was actually liberalizing its gun laws when Hitler came to power.

On the question of whether guns or institutions safeguard liberty, advocates of each position, however differing, often invoke the US experience as evidence for their side. But America makes an ambiguous case, for it has both strong democratic institutions and traditions *and* hundreds of millions of firearms in private hands. Which one is holding the nation together after more than two centuries is a matter of opinion, not science.[45]

3

THE HARM DONE BY GUNS

How Many Americans Are Killed or Injured by Gunfire?

Approximately 1 million Americans have died from gunshot wounds in homicides, accidents, and suicides during just the last three decades—more than all combat deaths in all wars in US history. In 2017, the National Center for Health Statistics tabulated 39,773 firearms deaths, including 15,095 homicides, 23,854 suicides, and 486 unintentional killings. As a point of reference, there were as many gun deaths as traffic deaths in 2017. Another point of reference is the years of potential life lost before age 65: Gunshot injuries account for 1 of every 13 years lost to early death from all causes.[1]

Of course, not all gunshot injuries are fatal. The homicide victims are just the tip of the violence iceberg. In most cases of gun robbery and assault the victim is not injured—the perpetrator threatens the victim without shooting or shoots and misses. If the victim is shot, the chances are only about one in six that it will prove fatal—in which case the assault becomes a homicide.[2]

Emergency rooms treated 85,000 nonfatal gunshot injuries in 2015, including 63,000 from criminal assaults.[3] In the same year, the police recorded more than 300,000 assaults and robberies in which the perpetrator used a gun to threaten or shoot the victim.[4]

While homicides and suicides are committed with a variety of weapons, firearms predominate. Three of every four homicides, and half of suicides, are committed with a firearm. Other prominent means of committing suicide include suffocation (28%) and poisoning with drugs or other substances (14%). Cutting and stabbing account for just 2% of suicides and 9% of homicides.[5]

Finally, it should be pointed out that not all of the 15,095 homicides in which one person fatally shot another were criminal. The Vital Statistics system identifies 553 of them as "legal intervention," which is to say that the shooting was by a law-enforcement agent during an encounter with a suspect. (As it turns out, this figure represents a substantial undercount, due to the fact that death certificates often fail to record officer involvement—the true number of fatal shootings by law enforcement officers in 2017 was about 1,000.[6]) Furthermore, some fraction of the homicides committed by civilians are considered legally "justified" in the sense that the shooter was acting in self-defense.[7]

Is Gun Violence Rising or Falling in America?

To note the obvious, gun violence is violence perpetrated with a gun. Gun violence rates are high when and where both guns and violence are plentiful. For the nation as a whole, the trend in gun violence rates generally follows the trends in overall violence rates. That trend was strongly downward between the early 1990s and 2014, during which time the homicide rate dropped by half. In fact, the homicide rate in 2014 was comparable to what Americans enjoyed in the 1950s—before the national epidemic of violence that began in 1963 and persisted for three decades. This remarkable history is depicted in figure 3.1. The figure indicates the number of homicides each year divided by the US population in millions. The overall rate ranges from about 40 victims per million up to more than 100 victims per million.

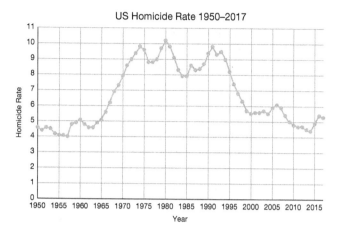

Figure 3.1 US homicide rate, 1950–2017

One logical reason that homicide rates may be declining in recent years is that medical treatment of trauma victims is improving. Much has been learned from wartime experience with trauma treatment in Vietnam, Iraq, and Afghanistan—and from treating gunshot victims here at home. Both emergency medical response and treatment after hospitalization have become more effective, so that some victims are saved now who would have been lost in previous times. Other things equal (such as the types of firearms in use by criminal assailants), the result is a decline in the "case-fatality rate"—the likelihood that a gunshot victim will die of his or her wounds. Unfortunately, there is a countervailing trend toward the use of more powerful and lethal firearms in criminal attacks, and the net effect on survival is not clear.[8]

In fact, there have been sharp declines in all types of criminal violence since the early 1990s. The (nonfatal) robbery and assault rates recorded in police records, or from the National Crime Victimization Survey, have declined even more than the homicide rate, and these declines have nothing to do with improved medical practice. Our belief is that the homicide decline is closely linked to this larger picture of reduced violence. The main reason that fewer people are dying from homicide is that there is less violence.

What about suicide? During the post–World War II era there has been no clear trend in overall suicide rates; the suicide death rate was 114 per million in 1950, and 104 in 2000, with a steady increase since then. By 2017 the rate had reached 145.[9]

Firearms used to figure even more prominently in suicide than they do today. In 1990, 61% of suicides were committed with firearms. Twenty-five years later the figure had dropped to 51%.[10] The drop in the percentage of suicides involving guns goes hand in hand with the declining prevalence of guns in the home during this period.

Why Are Guns of More Concern Than Other Weapons?

A popular slogan claims that "guns don't kill people, people kill people." The intent is no doubt to suggest that if "people" were deprived of guns, they would find some other means of killing each other—that what matters is the intent, not the type of weapon. What is missing from this argument is that without a gun, the *capacity* to kill may be greatly diminished. The bumper sticker is right: "Guns don't kill people. They just make it easier."

Slogans aside, the true causal role of guns in homicide is one of the fundamental issues in gun violence research and evidence-based policymaking. In some circumstances the claim that the type of weapon matters seems indisputable. There are very few drive-by knifings or people killed accidentally by stray fists. When well-protected people are murdered, it is almost always with a gun: More than 90% of lethal attacks on law-enforcement officers are with firearms, and all assassinations of US presidents have been by firearm. When lone assailants set out to kill as many people as they can in a house of worship, at a business, or on campus, a gun is the most readily available weapon that will do the job. But what about the more mundane attacks that make up the vast bulk of violent crime?

The first piece of evidence is that robberies and assaults committed with guns are more likely to result in the victim's death than are similar violent crimes committed with other weapons. In the public health jargon, the case-fatality rates differ by weapon type. Take the case of robbery, a crime that includes holdups, muggings, and other violent confrontations motivated by theft. The case-fatality rate for gun robbery is 3 times as high as for robberies with knives, and 10 times as high as for robberies with other weapons.[11] For aggravated (serious) assault it is more difficult to come up with a meaningful case-fatality estimate, since the crime itself is in part defined by the type of weapon used. (In the Federal Bureau of Investigation [FBI]'s Uniform Crime Reports, a threat delivered at gunpoint is likely to be classified as an "aggravated" assault, while the same threat delivered while shaking a fist would be classified as a "simple" assault.) We do know that for assaults from which the victim sustains serious injury, the case-fatality rate is closely linked to the type of weapon. Using data from visits to the emergency department, it appears that the case-fatality rate for gunshot assaults is 12 times the rate for assaults with a knife.[12]

Case-fatality rates do not by themselves prove that the type of weapon has an independent causal effect on the probability of death. It is possible that the type of weapon is simply an indicator of the assailant's intent and that it is the intent, rather than the weapon, that determines whether the victim lives or dies. This view was offered as a reasonable possibility by the famed criminologist Marvin Wolfgang, who in his 1958 study of homicide in Philadelphia contended that "few homicides due to shooting could be avoided merely if a firearm were not immediately present, and that the offender would select some other weapon to achieve the same destructive goal."[13] The same claim has shown up in the writings of some other criminologists; the gun makes the killing easier and is hence the obvious choice if the assailant's intent is indeed to kill. If no gun were available, the reasoning goes, most would-be killers would still find a way. In this view, fatal and nonfatal attacks form two distinct sets of events with little overlap, at least in regard to the assailant's intent. But the evidence suggests otherwise.

The speculation that the intent is all that matters seems far-fetched. When a tool is available to make a difficult task much easier—say, killing a person—then we expect that the task will be undertaken with greater frequency and likelihood of success. Legal scholar Franklin Zimring developed perhaps the most telling empirical evidence on how this calculus applies to violence. He demonstrated that there is actually a good deal of overlap between fatal and nonfatal attacks. Even in the case of earnest and potentially deadly attacks, the victim usually survives. This fact suggests that the assailant has ambiguous or unsustained intention at the time of the attack, as would be expected of someone who is intoxicated or enraged. Whether the victim lives or dies then depends importantly on the lethality of the weapon with which the assailant strikes the first blow or two.[14]

Zimring's studies of wounds inflicted in gun and knife assaults suggest that the difference between life and death is often just a matter of chance, determined by whether the bullet or blade finds a vital organ. It is relatively rare for assailants to administer the coup de grâce that would ensure their victim's demise. For every homicide inflicted with a single bullet wound to the chest, there are two survivors of a bullet wound to the chest who are indistinguishable with respect to the assailant's intent. It is largely because guns are intrinsically more lethal than knives that gunshot injuries are more likely to result in death than sustained attacks with a knife to vital areas of the body. Another of Zimring's studies provides still more compelling evidence by comparing case-fatality rates for gunshot wounds involving different-caliber weapons. A wound inflicted by a larger-caliber gun was more likely to prove lethal than a wound inflicted by a smaller-caliber gun. Assuming the choice of gun is not related to the intent of the assailant, it's the type of weapon that influences whether the victim lives or dies.[15] This study was recently replicated using five years of data on fatal and nonfatal shootings in Boston, with the same result. While the caliber of the gun is not correlated with indicators of the intent or skill of the shooter (such as number of shots and number of wounds), the likelihood of death rises sharply as the caliber of the firearm increases.[16]

The argument in a nutshell is that robbery–murder is a close relative of robbery, and assaultive homicide is a close relative of armed assault. Death is in effect a byproduct of violent crime. Thus, while the legal severity of the crime depends on whether the victim lives or dies, this outcome is not a reliable guide to the assailant's intent or state of mind.

One logical implication of this perspective is that there should be a close link between the overall volume of violent crimes and the number of murders, moderated by the types of weapons used. Where Zimring provided a detailed description of cases as the basis for his conclusion, tests based on aggregate data are also potentially informative. One study of robbery–murder trends in 43 large cities supported the "byproduct" claim: A tight connection was evident between variation in robbery and robbery–murder rates. An increase of 1,000 gun robberies was associated with three times as many additional murders as an increase of 1,000 non-gun robberies.[17] The type of weapon matters.

Zimring and Gordon Hawkins later published *Crime Is Not the Problem*, making the case that violent-crime rates in American cities are not particularly high relative to the rest of the developed world—with the notable exception of homicide.[18] American "exceptionalism" is the result of the fact that in the United States assaults and robberies are much more likely to be committed with guns, and that makes them more lethal. In this view, American perpetrators are not more vicious than those in Canada, western Europe, or Australia—Americans are just better armed.

The type of weapon matters in other respects as well. Consider the role of weapons in the crime of robbery. Use of a gun enhances the robber's power, making it relatively easy for him to control his victim and gain compliance. As a result, other things equal, robbers bearing guns are more likely to succeed than are their knife-wielding counterparts. And when robberies by firearm do succeed, the average value of the offender's "take" nearly doubles.[19] Further, the likelihood of injury to the victim depends on the type of weapon, with gun robberies the least likely to involve injury—the threat is sufficient to gain compliance. Of course, when the robber does fire his gun, it is quite likely that the victim will die, making gun robberies (as noted above) by far the most lethal type of robbery. In any event, that gun robberies are so much more lucrative than robberies with other weapons raises an interesting question—why are most robberies committed *without* a gun? One likely answer is that many robbers lack ready access to one.

In sum, the type of weapon deployed in violent confrontations is not just an incidental detail; it matters in several ways. Because guns provide the power to kill quickly, at a distance, and without much skill or strength, they also provide the power to intimidate other people and gain control of a violent situation without an actual attack. When there is a physical attack, then the type of weapon is an important determinant of whether the victim survives, with guns far more lethal than other commonly used weapons.

The most important implication of this so-called instrumentality effect is that policies that are effective in reducing gun use in violent crime would reduce the murder rate, even if the volume of violent crime were unaffected. As it turns out, about half of the states have incorporated sentencing enhancements for use of a gun in crime. These enhancements, most of which were adopted in the 1970s and 1980s, were intended to reduce gun use in violence. Systematic evaluations offer some indication that they have been effective.[20] In any event, the widespread adoption of gun enhancements by state legislatures is a clear indication of the commonsense appeal of the instrumentality effect.

Does the Availability of a Firearm Increase the Risk of Suicide?

There are millions of suicide attempts and gestures every year, and 500,000 that are serious enough to require emergency medical treatment. Even though relatively few suicide attempts involve a self-inflicted gunshot, guns account for fully half of all completed suicides.[21] As with assault, guns are simply more lethal than other commonly used means; the case-fatality rate is 85%.[22] Of course people who have a sustained determination to kill themselves may eventually find a way, but most suicides are a response to transitory circumstances. One study found that among people who make near-lethal suicide attempts, 24% took less than five minutes between the decision to kill themselves and the actual attempt, and 70% took less than one hour.[23] Teen suicide is particularly impulsive, and if a firearm is readily available, the impulse is likely to result in death. It is no surprise, then, that households that keep firearms on hand have an elevated rate of suicide for all concerned—the owner, spouse, and teenaged children.[24] While there are other highly lethal means, such as hanging and jumping off a tall building, suicidal people who are inclined to use a gun are unlikely to find such a substitute acceptable. Studies comparing the 50 states have found gun suicide rates (but not suicide with other types of weapons) are closely related to the prevalence of gun ownership.[25]

It is really a matter of common sense that in suicide, the means matter. For families and counselors, a high priority for intervening with someone who appears acutely suicidal is to reduce his or her access to firearms, as well as other lethal means.

Who Is at Risk of Being Shot?

For assault and homicide, young men are vastly overrepresented in the gunshot victimization statistics. Males aged 18 to 34 are the victims of half of all murders.[26] Within this group lie large differences by race. Homicide victimization rates in 2017 (consistent with earlier years) were 16 times as high for African Americans as for non-Hispanic whites. Indeed, homicide is the leading cause of death for African Americans in this age group and the second-leading cause of death for Latino males. For all men in this age range, most (89%) homicides are committed with guns.[27]

Unsurprisingly, the shooters tend to be similar to the victims, with even greater concentration among young men. The violence is engendered by routine altercations or turf contests or underground-market transactions that go wrong. In cities where gangs are prevalent, such as Boston, Chicago, and Los Angeles, the bulk of the deadly violence by youths can be attributed to gang members, since they often have access to guns and may be involved in the underground economy.

Police long have been aware that gun violence is concentrated in certain neighborhoods and among certain groups of people, but only recently have officers begun using sophisticated statistical methods to document this impression and adjust their strategies accordingly. The Chicago Police Department in particular has invested in "predictive policing" as a guide to deployment and intervention. In 2013, statisticians at the Illinois Institute of Technology helped develop the Strategic Subject List (also known as the "heat list") to identify which residents with a criminal record had the greatest chance of being involved in gun violence, either as a victim or a shooter. Those individuals who had been victims of serious assault or had violence arrests or arrests for unlawful weapon use rose to the top of the list, after an adjustment for age.[28] The use of this information in guiding police priorities is controversial and so far of uncertain value.

About one in five homicides involves women as victims. For women, unlike men, the greatest danger lies within the family, especially spouses or intimate partners. That said, the long-term trend for domestic violence has been favorable. The increasing independence of living arrangements gets much of the credit. Women are now far less likely to live with a man, and if they do, can more easily move out if the relationship becomes violent.[29] As a result, they are less likely to be killed— and much less likely to kill.[30] In the mid-1970s there were about the same number of male and female domestic homicide victims, but now the victimization rate for women, while lower, is three times that of men. An enduring pattern is that when there is a gun in the home, domestic violence is more likely to escalate to murder—usually of the woman.[31]

Suicide presents a different picture. The most obvious similarity with homicide is with respect to gender. Once again, just one in five victims is female. The male–female difference in suicide rates is surely influenced by the differential access to and familiarity with guns. While females are more likely to attempt suicide than males, women are much less likely than men to use a gun.[32]

Suicide, unlike homicide, is concentrated among whites. For white men the rates are high and reasonably uniform across the age spectrum from 20 to 80. Other less obvious characteristics actually bring the suicide picture closer to homicide victimization: Suicide victims are disproportionately unmarried, unemployed, low income, and educated at the high school level or less.[33] There is also a high prevalence of mental illness associated with suicide, most commonly depression and substance abuse.[34]

How Has Gun Violence Touched National Political Life?

Four US presidents have been assassinated—Abraham Lincoln (1865), James A. Garfield (1881), William McKinley (1901), and John F. Kennedy (1963). All of them were shot. Lincoln's assassin, John Wilkes Booth, was angry at Lincoln's pursuit of the Civil War and an end to slavery. Garfield's assassin, Charles Guiteau, was disappointed that he did not receive a federal patronage job. McKinley's assassin, Leon Czolgosz, was an attention-seeking anarchist. Kennedy's assassin, Lee Harvey Oswald, was a former US Marine and temporary defector to the Soviet Union whose motives for killing the president remain widely debated.

Besides the four presidents who died, one—President Ronald Reagan—was severely wounded in a 1981 assassination attempt by a mentally ill man who was seeking to impress the actress Jodie Foster. Former president Theodore Roosevelt was shot in the chest while on the campaign trail in 1912 but finished his speech before seeking medical care. Other presidents have had close calls with gun-wielding assailants but have escaped injury. They include Andrew Jackson (1835), Franklin D. Roosevelt (1933), Harry S. Truman (1950), Gerald Ford (1975, twice), and Bill Clinton (1994).

Thus, nearly one-quarter of sitting US presidents—10 of 44—have been shot or shot at by would-be assassins. Other prominent figures who have been shot to death in recent decades in the United States include civil rights leaders Medgar Evers (1963) and the Reverend Martin Luther King Jr. (1968); Senator Robert F. Kennedy (1968); and musicians John Lennon (1980), Tupac Shakur (1996), Biggie Smalls (1997), and Nipsey Hussle (2019).

What Is a Mass Shooting, and How Frequent Are They?

There is no widely agreed-upon definition of a mass shooting. The frequency of such events is very sensitive to the precise definition used.

Several private organizations have taken on the task of collecting and reporting mass shootings. The Gun Violence Archive (a nonprofit, unaffiliated organization) scans multiple sources for information on mass shootings. Any incident in which four or more victims are shot is included, regardless of location or circumstance. For the years 2015 to 2018, the Archive reports about 350 such incidents per year, averaging about one death and four injuries.[35]

A much more restrictive definition is used by *Mother Jones* magazine. For inclusion in its tabulation, an incident must result in four or more victims killed and occur in a public place such as a school, workplace, or commercial area. Further, the killing must in some sense be indiscriminate, excluding robberies and gang fights. This definition yields just 12 incidents in 2018, compared with 340 in the Gun Violence Archive for that year.[36]

So which definition is right? Surely the *Mother Jones* definition better captures the mass shootings that have galvanized such public outrage in Littleton, Newtown, Charleston, Orlando, Las Vegas, and Parkland, to name but a few. The broader definition utilized by the Gun Violence Archive is useful for tracking the near-daily occurrence of shootings with multiple victims.

It may seem surprising that there is no regular report by the FBI or other federal agency on the number of mass shootings. The Congressional Research Service did produce a one-time report on mass shootings between 1999 and 2013, using FBI data to identify incidents in which four or more victims were killed.[37] The FBI tabulates "active shooter" incidents, but the definition is vague and difficult to apply consistently.

There has been much debate about whether the number of mass shootings is increasing. The answer may well depend on the particular definition. In any event, the longer-term trends cannot be reliably documented from existing data sources. What is clear is that four of the five most deadly mass shootings in US history have occurred since 2012.

What Are the Worst Mass Shootings in History?

In the United States, the most lethal mass shooting (through mid-2019) occurred on the Las Vegas Strip on October 1, 2017 (Table 3.1). The shooter, a 64-year-old retiree, had spent a week accumulating an arsenal of assault weapons in his rooms on the 32nd floor of the Mandalay Bay Hotel. He equipped the semiautomatic AR-15–style weapons with bump stocks, which had the effect of making it possible for him to fire continuously with a single pull of the trigger, using large magazines with 100-round capacity. He fired more than 1,100 rounds in 10 minutes into a concert-going crowd on the Strip below, killing 58 people and leaving 851 injured—more than 400 of them by gunfire and hundreds more in the ensuing pandemonium. He then shot himself. His motive remains unknown.

Table 3.1 The Ten Most Deadly Mass Shootings (Through Mid-2019) in the United States

Incident	Year	Deaths*	Injuries
Las Vegas Strip, NV	2017	58 + 1	422
Pulse nightclub, Orlando, FL	2016	49 + 1	53
Virginia Tech, Blacksburg, VA	2007	32 + 1	17
Sandy Hook Elementary School, Newtown, CT	2012	27 + 1	2
First Baptist Church, Sutherland Springs, TX	2017	26 + 1	20
Luby's Cafeteria, Killeen, TX	1991	17 + 1	27
Walmart, El Paso, TX	2019	22	24
McDonald's restaurant, San Ysidro, CA	1984	21 + 1	19
University of Texas clock tower, Austin	1966	17 + 1	31
Marjory Stoneman Douglas High School, Parkland, FL	2018	17	17

*If the shooter was killed, it is noted as +1. Injuries refers to gunshot injuries only.
Source: Wikipedia.

Second on this list of infamous events is the attack on the Pulse, a gay nightclub in Orlando, by a 29-year-old American security guard. He shot 102 people over the course of an extended siege. He himself was then shot dead by an Orlando police officer. The FBI deemed this shooting to be a terrorist attack based in part on statements the killer made in a 911 call during the attack, in which he claimed allegiance to the Islamic State of Iraq.

Among the mass shootings on campuses, the most deadly occurred at Virginia Polytechnic and State University, better known as Virginia Tech, on April 16, 2007. In two closely timed sprees, a university senior killed 32 students and teachers and wounded 17 others before killing himself. The killer, a South Korean national who had moved with his family to Virginia when he was in third grade, had a history of mental illness. In 2005 a Virginia court had found him to be a danger to himself and ordered a psychiatric evaluation. While that order was a disqualification for gun ownership under federal law, he subsequently succeeded in passing a background check for purchasing the guns he used in the attack.

The first mass public shooting in the modern era occurred at the University of Texas in 1966, when an engineering student and former Marine opened fire from the campus clock tower, killing 14 people. One more person died years later of complications from his injury. Before the rampage, the gunman had murdered his wife and his mother. Another 31 were wounded that day.

As gripping as they are, mass shootings rarely lead to significant changes in gun policy. The ones that do typically involve schoolchildren. On April 20, 1999, in suburban Denver, two Columbine High School students shot to death 12 of their classmates and a teacher and wounded 21 other students before killing themselves. The Columbine massacre was the fifth—and by far the most deadly—multiple-fatality shooting that had unfolded in American public schools over roughly a two-year period. Columbine, along with a shooting in Springfield,

Oregon, one year earlier, led voters in those states to approve popular referenda requiring all firearm buyers at gun shows to undergo a background check.

The deadliest firearms massacre at a K-12 institution occurred on December 14, 2012, at Sandy Hook Elementary School in Newtown, Connecticut. After a mentally ill 20-year-old who had briefly attended the school years earlier completed his rampage, 20 first-graders and 6 educators were dead. The assailant also killed his mother and himself that day. Like Columbine, the Sandy Hook massacre was the culmination of a string of especially high-profile mass shootings, including that of Congresswoman Gabrielle Giffords (D-AZ) and 19 others in 2011 and that of 70 Aurora theater patrons, 10 Sikh worshippers, and 8 signage-company employees just in the prior five months of 2012. Following Sandy Hook, President Obama, who had just been reelected, made gun violence prevention a personal priority. A number of states adopted more stringent regulations on guns, but others acted to deregulate guns. Congress passed no legislation either way. More recently the 2018 massacre of students at Marjory Stoneman Douglas High School helped mobilize support for gun regulation during the November midterm elections and led to stricter gun laws in Florida and elsewhere.

A historical footnote: America's worst school massacre did not involve firearms, but rather dynamite. In 1927, a farmer and school board treasurer in tiny Bath, Michigan, blew up the local consolidated school and killed 38 children. Six adults, including the farmer and his wife, also died in his killing spree, while 58 were injured. As a news account reported at the time, "Hardly a family in the village did not have at least one child enrolled among the school's normal attendance of about 200."[38]

Mass shootings are more common in the United States than in other advanced industrialized democracies, but other such nations have experienced their own such "lone wolf" attacks in recent years. The most lethal such shooting took place in peaceful Norway in 2011. In that attack, a 32-year-old anti-Islamic extremist exploded a bomb outside the government headquarters in downtown Oslo, killing 8, then took a ferry to a Workers Youth League summer camp on an island 25 miles away and shot 69 people dead, mostly teenagers. While an initial court-ordered psychiatric assessment found him suffering from paranoid schizophrenia, a second assessment found him to be sane enough to stand trial.

American observers can only marvel at the legislative response triggered by several high-profile mass shootings abroad. In March 2019, a lone gunman attacked worshippers in two mosques in Christchurch, New Zealand, killing 50. The government responded immediately with new gun regulations, banning the possession of assault weapons and requiring current owners to turn in these firearms. The government offered compensation. This chain of events was reminiscent of Australia's experience in 1996 when a massacre in Tasmania killed 35 people. After the shooting, the Australian government imposed a near-ban on semiautomatic firearms and required owners to turn in the newly banned weapons in exchange for compensation. About 1 million weapons were ultimately confiscated and destroyed. In the same year, a man entered the Dunblane (Scotland) Primary School and proceeded to murder 16 children and 1 teacher before killing himself. Parliament quickly banned private possession of most handguns.

In addition to these lone wolf attacks, there also have been organized terrorist attacks on civilian populations. In the Western world, the most notable was the November 2015 massacre of 130 people by three groups of men operating in several locations in Paris, using guns and bombs. We view such attacks as qualitatively different than the mass shootings in the United States, more akin to a militia action.[39]

Are There Common Elements in Mass Shootings?

Some common aspects are apparent. First, shooters are almost always male, and they tend to operate alone. Second, random shootings are often not as random as they seem. For example, 33% of mass public shootings between 1983 and 2012 occurred at the shooter's current or former workplace.[40] In 54% of mass shootings between 2009 and 2017 the shooter killed a current or former intimate partner, along with others.[41] In particularly media-worthy mass shootings, at least two-thirds of the time the shooter had an immediate connection to the location—he had worked, studied, done business, or prayed there, or he was targeting a family member on the job. It is quite common for mass shooters to take their own life at the scene.

In some of the most deadly shootings—at Virginia Tech, the Aurora movie theater, and the Sandy Hook school, for example—the perpetrator turned out to have had either documented mental illness or clear warning signs. A further indication of mental illness is found in an analysis of 160 "active shooter" events documented by the FBI; in 40% of these cases, the shooter ultimately committed suicide.[42]

A particular concern during the 1990s was the epidemic of mass shootings in secondary schools, culminating in the April 1999 incident at Colorado's Columbine High School, where two seniors shot three dozen people, killing a dozen of their classmates and a teacher and then themselves. In response to this event and others like it, the US Secret Service and US Department of Education conducted an analysis using the "threat assessment" approach developed for protecting public figures. Among their findings:[43]

- "Incidents of targeted violence at school rarely were sudden, impulsive acts."
- Before most incidents other people—usually classmates—knew about the attacker's plans.

- "Most attackers had difficulty coping with significant losses or personal failures. Moreover, many had considered or attempted suicide."
- "Many attackers felt bullied, persecuted or injured by others prior to the attack."
- "Most attackers had access to and had used weapons prior to the attack."

The report encouraged school officials to develop better sources of information, as most of the serious rampages could have been stopped if one of the students who was in the know had thought to tell an adult.

Beyond this sound advice, policymakers have struggled with how to prevent mass shootings. Predicting violent behavior is difficult, even when mental illness is present, and the difficulty is compounded for rare events such as mass shootings. (One leading violence researcher likened predicting massacres to "trying to find a very small needle in a very large haystack."[44]) Federal gun laws allow all but a small fraction of the most severely mentally ill to possess a firearm, and the system that is supposed to flag those prohibited purchasers is subject to uneven reporting and missing records. Medical privacy and civil liberties protections often prevent preemptive action by family members or authorities, however well meaning.

An increasing number of states have responded to the threat by putting more armed guards in schools and even allowing (or encouraging) teachers to carry guns. As with keeping a gun in home to repel home invaders, the problem with arming teachers is that in preparing to respond to one threat, it introduces a new one. Putting more guns in school enhances the risk that students will abscond with the weapon, that it will be accidentally discharged, and that school personnel will use it unnecessarily to break up fights among students. These new dangers must be balanced against the objective risk of a mass shooting, which is on the order of 1 in 100,000 per year.

Does the US Have More Violent Crime Than Other Countries?

Yes, but. When the US violence rates are compared with those of other high-income countries, the United States ends up on the high end of the spectrum. But where the US rates are really off the scale is with respect to homicide, and these high homicide rates are largely the product of America's outsized rates of *gun* homicide. In turn, as we discussed earlier, the elevated rates of gun homicide in the United States are a byproduct of assaults and robberies that kill the victim because a gun is involved. A comparison between the United States and Canada is illustrative. The US non-gun homicide rate in 2017 was 42% higher than Canada's, but the US gun homicide rate was a staggering 510% higher.[45] Similar comparisons can be made with Europe, Australia, and other wealthy nations, with similar results. The US non-gun homicide rate is relatively high, which tells us something about underlying violence rates. But the huge difference involves gun homicides, which tells us a lot about the difference in availability of guns, particularly handguns.

In any event, while the United States looks like a dangerous place to live in comparison with other wealthy nations, some of the poorer nations have far higher homicide rates. In particular, a number of nations in Latin America and the Caribbean have much higher rates of violence and murder than the United States. Much of that violence comes from conflict around the illicit drug trade, which also provides the means to arm the combatants with deadly weapons.

How Much Does Gun Violence Cost America?

Generating a comprehensive measure of the societal impact of gun violence requires accounting for all the ways in which it affects the quality of life. The elevated rate of homicide, as important as it is, provides just the beginning of the calculation.

The traditional approach for valuing disease and injury is the "cost of illness" method, which misses or misconstrues much of what is important about gun violence. In essence, the cost-of-illness approach values people the way a farmer would value livestock, based on their productivity and the market value of their "output." (In recent years, analysts have added an estimate of the monetary value of lost enjoyment of life, as determined by the courts in wrongful injury or wrongful death lawsuits.) The result is a figure that is nearly proportional to the number of deaths, regardless of the circumstances of the death. The estimate does not make a distinction based on whether the victim committed suicide, for example, or was killed by a home intruder. Fortunately, there is an alternative approach, one generally favored by economists, that is forward looking and places a value on individuals' sense of safety as opposed to calculating the economic value of lives lost.[46]

In the individual-safety perspective, gun violence is like pollution, traffic, or poor schools. Anyone living in a neighborhood where gunshots are commonly heard is likely to be negatively affected. The possibility of being shot, or of a loved one's being shot, engenders fear and costly efforts at avoidance and self-protection—as when mothers keep their children from playing outside for fear of stray bullets. Property values suffer as people with sufficient means move to safer neighborhoods, and businesses suffer (and pull out of the neighborhood) as customers gravitate to shopping areas where they feel comfortable. Tax revenues are diverted to cover the financial costs of medically treating gunshot victims (usually at public expense) and of law-enforcement needs.

The costs of fear induced by gun violence are subjective, but they induce avoidance and prevention choices that have immediate financial costs. The value of safety is reflected in what people and agencies are willing to pay to reduce the perceived threat. In the public domain, we need only point to the Secret Service, with its multi-billion-dollar budget to protect the president and other top officials—primarily against being shot. No president has actually been shot since Ronald Reagan in 1981, but protection against the threat entails a real cost. An even more vivid example would be the expensive efforts undertaken by primary and secondary schools to protect against rampage shootings; such measures include everything from installing metal detectors, to regulating the kinds of backpacks that kids can carry, to spending classroom time in active-shooter drills.

With respect to private actions, the real-estate market provides some guidance about cost. We can in principle infer the value of safety from property values, comparing neighborhoods that are differentially affected by gun violence while controlling for other factors that may be relevant in the real-estate market. That approach is bound to be incomplete (since at best it can capture only the local place-related effects of gun violence) and poses an almost insurmountable statistical challenge (since other neighborhood problems are highly correlated with gun violence).

But those who are exposed to gun violence on a regular basis have a clear idea about the consequences. A research team from the Urban Institute interviewed residents and other stakeholders of high-crime communities in six cities. There was consensus that gun violence hurts housing prices, induces people to relocate when they can, and discourages new households and businesses from moving in.[47] Those who remain must adapt their daily routines and lifestyles to avoid violence. Specific actions might include staying home after dark and investing in various security measures. Retail businesses may have to lock their doors during business hours. As just one example, a Minneapolis stakeholder mentioned a beauty salon that had been a 25-year mainstay of a community but considered closing after a stray bullet came through the window and grazed the head of a customer.

The most striking evidence for the effect of gun violence on the local economy is in the revitalization of a number of cities that coincided with the great crime drop starting in the early 1990s.[48] New York is the most visible exemplar; the city was dangerous and declining in the 1970s and 1980s, and now has become safer than perhaps any time in its history. Harlem, Brooklyn, and the Bronx have been transformed with inflows of new residents and massive investments in real estate and retail businesses. It is only reasonable that safety is a precondition for economic success.

This sort of qualitative information is suggestive, but to quantify the costs of gun violence, a different sort of survey has been developed by economists. The goal is to estimate the public's willingness to pay for increased safety. The method, known as "contingent valuation," is widely used in valuing different aspects of the environment.

The first contingent valuation of the cost of gun violence asked respondents to a 1998 national survey whether they would be willing to vote for a measure that would reduce gun violence in their community by 30%, if it were going to cost them a specified amount (which was randomly varied across respondents).[49] The pattern of answers was interesting and quite reasonable; for example, respondents with children at home were willing to pay more than those without. The overall estimate was that such a reduction in gun violence would be worth $24 billion.[50] Multiplying up to a hypothetical 100% reduction suggests that interpersonal gun violence was at the time an $80 billion problem, and that the subjective costs were by no means confined to the people and communities that were at highest risk of injury—indeed, the willingness to pay for this reduction actually increased with income.

In sum, the threat of gun violence degrades the quality of life in affected communities. A reduction in gun violence has tangible value: not only more life, but also a higher quality of life. And that is worth a great deal.

How Does Exposure to Gun Violence Affect Mental Health?

Exposure to gun violence may have long-term detrimental effects on the well-being of survivors, witnesses, and even people who just feel a close connection to those directly affected. These impacts have been well documented among armed-services members. A particular focus has been post-traumatic stress disorder (PTSD), a lingering anxiety disorder characterized by having nightmares, reliving the experience, becoming hypervigilant, and feeling distant from friends and family members. The US Veterans Administration estimates PTSD prevalence rates of 30% for Vietnam veterans, and 10% to 15% for veterans of subsequent wars.[51] On the home front, the evidence is accumulating that people exposed to intensive violence, especially as children, may incur serious psychological problems, including PTSD. Anxiety, fearfulness, distrust, difficulty in concentrating—these traits, which obviously impede development into a successful adult, constitute a difficult-to-measure but important part of the social burden of gun violence.[52]

Exposure to violence can come in many forms. First, there are the survivors of gunshot assault. In recent years, about 1 in 100 black males have suffered a gunshot wound in a criminal attack before age 18, with lower rates for other demographic groups.[53] Most of these shootings will have a direct impact on others as well, including eyewitnesses, family members, and classmates. Of particular public concern has been the effect of mass shootings at schools and universities, where a high percentage of witnesses have been found to develop stress disorders, including PTSD.[54] A consistent finding is that the same exposure has disparate effects, with some victims more resilient than others. Among the most vulnerable are those with a preexisting anxiety disorder or depression.[55]

Since the Columbine massacre in 1999, approximately 200,000 students in elementary, middle, and high school have been directly exposed to mass shootings in their schools.[56] Far more common has been exposure to street violence by children in heavily impacted neighborhoods. Growing up with persistent fear and anxiety due to the routine sound of gunshots and direct knowledge of victims can have profound effects on children's mental health, not to mention their behavior and ability to learn. The same is true of exposure to violence at home. For young children especially, "Chronic activation of the body's stress response systems has been shown to disrupt the efficiency of brain circuitry and lead to both immediate and long-term problems in learning, behavior, and physical and mental health." [57] Children growing up in such environments are susceptible to school failure and later recruitment into risky activities, such as carrying guns.[58]

The consequences of chronic exposure to community violence during childhood are mediated by other circumstances. Identifying and quantifying a particular causal pathway is a challenge, since there is little possibility of experimentation. But sometimes natural experiments can provide good evidence. To give one example, social scientists at New York University investigated the effect of a nearby violent crime on students' performance on standardized tests that same week. They compared students who lived on a block where a violent event occurred just before the exam to students who lived on a block where a violent event occurred just after the exam. The two groups were similar in other respects, and the authors were able to demonstrate that those who had been exposed prior to the exam had a lower score on the English portion of the test; there was no effect on the math performance.[59] If a single event of this sort can affect academic performance, it is all too plausible that chronic exposure has broader and long-term effects.

A large percentage of children who grow up in violent communities are damaged by the experience. It is no surprise that some of them become violent and criminally active adults. This is but one pathway by which violence begets violence.

4

CAUSES OF GUN VIOLENCE

Who Can Be Trusted with a Gun?

A simplistic but common understanding of crime is that the population can be divided neatly into two groups, good guys and bad guys. In this view, the bad guys commit crime unless they are locked up, and the good guys are reliably law-abiding. This is a familiar storyline of the old movie Westerns, with the actors handily identified by whether they wore a white hat or a black hat. The "white hat, black hat" myth continues to permeate the discussion of gun violence and gun regulation. As National Rifle Association (NRA) chief executive Wayne LaPierre asserted: "The only thing that stops a bad guy with a gun is a good guy with a gun."[1]

Like most myths, this one has some element of truth. Serious criminal activity tends to be quite concentrated. If we could keep guns out of the hands of gang members, predatory criminals, and violence-prone people (including domestic batterers), then the number of murders would be substantially reduced. But how are these and other high-risk people to be identified in advance of their shooting someone?

The federal Gun Control Act of 1968 attempts to accomplish just that. It specifies 10 categories of people who are banned from buying or possessing a firearm. The list includes anyone who has been convicted of a felony (e.g., a crime with possible sentence exceeding one year), is under indictment for a felony, is a fugitive from justice, has been convicted of a misdemeanor crime of domestic violence or is under a restraining order, is an illegal alien, has been adjudicated as a "mental defective" (the unfortunate term in the law for those with severe mental disability or illness), is a drug abuser, or has been dishonorably discharged from the military. There are also age restrictions on purchase and possession.

One problem is that this list misses a large share of those who end up committing serious crimes with guns. For example, a study of adult murder defendants in Chicago found that while most of them had extensive records of arrests and convictions for minor crimes, only 40% of them had actually been convicted of a felony.[2] Most of the others were not disqualified by federal law from buying a gun legally. So in practice it is not so easy to tell the white hats from the black hats based on official records.

The list of prohibited categories could be extended to include, say, conviction of any violent misdemeanor or drug violation or one or more driving-under-the-influence (DUI) convictions. Perhaps we could think of those as the "gray hats." A broader list of disqualifications would ensure fewer dangerous people could legally possess a gun but would come at the cost of denying gun ownership to some people who are relatively reliable.

We can also imagine reversing the presumption about gun rights. Federal law is guided by the premise that owning a gun is a right granted to all adults who are legal residents of the United States, *unless* they are disqualified. A quite different approach would be to treat gun ownership as a privilege to be reserved for those who can demonstrate that they are trustworthy. This approach has been incorporated in state law for handgun permits. For example, in North Carolina a law dating back to 1921 required that anyone buying a handgun would have to get a permit from the sheriff and that the permit would be issued only to those who could produce two character witnesses and demonstrate a home-defense need for the gun.[3] (These specific requirements are no longer in force.) There has been a broad retreat from such stringent requirements in the last three decades. A remaining exception is New York City, where residents must obtain a license to possess a handgun, and only those of good moral character (as determined by a background investigation) qualify for the permit. The Supreme Court's 2008 decision in *District of Columbia v. Heller* made clear that gun ownership is not an unfettered right but that it demands a higher standard of legal protection than a mere privilege would garner.

The question of who can be trusted with a gun tends to play out differently in the regulation of hunting. States often require that hunters pass both written tests and field tests demonstrating their knowledge of the rules and of weapons handling. Such requirements are nonexistent for buying a gun—and in most states for carrying it in public.

Incidentally, the question of who can be trusted with a gun is not just a matter for state and federal law; it is also an issue for family and friends. Should you let your child visit a home where you know guns are stored? Should Granddad be encouraged to give up his gun now that he is becoming senile or depressed? Can a wife whose husband often threatens her with his gun persuade him to give it up? Will old friends continue to go hunting together when one of them has started to drink too much in the duck blind?

Do More Guns Cause More Crime—or Less?

Criminals rarely buy their guns from a licensed dealer—most obtain them by buying or borrowing from family members or friends, by stealing, or by making a connection in the underground market. (Fewer than 10% of prisoners in national surveys who admit to having a firearm indicate that they purchased it from a store.[4]) Where firearms ownership is widespread, it will be easier for delinquents and gang members and predatory criminals to obtain a gun. A teen looking to appropriate a firearm in Mississippi, where 60% of the households have at least one, probably need look no farther than his parents' closet or dresser drawer; the search may take a lot longer for a teen in Massachusetts, where just 13% of households are armed. The same differences show up in other informal channels by which guns find their way into the hands of youths or felons or others who are disqualified from buying them from a gun store.

So we expect that dangerous people will find it easier to obtain a firearm in a gun-rich environment than in one where gun ownership is relatively unusual. This "availability" hypothesis finds support in a variety of scientific studies. Among the findings: There is a positive statistical association across urban jurisdictions between the prevalence of gun ownership and (1) the theft of firearms in burglary,[5] (2) the likelihood that teenage males carry guns,[6] and (3) the percentage of robberies committed with guns.[7]

However, the interpretation of such results is in some doubt. Gun-rich jurisdictions, such as Mississippi, are systematically different in various ways from jurisdictions with relatively few guns, such as Massachusetts. These differences make it difficult to demonstrate that it is gun density per se that accounts for the differences in criminal use of guns. The usual approach for addressing this problem has been to statistically control for a few other state characteristics, such as population density, poverty, and the age and racial composition of the population. But these variables never explain very much of the geographic variation in crime rates, suggesting that the list of available control variables is inadequate to the task. Also unclear is whether widespread gun ownership is the cause or effect of an area's crime problem, since high crime rates may induce residents to buy guns for self-protection.

Some of the problems with cross-sectional studies can be overcome by using panel data—measurements at multiple points in time—to compare *changes* in gun ownership with *changes* in crime across jurisdictions. Compared with Massachusetts, Mississippi may have much higher homicide rates year after year for reasons that cannot be fully explained from existing data sources. But by comparing changes rather than levels, we implicitly control for any unmeasured differences across states that are relatively fixed over time, such as a "Southern culture of violence." The best available evidence suggests that a change in gun prevalence has a direct effect on weapon choice in robbery and assault, and most importantly, that the presence of more guns leads to more gun homicides (and more homicides overall).[8]

Finally, it is worth emphasizing that the conclusion is not "more guns, more crime." Research findings have been quite consistent in demonstrating that gun prevalence has little if any systematic relationship to the overall rates of assault and robbery. The strong finding that emerges from this research is that gun use *intensifies* violence, making it more likely that the victim of an assault or robbery will die. The positive effect is on the murder rate, not on the overall violent-crime rate. In other words: more guns, more deaths.

Is Gun Violence Linked to Other Types of Violence?

Yes. And it follows that if we could curtail the underlying causes of criminal violence, then guns would do less damage. In fact, that is precisely our experience with violent crime during the last generation. A sharp drop in overall rates of violence has been coupled with a similar drop in gun violence. Robberies, rapes, and aggravated assaults declined by 82% between 1993 and 2017, from 20.7 per 1,000 persons age 12 or older to 3.8 per 1,000.[9] The use of firearms in violent crime followed the same trend during this great crime drop.[10]

The same point could be made by comparing different neighborhoods. Gun crime is a devastating problem in Chicago's high-poverty inner-city neighborhoods and a relatively minor problem in its wealthier neighborhoods. The difference is not so much in the availability of guns, but rather in the overall amount of violence. It is the combination of violence and guns that produces a high murder rate.

Without a doubt, then, one strategy for reducing gun violence is to reduce criminal violence generally. If we would take steps to reduce alcohol and drug abuse, offer better treatment for mental illness, reduce school dropout rates, and deploy police resources more strategically, crime rates would fall further and guns would be of correspondingly less concern. But when and where violent crime is a problem, we cannot afford to ignore the role that guns play in intensifying that violence.

Suicide is also an important concern closely associated with gun availability. And as in the case of criminal violence, it is true in principle that we could reduce the gun-suicide problem by addressing the conditions that lead people to give serious consideration to ending their lives—or bring into counseling those who do consider suicide. The US military has given increasingly high priority to suicide prevention (with uncertain results) as rates have climbed during the many years of war in Iraq, Syria, and Afghanistan. The stresses of serving in war zones lead to post-traumatic stress disorder, drug abuse, and other risk factors for suicide—and the ready availability of firearms translates these risks into high death rates.

What Do Israel and Switzerland Teach Us About Guns and Violence?

Switzerland and Israel are often used by pro-gun advocates as evidence of the effectiveness of a heavily armed public in combating crime and terrorism. A variety of claims are made about these countries to the effect that firearms possession is prevalent and largely unregulated or (in the case of Israel) actively promoted. But the reality is quite different. In fact, firearms are more closely regulated and scarcer in these countries than in the United States. Gun policy in both countries recognizes that civilian firearms possession and carrying pose a threat to public safety.

It is true that both countries have a large military presence. In Israel most citizens are obligated to serve in the military—32 months for men, 24 months for women—and afterward many are obligated to serve in the reserves, depending on need. But this high level of mobilization has little effect on gun availability away from military bases. Beginning in 2006, the Israeli Defense Forces changed their policy so that most personnel do not carry their weapons while on weekend leave. The intended result, apparently achieved, was to reduce the rate of suicide. Otherwise, Israel has a low rate of firearms ownership and possession, indicated by the fact that less than 10% of suicides nationwide are committed with firearms compared with 50% in the United States.[11] The government requires all civilian gun owners to be licensed and issues permits only to those with a demonstrated need. The government keeps a registry of licenses, which must be renewed every three years. All gun transfers are to be registered with the government. Gun carrying, either concealed or in the open, requires a permit.

In Switzerland, gun ownership is more common than in Israel but still comprehensively regulated. All able-bodied Swiss men are required to perform military service from age 19 to 34 (up to age 50 for general officers), which for the most part consists of reserve duties. The commitment to national preparedness is reflected in the fact that target shooting is a national sport. (The celebrated purpose of good marksmanship is national defense, not self-defense.) While in the reserve, men are issued a personal weapon, in most cases an assault rifle, to be stored at home or (if they choose) in the local armory. They are entitled to keep their military weapon after leaving service, but only after it is converted to semiautomatic firing mode and registered with the federal government. The army stopped issuing ammunition to reservists for home storage in 2008.

Civilian weaponry is regulated by the Swiss federal government and the cantons. Automatic weapons are banned, a government-issued acquisition permit is required to purchase a handgun from a dealer, and private transfers require that the seller determine the identity of the buyer and keep detailed records about the transaction. Those seeking a permit to carry for self-defense purposes must pass a series of tests demonstrating their knowledge of gun safety and use and make an argument that the firearm is needed in response to a specific risk.

The relative scarcity of available firearms, especially handguns, in Switzerland is indicated by the fact that only 20% of suicides are committed with firearms, as compared with half in the United States.[12]

Switzerland and Israel have lower rates of violence than the United States, but it is not because they have more guns or more gun carrying. Just the reverse is true. These countries illustrate the general point made previously: Gun violence requires both guns and violence. Violence rates in these countries are much lower than in the United States, regardless of weapon type. Guns are comprehensively regulated, and the prevalence of gun ownership is lower than in the United States.

Do Cultural Differences Help Account for Differences in Gun Violence?

For more than a century, "culture" has been invoked to explain different levels of violence within the United States and between the United States and other nations. But what does it mean to blame "culture" for differing levels of violence in general and gun violence in particular? And how might we evaluate cultural explanations against other types of explanations?

In the present context the term "culture" is akin to widely shared belief systems—or in the words of the historian David Hackett Fischer, "folkways"—governing the appropriate response to threats to one's person and to the social order generally. As we discuss in Chapter 8, there is a strong American tradition of associating guns with protection, and these ideas took root early. In Appalachia, Fischer argues, eighteenth-century Scotch-Irish settlers brought with them a belief that violence was necessary to "conquer their own peace."[13] In the Deep South, violent folkways emerged from a plantation system in which individual status depended on the often violent domination of others. Westward expansion brought lawlessness among cattlemen, frontiersmen, and miners, and violence among Anglos, Native Americans, and Hispanics. Even after slavery was abolished, the frontier was settled, and Southerners moved north and vice versa, these folkways persisted.

Cultural explanations tend to be deployed not to explain crime in general (rape, robbery, domestic violence, etc.) but rather to account for particular *types* of crime, namely assaults and homicides arising from personal disputes between unrelated people. These encounters are said to stem from a "culture of honor" that originated in the South and is rooted in age-old status grievances exacerbated by a "siege mentality."[14] How else to explain why, historically, rates of suicide and property crimes have been lower in the South but rates of homicide have been higher? "It is the 'personal difficulties' with deadly weapons, street-fights, and affrays in the Southern States that swell the number of homicides out of all proportion," wrote the journalist H. V. Redfield in his classic 1880 study, *Homicide: North and South.*[15]

Culture-based theories have great intuitive appeal, but they are tricky to prove empirically. One problem is that belief systems are hard to quantify and often seem to go hand in hand with other factors that facilitate violence, such as disadvantage and the breakdown of order. Thus, while early studies blamed high rates of violence on Southern culture, later scholars found that effect was just a product of the South's unusually large rates of poverty, illiteracy, lack of education, and other afflictions. (More recent work has insisted that, even after accounting for these problems, the "Southern effect" persists.[16]) Even at the individual level, it is hard to sort out cultural folkways from other drivers of violent encounters. Take the paradigmatic nineteenth-century Southern ruffians squabbling over an insult or the modern gang member who pulls his weapon in response to a sideways glance. If shots are fired, what was the underlying cause? A widely accepted cultural understanding of how men are to resolve disputes? An instinctive psychological reaction? A quick cost/benefit calculation about how best to survive the encounter? A subconscious adaptation to ineffective systems of law and order? It's hard to know.

Muddling things further, violence rates can be very different across regions that look pretty similar. Take the filmmaker Michael Moore's examination of the United States and Canada, neighboring nations that share a British heritage and frontier traditions, high levels of economic development, open democratic governance, even popular culture—but have very different levels of gun violence. In *Bowling for Columbine*, Moore suggests that Canadians have less gun violence because they are less volatile and more deferential to collective, consensus approaches to problem solving, a common characterization. But it's also true that Canada has much stricter gun laws than the United States and much lower rates of handgun ownership. So is Canadian cultural "niceness" keeping the gun homicide rate low? Or are Canada's gun laws keeping matters in check? Or is it both—the culture gave rise to the laws, which reinforce the culture?

No one can say for sure, at least as of now. But circumstantial evidence leads us to question "culture" as the overriding explanation for violence (though we believe it may matter in certain circumstances). Our general skepticism stems from the fact that while the US non-gun homicide rate in 2017 was 42% higher than Canada's, the US gun homicide rate was fully 510% higher (see Chapter 3). Likewise, within the United States, the exceptional rate of Southern violence is really a problem of gun violence, not violence by other means. (The 2017 homicide rate was 48% higher in the South than elsewhere, a gap almost entirely due to the difference in gun homicide rates.[17]) If cultural predispositions were to blame for violence, we would expect to see disparities between the United States and peer nations, and between the American South and other regions, in *non-gun* assaults and homicides. But where these differences exist, they tend to be relatively small.

Another challenge to culture-based theories is that, while folkways are supposed to stick around from generation to generation, homicide rates have fluctuated greatly *within* geographic areas, and *between* them, over time. For example, within the United States, homicide rates were comparatively high in the years around the American Revolution, hit an all-time low in the decades after the War of 1812 (at least outside the slave South), rose again in the Civil War era, then declined, then rose again.[18] Between 1993 and 2014, the homicide rate declined by half, even though American culture has changed little. Making matters more complicated, these broad trends mask large, often divergent, patterns between regions and racial groups that are inconsistent with "sticky" cultural explanations. Looking across nations, the role of culture becomes even more puzzling. The United States now has a homicide rate 7 times that of other wealthy nations (and a gun homicide rate that is 25 times as high).[19] But in the first half of the nineteenth century, US rates, at least in the North, were on a par with, or even lower than, Canada's and western Europe's.[20]

So culture is an inadequate explanation for different levels of violence in general, or gun violence in particular. But we are persuaded that there is something to these theories, in part because of creative recent work on the longstanding puzzle of Southern homicide and gang violence. Most straightforwardly, while white Southern men (the honor culture's standard-bearers) don't differ much from their non-Southern brethren in general attitudes toward force and violence, these Southerners are comparatively supportive of using violence in particular situations where honor is at stake—for example, in defense of the home and in response to an affront.[21] Southern males attending college in the North are more likely than their classmates to get measurably angry when provoked.[22] And cities and rural areas with large numbers of Southern white transplants have unusually high rates of argument-based homicides, all else being equal.[23] Careful research on Northern urban gangs makes a persuasive argument that cultural codes of preemptive aggression can spread quickly within these tightly knit groups.[24]

So where does this leave us? Culture—understood in this context to signify beliefs about, and ways of handling, personal threats—probably does account for some of the "excess" lethal violence that we see in the American South and in urban areas. Cultural folkways may also account for differences in lethal violence across nations, though other factors—such as economic development, governance structures, and access to guns—no doubt play a much stronger role. We are inclined to see cultural beliefs as one of an interlocking and mutually supportive constellation of factors that influence how violent or peaceful a community, state, or nation is.

Does Violence on the Screen Cause Violence in the Real World?

As early as the 1920s, commentators debated whether movies—then called "talkies" because sound had just been introduced—were "lowering the moral consciousness of youth" and contributing to delinquency, homicide, and crime waves generally.[25] Scholars undertook studies and concluded that movies probably had little if any effect on misbehavior.[26] These researchers surmised that delinquents naturally liked violent movies. Of course, much has changed since then—including the advent of television, video games, streaming video, and online do-it-yourself video platforms, such as YouTube and Facebook. Interestingly, however, the debate over "talkies" in the early twentieth century identified the core questions that bedevil us to this day and foreshadowed a general takeaway: It's complicated.

As with any question of cause and effect, it's important to understand the story. In social science, we sometimes think of "cause" as meaning "heightens the likelihood of."[27] If factor X heightens the risk of behavior Y, we want to know whether the impact is statistically meaningful (that is, unlikely to be a chance result), and if so, how large the effect is (which might tell us whether a policy intervention is worthwhile). Further, we want to know *why* X is associated with Y—what mechanisms explain the relationship? In this regard studies of so-called media effects have identified a number of possibilities. The media decide who is worthy of public attention. If you're feeling left out, you can dress up like another "loser" who has gained notoriety, perform your own version of his violent action, and bask in the fame. Another related possibility is that the media can create "scripts" or "schemas" that provide guides to troubled people in resolving their problems. If you're being bullied, you don't go to the counselor—you shoot up the school. If your wife leaves you, you don't drown your sorrows—you shoot up her workplace. A third possibility is that violent media actually change the way you think, feel, and behave—especially after prolonged exposure.[28] If you shoot a lot of people through video games, eventually you will become desensitized to violence, see aggressive responses as normal, and lose any moral qualms about using violence in your own life.

These mechanisms purportedly link media violence to actual violence. The mechanisms are plausible enough, but it's harder than one might imagine to validate them, let alone to establish that they explain a significant amount of gun violence in America or the world. Establishing a conclusive link between media violence and real-world violence is complicated, for several reasons.

First, and most obviously, many forces operate on and through individuals to increase their chances of behaving aggressively or violently. These risk factors may involve psychiatric disorders, socioeconomic disadvantage, substance abuse, abusive or neglectful parents, exposure to community violence and violent peers, and so forth. Consumption of violent media may be one of many risk factors connecting an individual to a violent act. But most researchers believe that a cumulation of risk factors—perhaps moderated by positive influences such as caring mentors, parents, and communities—turns out to make the difference in individual behavior.[29]

A second complication is what we mean by "media" when we talk about media effects on violence. Studies often lump them together, but television, online platforms, and video games differ in important ways. They attract different audiences, are subject to different rules about the presentation of violence, and command different amounts of attention. The 1950s TV Western *Gunsmoke* is not the same as the twenty-first-century video game "Postal 2." Presumably they have differing effects on viewers.

Third, so-called media effects are hard to measure. Typically, a researcher can't just round up a bunch of young people (we are usually concerned about violence among young people), put them in a study that randomly exposes them to violent (or nonviolent) television or movies, and track them over long periods of time to see how aggressively they behave. If the researcher takes a different route—by asking people about their media consumption and aggressive behaviors—she can't be sure that either will be reported accurately. And even if the researcher trusts the young people's self-reported answers and finds a relationship between media use and behavior, it's hard to tell what is causing what. Maybe violent media consumption causes aggressive behavior, or maybe people who are disposed to being aggressive seek out violent media. Statistical methods can help sort out the direction of these relationships, but even sophisticated techniques are imperfect.

Fourth, the best studies by the leading researchers reach conflicting results.[30] One of these conflicting results is whether the results, in fact, conflict.[31] There is actually a lively debate among experts about whether media affect violence, and if so, by how much. In part the debate hinges on what kind of violence we're talking about and over what period of time. If spending lots of time playing violent video games makes a young person more likely to lash out in the moment, that's of some concern. If it makes him more likely to get into the occasional fistfight, that's of greater concern. If it turns him into a chronically belligerent adult, that's of even greater concern. If it causes him to snap and massacre large numbers of people at the local school, then we are beyond the level of "even greater concern." To oversimplify a complex and rich body of work, the research on the links between (some kinds of) media and low-level aggression is persuasive, while there is no real reason to draw a direct line from violent-media consumption to mass shootings.

Fifth, even when laboratory studies find media effects on individual aggression, the finding may not translate to the real world or explain much of its violence.[32] A belligerent answer that a subject might give to a researcher, in the moment, after a media message in an artificial setting, may not be the same response he would have after watching a violent movie with his friends in a college dorm room. Laboratories are not homes or neighborhoods, and experimental subjects are not people operating in the real world. The vast majority of gun violence consists of disputes over turf and drug markets, attacks on romantic partners, and suicides. The role of violent television or other media in contributing to these situations remains difficult to identify.

Finally, the question of whether violent media exacerbate real-world violence depends on the level of analysis, whether individual or aggregate. Studies that look at subjects in a laboratory setting may find that exposure to violent content increases aggressive thoughts or feelings. Likewise, studies that survey people on their consumption of violent media might find that more consumption is associated with a greater likelihood that the person will act aggressively, especially if provoked. But studies that look beyond the individual to society-level trends—for example, in video game usage and violent crime—may find no relationship between them, or even a counterintuitive trend in which violent media usage increases while violent crime decreases.[33]

As we said, it's complicated. In the next few sections, we talk about a few specific findings that may help you understand why.

Does Violent Entertainment Contribute to Real-World Violence?

The evidence is inconclusive for all the reasons discussed above. With that warning, we find that most of the research suggests that watching violent television has a modest effect on aggression, more so in children than in adults and more so in the short term than in the long term. What accounts for these effects? We can only speculate. Watching dramatic violence on TV may encourage actual violence by teaching kids that aggression is an acceptable means of solving problems and providing examples for them to follow. Televised violence may also numb viewers to the effects of real-life violence on others, making such violence easier to commit.

One study looked at the home lives, peer interactions, and TV viewing habits of 550 elementary-school children who came of age in the 1970s and 1980s, then tracked most of them down in the early 1990s to see how their lives had turned out.[34] The scholars were interested in whether childhood TV viewing would predict later abusive or even criminal behavior. They found that the amount of violent TV the study subjects had watched as a child—and the degree to which they identified with violent characters and viewed TV as reflective of real life—significantly predicted violent behavior in adulthood. These relationships held up even after the authors statistically "controlled for" the effects of some other influences, such as violence and poor parenting in the childhood home, childhood poverty, and adult viewing of violent TV.

Another study looked at consumption of violent media around the world. One critique of media effects research has been that these effects are culture specific—violent television in Japan, for example, might play out differently, and have different impacts on viewers, than violent television in the United

States. Contrary to this hypothesis, the study found that media effects on adolescent aggression are broadly similar across countries as diverse as China, Romania, and Australia.[35]

The evidence that violent media affect aggression is suggestive. But nonexperimental studies such as these must be viewed with skepticism, as they aren't equipped to capture the full range of individual characteristics that might drive both media consumption and violent behavior. Quasi-experimental studies looking at changes in violence levels after television was introduced into a society have found mixed results—in some places, TV appeared to increase societal violence, while in other places there was no effect.[36] And counterintuitively, at least one study has suggested that watching violent television might actually insulate kids from criminal activity—since they're home watching TV instead of carousing with the local street gang.[37]

That said, we take seriously the findings that TV adds a bit of fuel to a fire that, as any comparison with America's peer countries makes clear, needs no additional stoking. Policymakers have acted accordingly by introducing a TV rating system that guides parents away from shows inappropriate for kids. In Chapters 7 and 12, we discuss policy interventions that are arguably more consequential for reducing gun violence.

Should We Worry About Violent Video Games?

When teenaged boys shoot up schools, the question invariably arises: Are violent video games partly to blame? The claim is plausible enough, in part because the timing works. Highly graphic games, including the "first-person shooter" genre, became popular in the mid- to late 1990s, around the time of the first wave of mass shootings in otherwise quiet schools. Several rampage shooters, including those at the Columbine, Sandy Hook, and Marjory Stoneman Douglas schools, were reportedly gamers, in some cases obsessively so. And the connection between video and real-life violence is easy to imagine. First-person shooter games absorb youngsters in a fantasy world where guns mean power, and violence has neither costs nor consequences. In a 2017 poll, 60% of Americans thought gun violence in video games contributed to real-life gun violence.[38]

On the other hand, skeptics look at larger trends and wonder how bad video games really could be for society. Gaming has taken hold in America over the last three decades, roughly coinciding with the remarkable drop in youth violence that began in the early 1990s.[39] And gaming is wildly popular in countries such as the Netherlands and South Korea, which have very little violence. Indeed, a *Washington Post* analysis found no relationship between per capita gaming expenditures and violent crime rates across 10 advanced industrialized nations.[40] Then there's the obvious fact that millions of kids play violent games and manage to lead peaceful lives. Even scholars who worry about video games would agree that students who shoot up schools have problems far more serious than an unsavory choice in recreation.

What does the research say? Evidence is growing that violent video games may have some effect on antisocial behavior. One review of 350 studies involving 130,000 total participants found that intensive engagement with violent video games increases an individual's risk of aggression and adversarial thoughts and beliefs, while also reducing empathy and helping behaviors. The size of the effect varies depending on how the question is studied, but the cumulative evidence is fairly consistent and compelling.[41] Other work has found that intensive violent gaming reduces empathy toward others, desensitizes people to violence at least in the short term, increases the likelihood of wrongly interpreting others' behavior as hostile, and exacerbates bias against ethnic groups represented as on-screen villains.[42] Some research suggests that intensive playing of violent video games can lead to more than casual aggression, including hitting others and fighting,[43] dating violence,[44] and juvenile delinquency.[45]

Although these findings are consistent and the studies rigorous, it's important to note that the academy sometimes suffers from "publication bias," the tendency of scholarly journals to publish studies that find causal effects (for example, video games cause aggression) and to decline to publish studies finding no such effects. Some scholars have suggested that publication bias is a significant problem in the field of media violence and that if studies with null findings were more readily published, the case for media effects would be very weak indeed.[46]

Nevertheless, since 1994 video games have been subject to a rating system similar to the one used for movies to help guide parents toward age-appropriate products. In 2005 California went further, passing a law banning sales or rentals of violent video games to minors. The Supreme Court overturned the law in 2011 on the grounds that it violated the First Amendment. In the majority opinion, Justice Antonin Scalia noted that the wicked queen tries to poison Snow White, and Hansel and Gretel off their captor by baking her in an oven, but we don't ban *Grimms' Fairy Tales*.[47]

As the discussion above suggests, the question of whether on-screen violence contributes to real-life violence divides scholars into different camps. The debate hinges in part on whether the researcher is looking at broad social trends or individual-level behaviors. For purposes of the gun debate, it's perhaps helpful to distinguish among low-level aggression (pushing back when you get shoved), low-level violence (fighting), and serious violence (criminal assault, rape, etc.). There is a persuasive body of evidence that consuming violent media is a modest risk factor for casual aggression, and some evidence that violent media contribute to low-level violence—particularly in kids already at risk. But as yet there is no persuasive evidence that video games or other graphic media are causing the sort of social mayhem for which they are blamed in moments of national trauma.

No doubt studies will continue to look for linkages between gaming and violence. As we discuss in Chapter 6, however, policies aimed at other aspects of America's gun violence problem are likely to have a greater impact.

Does News Coverage Encourage Copycat Crimes? Suicides?

A week after the Sandy Hook school shooting, the NRA's Wayne LaPierre, excoriated the mass media for their coverage of the tragedy: "How many more copycats are waiting in the wings," he asked, "for their moment of fame from a national media machine that rewards them with wall-to-wall attention and a sense of identity that they crave, while provoking others to try to make their mark?"[48] LaPierre may have had many reasons to take the spotlight off the Sandy Hook tragedy, but his concern that it could inspire others is grounded in a long history of scholarly research.

In pioneering work conducted in the 1890s, the French sociologist Gustave Le Bon argued that misbehavior is contagious. Like a bad cold, it spreads from person to person. The media can help the contagion to spread far and wide. As early as the 1920s, people worried that sensationalist journalism was breeding "an unwholesome curiosity about criminals" and contributing to "the growth of criminality."[49] In the modern era, social scientists have found the copycat phenomenon to be a factor in airline hijackings, fire setting, product-tampering hoaxes, and crime generally. However, most work in recent years has focused on two phenomena: mass shootings and suicides.

Scholarly research, as well as a growing amount of anecdotal evidence, suggests that mass shootings follow a pattern suggestive of a contagious disease. And in this contagion, the 1999 attack at Columbine High School—in which 2 students killed 12 classmates and a teacher, as well as themselves—serves as a sort of Patient Zero, the one that infected many others.[50] One study estimated that as of 2015, the Columbine attack had "inspired at least 74 plots or attacks across 30 states."[51] About two-thirds of these planned attacks were thwarted, but in the 21 carried out, 89 people were killed and another 126 wounded. The study found that "in at least 14 cases, the suspects aimed to attack on the anniversary of Columbine. (Twelve of these plots were thwarted; two attacks ultimately took place on different dates.) Individuals in 13 cases indicated their goal was to surpass the Columbine body count. And in at least 10 cases the suspects referred to [the Columbine shooters] as heroes, idols, martyrs, or God."[52]

The list of Columbine-inspired events includes some of the nation's most deadly school shootings, including those at Virginia Tech (2007), Sandy Hook (2012), and Santa Fe, Texas (2018).[53] So-called Columbiners, plotters who modeled themselves in some way on the 1999 shooters, constitute what one security professional called "a cult following unlike anything I've ever seen before."[54] The Columbine shooters are not alone in this regard; other rampage shooters also have served as "role models" for subsequent assailants.[55]

The most-studied copycat phenomenon is suicide. Here, the evidence is strong and consistent, both within the United States and internationally: Reports of suicide in the media lead to spikes in suicide rates in patterns hard to explain by random chance. In an analysis of more than 50 studies, one scholar found that factors most likely to set off copycats include media coverage of celebrity suicides and suicides by women.[56] Tellingly, one study found that suicides declined during a long newspaper strike.[57] In Austria, after a spike in suicides committed by jumping in front of subway trains, the media tempered their coverage, and these incidents dropped and remained low.[58]

In response to consistent research findings, US public health agencies, along with public-health–oriented nonprofits, have endorsed guidelines that discourage using "suicide" in the headline, reporting on suicide "epidemics," or showcasing grieving relatives or suicide survivors—all types of coverage that could encourage suicidal behavior.[59] Instead, the guidelines suggest that the media avoid glamorizing the victim and focus on how treatment can be effective. Likewise, gun violence prevention groups have begun a "No Notoriety" campaign, initiated by the parents of a young man killed in the 2012 Aurora theater attack, to urge the press not to name assailants in mass shootings.

Although studies of media effects typically look at copycat crimes, one study examined how news coverage of traumatic events—in this case the 2013 Boston Marathon bombing and the 2016 Pulse nightclub massacre—affect people who follow the news.[60] The study found that coverage of these events can create a cycle of distress, whereby people become increasingly anxious with each succeeding event.

What Do We Know About the Connection Between Mental Health and Gun Violence?

The relationship between violence and mental illness is a complicated and sensitive topic—one that is receiving long-overdue attention from policymakers and gun violence prevention groups.[61]

Making sense of this topic requires clarity regarding definitions. Most broadly, to say that someone is "mentally ill" could refer to any one of the hundreds of conditions that the American Psychiatric Association defines in its *Diagnostic and Statistical Manual of Mental Disorders* (DSM). These conditions vary widely in their severity and types of symptoms—from anxiety, to eating problems, to compulsive internet gaming, for example. Alternatively, in discussions related to gun violence prevention, the term "mental illness" usually refers more narrowly to a short list of serious conditions that greatly impair normal thought, mood regulation, and social functioning over the life course if not treated successfully. Among these are schizophrenia-spectrum disorders, severe bipolar disorder, and major depressive disorder. Alcohol and drug use disorders are also included in DSM, and often co-occur with other major psychiatric disorders, but historically have been viewed differently—sometimes as a personal failing rather than an illness. In any event, a discussion of the importance of "mental illness" in gun violence requires clarity regarding just what is included in the mental illness category.

To understand the importance of mental illness and substance abuse as contributing factors to gun violence, it is useful to ask two questions. One is whether some or all of these conditions cause elevated rates of gun violence. A second question is what fraction of gun violence is accounted for by mental illness. The two questions are logically related according to how common the illness is within the general population. People with schizophrenia have higher rates of violence than people without mental illness, but since schizophrenia is a rare disorder in the population—affecting less than 1% of adults—the impact of schizophrenia on the overall volume of violence is low.[62] Substance use disorders are associated with higher rates of violence, and since these conditions are also more common than illnesses such as schizophrenia, a larger percentage of serious violence is committed by people with substance use disorders.

Finally, there is the question of policy: How should mental illness be considered in deciding whether a person is too at risk of violence to possess a firearm? Answering this question involves weighing the likely benefits to society against the costs to individuals. Prohibiting all persons with a psychiatric diagnosis from possessing guns would prevent some suicides and homicides—but at the cost of restricting the rights of millions of law-abiding, non-dangerous individuals. Such a policy could also add to the stigma associated with mental illness by reinforcing the false belief among the general public that mentally ill individuals are generally dangerous. Using much narrower criteria, the federal Gun Control Act specifies lifetime disqualification for gun possession by people who have been involuntarily committed to a hospital for treatment of mental illness. The logic of such a prohibition is that dangerousness to self or others is embedded in the criteria for involuntary commitment, and there is also legal due process—a court hearing—when a person is subject to involuntary commitment. A number of states have adopted "extreme risk protection orders," or "red-flag laws," which authorize a judge to temporarily remove guns from a person who is deemed to be going through an episode making him unsafe to self or others.[63] The removal typically follows a petition by a family member or police officer. For policymakers, the question is how well these regulations address the underlying goal of gun violence prevention and at what cost.

Here we provide a brief review of the best work on these complicated questions, with the caveat that researchers have much to learn and the findings are nuanced and sometimes inconsistent.

Studies have found that people with certain types of serious mental illness, including schizophrenia, bipolar disorder, and major depression, are at increased risk of committing violence against others.[64] A review of more than 20 studies estimated that seriously mentally ill people are three to five times more likely to engage in violent behavior than are people without such a diagnosis.[65] The risks are further increased if the individual is not undergoing medical treatment, is facing stressful life issues such as unemployment and poverty, is exposed to violence in his current social environment, was a victim of violence during early life, or is abusing drugs or alcohol. Indeed, alcohol and drug misuse are not uncommon in people with other psychological disorders. In people who both abuse substances and have another major mental disorder, research suggests that the substance abuse typically contributes more than the other disorder does to violent behavior.[66]

Even though mental illness may be an independent contributor to violent behavior, other personal characteristics—such as a person's age, socioeconomic status, and history of criminal behavior—are stronger predictors of whether he will harm others.[67] People with serious, diagnosed mental illness commit only a small fraction of violent crime—perhaps 5% or less[68]—and the vast majority of people with such disorders who aren't abusing substances will never run afoul of the law.[69] A study of nearly 1,000 former mental-hospital patients found that just 2% committed a violent act with a gun after their release, and just 1% used the gun on a stranger.[70] Those rates are far higher than for the population at large, but this group does not account for a large share of the gun violence problem simply because relatively few people have been in a mental hospital. In other words, if we could cure everyone hospitalized for serious mental illness, we would notice very little reduction in violent crime.

The link between mental illness and gun violence is greatly affected by environmental factors. In comparing the United States to other wealthy nations, the most obvious environmental factor is the availability of guns. There is no reason to believe that the United States differs from, say, the United Kingdom when it comes to the prevalence of mental illness, yet the United Kingdom has only a few dozen gun homicides per year compared to 15,000 in the United States. The rate of gun homicide in the United States is more than 100 times the United Kingdom's. The obvious difference is the relative scarcity of guns in the United Kingdom. The same comparison, with the same general conclusion, could be made with every other wealthy nation. In the United States, violence associated with mental illness (including alcohol and drug use disorder) is far more likely to involve guns because guns are so readily available.

The topic of mental health typically arises in the aftermath of a mass shooting. An indiscriminate killing spree in a school, theater, or other public place is not the behavior of a normal person. That many of these killers are psychologically troubled is reinforced by the fact that most of them commit suicide or continue shooting until they themselves are shot. But a comprehensive study of 63 mass-casualty events from 2000 to 2013 found that most of the perpetrators (up to 75%) had not been diagnosed as mentally ill before the shooting.[71] This finding may reflect an important aspect of the problem, which is that for the most part, people are not provided with a psychological assessment unless they choose to seek one. Treatment can only prevent gun violence for those who volunteer for treatment or somehow come under court order to seek treatment.

People with serious mental illness are more likely to be victims of violence than perpetrators of it.[72] A Swedish study, for example, found that people with mental illness had a fivefold risk of death by homicide relative to the general population.[73] Likewise, suicides in the United States outnumber homicides by more than two to one. Depression, substance abuse, or other psychiatric disorders are estimated to be a factor in some 80% to 90% of self-inflicted deaths.[74] Indeed, the connection between mental illness and suicide is more pervasive and profound than for interpersonal violence.

Scholars who study the connection between violence and mental health have begun to question whether US public policies are well designed to balance society's interests in both individual rights and public safety.[75] Some experts have raised concerns about the longstanding federal law imposing a lifetime ban on gun possession by people who have been involuntarily committed to a mental institution at some point in their lives. These experts worry that the policy is too broad and too narrow at the same time. It prohibits many people from having guns even though they will never be dangerous, while doing nothing about a large number of people with behavior problems, such as impulsive anger combined with excessive alcohol use, that greatly increase the risk of violent behavior. In recent work, for example, Jeffrey Swanson and his colleagues found that roughly 9% of the population has both self-reported impulsive angry behavior problems (such as throwing tantrums, smashing things, or getting into fights) and access to firearms in the home.[76] Only a small fraction of these people had ever been hospitalized for mental health reasons—or ever would be, presumably—meaning that they are unlikely to be affected by the federal law on gun possession by people with a record of involuntary commitment.

The systematic evidence cautions us against seeing mental health services—as valuable and distressingly underfunded as they are—as a panacea for violence, including mass shootings. Serious mental illness is quite rare and does not account for a large share of interpersonal gun violence. Alcohol and drug abuse are much more common in the general population and are linked to violence. But even a thoroughgoing reform of behavioral health service systems to make treatment more available would not bring everyone with a substance use disorder into sustained treatment. For the most part, treatment is voluntary—and should be. What's more, involuntary inpatient and outpatient civil commitment have a limited role to play in the mental health care continuum, as well as in public policies to restrict firearms from risky people.[77] For the small group of adults with serious mental illnesses who need treatment to prevent them from harming themselves or others, yet are unwilling or unable to participate voluntarily in recommended treatment, court-ordered mental health services may prove beneficial in reducing risk. Moreover, insofar as involuntary commitment confers loss of firearm rights until it can be demonstrated that the person (who was committed for danger to self or others) no longer poses a safety risk, this policy may prevent some firearm-related deaths or injuries.

The link between serious mental illness, especially depression, is more pervasive in the case of gun suicide, and substance abuse also plays an important role there. The large majority of people who die in gun suicide did not have a mental health adjudication or a felony record that would have disqualified them from possessing a firearm, and they could have passed a background check to purchase a gun on the day they died.[78] Current federal law is not well tailored to these realities.

A number of reformers have called for a shift in the focus of gun regulation from diagnosis to behavior. Someone who appears to be an imminent threat to self or others presents an acute problem requiring quick intervention to separate him from guns. Red-flag laws are intended to provide the courts with such authority. Alcohol and drug abuse linked to dangerous behavior could be identified through convictions for impaired driving, with a resulting disqualification from gun ownership. The result would be to reduce (though of course not eliminate) the threat of suicide or homicide. In Chapter 12, we discuss so-called risk-based approaches to public policy.

5

MANUFACTURE AND MARKETING OF GUNS

How Large Is the Gun Industry in America?

The gun industry itself is rather small by traditional measures. Only a handful of companies produce a significant number of firearms in the United States, and at most 150,000 people are employed in the industry—about 1 in 1,000 of all US workers.[1] By comparison, the health care industry employs approximately 13 million workers, or 85 times the gun industry's labor force.

As shown in figure 5.1, there has been a remarkable increase in the sale of new guns in recent years.[2] The figures include guns produced domestically and imported from abroad but exclude firearms exported to other countries. Manufacturers' shipments to domestic sellers increased from 5 million firearms in 2005 to 16 million in 2016. The big increase began in 2008 with the election of Barack Obama as president. The "Barack boom" reflected gun fanciers' worry that the federal government under Democratic leadership would push for stricter firearm laws. (We return to the politics of gun marketing below.) The gun market sagged in 2017, after the election of Donald Trump, a Republican who opposes gun regulation.

In the period since World War II, handguns have assumed an increasingly important share of the total firearms market. These guns went from one-quarter of new gun sales in 1960 to

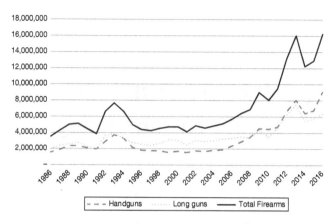

Figure 5.1 Annual shipments of new firearms to US dealers, 1986–2016

one-half of such sales in 1990, with minor variation since then. The surge in new gun sales since 2008 was led by handguns; in 2016, 56% of new guns were handguns. The relative popularity of different types of handguns has changed over this time as well. As recently as 1980, the domestic handgun market was dominated by revolver sales but now is primarily pistols. An increasing share of handguns has come from abroad, with imports rising from about 300,000 in the early 1980s to 3.7 million (40% of the domestic market) in 2016. American exports, on the other hand, constitute a small share of domestic manufacturers and are only about 3% as large as imports. The gun industry has a considerable trade imbalance.

How Is Firearms Production Organized?

Although hundreds of firms hold a firearms manufacturing license, the top 10 firearms manufacturers supply most of the weapons sold to civilian customers in the United States. (Many manufacturers produce fewer than 10 guns per year.) At the upper end of the spectrum are three firms that in 2018 accounted for half of all domestic manufactures: Sturm Ruger (primarily handguns and rifles), Remington Outdoor (rifles), and Smith & Wesson (handguns).[3]

Two foreign-owned companies, Glock and SIG Sauer, supply much of the market for pistols. Glock, an Austrian manufacturer, developed an innovative pistol in the early 1980s that caught on with police departments in the United States and also became identified with gangster life through rap lyrics. SIG Sauer is the brand name for handguns manufactured by a European company and distributed widely in the United States, including among law-enforcement agencies and in the US military.

O.F. Mossberg & Sons is the oldest family-owned gun manufacturer in the United States. It has long been known for its shotguns but is also active in the market for assault weapons and other types of firearms.

Several of the leading firms in handgun manufacturing in the 1980s and 1990s were Southern California's "Ring of Fire" companies. These companies (Lorcin Engineering, Bryco Arms, Davis Industries, Phoenix Arms, AMT, and Sundance Industries) produced low-quality weapons selling in some cases for $50 or less. These guns often are known by the pejorative term "Saturday night specials." By the early 1990s, Ring of Fire companies accounted for one-third of all US handgun sales and were heavily overrepresented in criminal use. Facing regulatory pressure and other problems, five of the six original Ring of Fire companies ended up declaring bankruptcy.[4]

Several manufacturers serving the high end of the market also have had their problems over the years, running afoul of the politics of the market. In March 2000 Smith & Wesson was the only major gun manufacturer to sign an agreement with the Clinton administration to voluntarily adopt safety and design standards. In response, pro-gun advocacy groups and gun clubs organized a boycott, leading to a steep drop in sales. The owners of S&W sold it at a fire-sale price to the Saf-T-Hammer Corporation; the new company canceled the agreement to make safe guns and was able to restore its reputation and sales position in the market. A similar story involves Colt, the company founded by Samuel Colt before the Civil War that popularized the revolver and dominated the firearms industry through World War I. In 1998 Colt took a hit following remarks by its chief executive officer to the effect that he favored a federal permit system with training and testing for gun ownership. A grassroots boycott of Colt products was successful in pushing down sales, and Colt is now a relatively minor player in the civilian market. Colt also lost its contract to supply the US military with the M4 carbine and briefly ended up in bankruptcy. Currently it sells high-end pistols and spinoffs of military weapons to the civilian market.

One of the largest firearms makers in the United States was created through a series of acquisitions by Cerberus Capital Management LP, a private-equity firm. In 2007, the year that Cerberus bought a controlling interest in Chrysler, it also began buying up a number of firearms manufacturing firms, including Remington, Marlin, and Bushmaster, assembling them in a private entity called the Freedom Group—later renamed Remington Outdoor. Cerberus attempted to sell its gun manufacturers following the massacre of children at Sandy Hook Elementary School in 2012; the killer had used a Bushmaster XM-15 assault weapon in that attack. Remington was reorganized under new ownership following bankruptcy in 2018. It is the defendant of a landmark lawsuit in Connecticut brought by parents of victims of the Sandy Hook massacre.

The most prominent industry trade group is the National Shooting Sports Foundation (NSSF). According to its internet site, its mission is "to promote, protect and preserve hunting and the shooting sports. Formed in 1961, NSSF has a membership of more than 12,000 manufacturers, distributors, firearms retailers, shooting ranges, sportsmen's organizations and publishers." NSSF runs the annual SHOT (Shooting, Hunting, Outdoor Trade) Show, the largest of its kind in the world. NSSF is active in representing members with respect to legal, regulatory, and legislative issues.

How Does the Industry Market Its Products?

The gun industry's volatile sales cycles are driven largely by politics. Peak sales in 1968 and 1993 coincided, respectively, with enactment of the Gun Control Act and the Brady Handgun Violence Prevention Act, both of which tightened federal regulation of firearms commerce. More recently, firearms sales started ramping up beginning in 2006, when a Democratic majority was elected to both houses of Congress, and continued sharply upward through President Obama's first term, and again in 2016 during the presidential campaign in which pro-regulation candidate Hillary Clinton appeared to be the frontrunner. Gun owners believed that the Democrats would take away their guns or at least make it more difficult to obtain the kind of gun they wanted. The irony is that nothing actually happened at the federal level. During Obama's first term the only change in gun policy was to ease restrictions, removing the ban on carrying loaded guns in national parks and transporting checked firearms on Amtrak. After his reelection and the Sandy Hook massacre, Obama called for a ban on assault weapons and universal background checks, but no new gun laws were forthcoming from Congress.

The fundamentals of the gun market have much to do with the decline of hunting. The traditional market for rifles and shotguns suitable for this activity has dwindled accordingly. The recent growth in gun sales reflects the success of the industry and pro-gun groups in reorienting demand from sporting weapons to guns designed for defensive purposes. Gun groups have stoked public fear of social chaos and government tyranny and have instigated a nationwide relaxation of laws governing the concealed carrying of weapons in public. Most states have either made it much easier to get a concealed-carry permit or removed the licensing requirement entirely. About half the states have adopted so-called stand-your-ground laws that further encourage a self-help mindset. These laws have increased the demand for readily concealable pistols and suitable accessories. The lobbying effort for such laws has been led by the National Rifle Association (NRA), which in turn receives financial support from the gun industry.

Another important trend that has helped the gun makers is the growing subculture that rests on doomsday narratives of social disorder, invasion by United Nations forces (to confiscate guns), and other claims that resonate with a large share of the gun market but strike others as far-fetched. The industry's marketing efforts have exploited the image of well-armed private citizens serving as the bulwark of freedom. The slogan of the NRA Business Alliance is "The Business of Freedom," and for several years the largest gun company in the United States called itself the Freedom Group. Indeed, the themes of patriotism, heroism, and liberty have become prominent in gun marketing. The message is complemented by the product mix, which increasingly consists of rifles that mimic the assault rifles used in military services in the United States and abroad, as well as high-capacity, high-powered pistols. (The industry has sought to rebrand knockoffs of military assault rifles as "modern sporting rifles" or "tactical rifles.") Beretta has been explicit about its marketing strategy for what became the M9 pistol adopted by the US military in 1990—win the military contract and then advertise it to the public as a military weapon. Glock had earlier succeeded with a similar strategy with the Austrian army. Assault weapons in the style of the Colt AR-15 (introduced to the civilian market in 1964) are semiautomatic versions of the M16 rifle used by the US military. These firearms are big sellers in the civilian market for rifles.

New guns are sold through brick-and-mortar retailers, including everything from small gun shops to Walmarts. While gun makers have an active online presence, federal law requires that new guns be sold in a face-to-face transaction with a licensed retailer. Amazon does not have a category for firearms, although it does sell accessories online.

Retailers have wrestled with how to balance the conflicting views of customers. With 4,600 outlets, Walmart is the largest retailer of firearms in the United States. While federal law allows sales of rifles and shotguns to 18-year-olds, Walmart has adopted 21 as the minimum age. It does not carry high-capacity magazines, handguns, or military-style rifles. Dick's Sporting Goods adopted similar restrictions in 2018 following the Marjory Stoneman Douglas High School massacre, and, in some of its outlets, Dick's has gotten out of the guns and ammo business entirely.

As of 2019, no retailer has been willing to sell personalized ("smart") guns, for fear of a boycott by pro-gun groups and individuals. Pro-gun activists worry that if such guns become available to customers, states might be inclined to require all new guns to be equipped with this technology. If this impasse can be surmounted, the industry presumably would welcome the chance to offer a new product line to customers.

What Is Required to Become a Licensed Firearms Dealer?

Anyone in the business of manufacturing, importing, or retailing firearms must obtain a federal license. Licenses are issued by the Bureau of Alcohol, Tobacco, Firearms and Explosives (ATF) in the US Department of Justice. For retailing ordinary firearms, the license fee is $200 for the first three years, with a $90 renewal fee thereafter. In addition to paying the fee, applicants must have a place of business with secure storage and not be disqualified from firearms possession because of, say, a serious criminal record. Only those with a federal license may legally receive shipments of firearms from distributors. Unlicensed individuals may sell firearms privately from their personal collection, but not as a regular business. (The legal line here is murky at best.)

With the privilege of being a firearms dealer comes a number of responsibilities: storing inventory safely, initiating background checks on would-be buyers, keeping records on all sales, providing information on specific sales when queried by

ATF's National Tracing Center, and generally obeying not only federal laws but also applicable state and local regulations.

As of 2019, there were about 57,000 dealers with a Type 1 (retail) license and 8,000 with a Type 2 (pawnbroker's) license. These figures constitute a considerable reduction from the early 1990s, when there were more than 200,000 licensees. At that time ATF was issuing licenses to almost anyone who chose to pay the trivial fee ($30), whether or not they had a place of business. A study by the Violence Policy Center pointed out at the time that there were more gun dealers than gas stations. In 1994 the federal government raised the fee to its current level, and the "place of business" requirement began to receive greater attention from ATF.[5]

How Many Guns Do Dealers Sell in a Year?

Licensed dealers sell both new and used firearms. As noted above, federal records indicate that in 2016 there were 16.3 million firearms manufactured for domestic use or imported, an all-time high. Retail licensees and licensed pawnbrokers also sell used guns. The number of used firearms sold by dealers nationwide is not recorded, but one credible estimate provides a ballpark estimate—15% of total firearm sales.[6] Thus, for 2016, total gun sales may have reached 18.7 million. That works out to an average of about 300 guns per retail dealer, about one per business day.

An average of 300 sales per year may sound too low to maintain a viable business, but most retail firearms licensees operate more as hobbyists than as storefront businesses. The relative handful of dealers who are seriously in the retail business account for the bulk of all sales. For example, an analysis of California handgun sales by dealers found that those that sold more than 100 per year constituted only 12% of all dealers but 81% of all sales.[7] (This study was made possible by the fact that California requires handgun sales to be reported to a state agency.)

How Are Dealers Regulated?

Lightly, if at all.

The federal agency responsible for regulating licensed dealers does not have the resources to do much enforcement. ATF's rather modest aim is to inspect all licensees at least once every five years, but it has fallen far short of this goal. In fact, the most recent internal review found that only 42% of licensees had been inspected for regulatory compliance between 2007 and 2012.[8] The reason is simple—Congress refuses to provide ATF with the necessary resources to do its job well.

In fiscal year 2017, ATF inspected 11,000 licensees of all sorts. Less than 0.5% were found to be so greatly in violation of regulations that the license was revoked or denied renewal, but minor violations were common: inadequate recordkeeping, failure to verify purchaser eligibility, and failure to report multiple sales of handguns. A number of researchers have explored the willingness of licensed retailers to sell to disqualified buyers. In one survey, licensees were asked what percentage of retailers knowingly participated in illegal sales. The average response was 3%.[9]

It should be noted that federal licensees are required to follow state regulations. Seventeen states in fact have their own licensing program for dealers. In several of these states, there is an active program of regulatory enforcement that supplements ATF efforts.

What Fraction of Gun Transactions Go Through Licensed Dealers?

In the national debate over gun control following the 2012 Sandy Hook school shooting, an oft-repeated claim was that 40% of all gun sales did not involve a licensed dealer and hence were exempt from the federal requirement for a background check. The point of citing the statistic was to demonstrate that the "private sale loophole" was very large and should be closed.

As it turns out, the 40% statistic, which was loosely based on the results of a national survey conducted in 1995, has been replaced by a more directly relevant and up-to-date estimate.[10] In 2015, the Harvard Gun Survey collected data from a nationally representative sample of Americans. The survey found that 78% of gun transactions during the preceding two years had involved a background check; the remaining 22% provided a best estimate of the private sale loophole.[11]

The 1995 survey had found that 60% of all transactions were purchases from a licensed dealer, and hence were required to include a background check by federal law. The Harvard survey, 20 years later, reached the same estimate of 60% for dealer sales. But between the two surveys, several states had instituted a background check requirement on private sales. The Harvard survey found that almost half of private transactions included a background check.

The statistic of greatest interest to law enforcement and policymakers involves the percentage of firearms used in crime that were obtained directly from licensed dealers. One important source here is a national survey of prisoners conducted in 2004. Of the prisoners who said that they had used a firearm in their most recent crime, just one of every nine indicated that they had obtained it from a gun store or pawnbroker.[12] Most guns used in crime come through private transactions.

What Are Gun Shows, and Why Might They Be Problematic?

Gun shows are weekend gatherings in public buildings organized by promoters to bring together buyers and sellers of firearms, ammunition, accessories, and related items. Exhibition space is rented to licensed dealers and private sellers. There is no comprehensive list of gun shows, but it appears that there are several thousand per year nationwide.

Gun shows are controversial in part because they facilitate sales by unlicensed individuals. Federal law requires anyone in the business of selling guns to have a federal license, conduct background checks on buyers, and keep records. But no license is required to sell guns out of one's private collection, and no federal rules regulate such sales except to ban transfers to an individual whom the seller knows is disqualified (as a felon, fugitive, domestic abuser, etc.). The seller can avoid legal liability by simply being careful not to ask any questions. Private sellers operate side by side with licensed sellers, but the latter are required to conduct background checks.

The situation is different in states that regulate private transactions. As of 2019, 20 states and the District of Columbia have some sort of background check requirement for private transactions.[13] Other states impose additional regulations on gun shows in particular.

Gun shows are one source of firearms to criminals and traffickers. What is not clear is how important gun shows are relative to other sources. Surveys of prison inmates suggest that very few of them acquired their weapons at gun shows.[14] But that only tells us something about the final transaction in what is typically a chain of transactions. It is possible that gun shows figure more prominently in the supply chain by which guns move from the legitimate market to the underground market and ultimately into criminal use.

Can Guns Be Sold on the Internet? Ammunition?

The internet helps connect buyers and sellers of all kinds of merchandise, including firearms and ammunition. Furthermore, shipments of ammunition are essentially unregulated. That fact came to the fore when it was discovered that the man who shot up a movie theater in Aurora, Colorado, in 2012 had legally obtained more than 6,000 rounds of ammunition by mail order.

The situation is a bit more complicated for shipping firearms. Unlicensed sellers can ship a firearm by a parcel service to a resident of the same state. (Ironically, such shipments are not allowed for licensed dealers, who must perform the transaction in person.) A 1927 law bans the US Postal Service from shipping handguns, but it can ship rifles and shotguns. Some other services, including FedEx and UPS, do not knowingly accept firearms for shipment between unlicensed parties.

As a result of these restrictions, there is no Amazon-style direct-sales operation for firearms. The internet does facilitate private sales, however. The largest site is ArmsList, a classified advertisements service that has thousands of listings of guns for sale by private individuals. When there's a deal, the buyer and seller are supposed to meet in person to complete the transaction.[15]

What Is the Supply Chain for Guns Used in Crime?

Almost all firearms that end up being used in crime originate with a sale by a licensed dealer. (The relatively rare exceptions are homemade guns, off-the-books imports, and thefts from manufacturers and shippers.) After the initial sale by the dealer, the firearm may undergo several more transfers before being used in a robbery or assault. Once in the possession of an active criminal or gang, the firearm may continue to circulate until confiscated by the police or discarded.

We can imagine at least three pathways from the gun's first retail sale to its illegal use. One path starts with the direct sale to the perpetrator. Here, a pistol might be purchased from a gun store, kept a few years for self-defense purposes, and then used in a domestic violence incident. Or perhaps an 18-year-old purchases a shotgun with the immediate intent of robbing a gas station.

More typical are cases that lie along the second and third pathways, in which the first sale by the dealer is just the beginning of a series of transactions. In the second scenario, a gun might be purchased from the dealer on behalf of another individual, who either cannot pass the background check (because of age or criminal record) or does not want to have his name on file in connection with a gun. Such a transaction, known as a straw purchase, is technically illegal but not uncommon. Guns obtained through straw purchases seem likely to go directly into criminal use.

The most common pathway to illegal use involves a firearm that has been in circulation for years before ending up as evidence in a crime. During that time, it may be given as a gift, loaned to a family member or friend, stolen, sold to an acquaintance or at a gun show, or kept in a gang's inventory to be doled out to youthful members when they need protection. In some cases, there are unlicensed middlemen involved in this supply chain, who seek to make a profit by acquiring a number of guns with the intent of reselling them off the books—an activity known as "trafficking."

Available sources of information on the supply chain are incomplete and require a good deal of interpretation. One source has been surveys of prisoners or arrestees, who tell us about the immediate transactions by which criminals obtain guns.[16] A variation on this approach has been ethnographic research asking gang members or others operating in the underground economy about their experience with guns.[17]

Also useful are data generated from attempts to trace firearms confiscated (or otherwise obtained) by law-enforcement agencies. These traces are conducted through a cumbersome process by the ATF's National Tracing Center, which uses the make, model, and serial number of the firearm to identify it and then trace it from the manufacturer or importer, to the distributor, and then to the retail dealer.[18] If the chain of paperwork is not broken, the dealer should have a record of sale (the 4473 form) that identifies the original buyer. ATF is also the source of other useful information pertaining to the hundreds of firearms-trafficking investigations the agency initiates each year.

One important finding from ATF's trace data is that a large percentage of firearms travel across state lines after the first retail sale. The interstate flow is far from random—guns tend to move from states where they are plentiful and easily accessed (because of lax state and local regulations) to states where they are tightly regulated and scarce.[19] While nationwide about 30% of traced guns were first sold at retail out of state, this percentage tends to be far higher in states such as New York and Massachusetts that have stringent regulations. The so-called Iron Pipeline along the eastern seaboard illustrates the point. Guns flow from Georgia, the Carolinas, and Virginia up to the more tightly regulated states of the Northeast. Similarly, a large percentage of the guns confiscated in Chicago originate in nearby Indiana and Wisconsin, which have little regulation of transactions.

Systematic trafficking is one part of this story. Evidence from ATF investigation files suggests that traffickers are typically small operators who are not making a living off of moving guns. Instead of a "gun kingpin," the right image is of some guy in Boston with a cousin from South Carolina who occasionally drives north with a few guns in his trunk, making both of them a small profit.[20] Larger operations typically involve licensed dealers who exploit their ability to obtain shipments of guns wholesale.[21] It should also be noted that not all the guns that arrive from out of state are trafficked. Much of this movement may be entirely legal, as when someone moves her household, including the gun collection, from one state to another.

Regulation also affects local movements of firearms. One example comes from state *de*regulation. Until 2007, Missouri required all handgun buyers to obtain a purchase permit from the local sheriff. Then the permit requirement was repealed, with the result that private sales were unregulated and sales by dealers were subject only to the federal requirement of a background check. After the law changed, Missouri saw an abrupt change visible in the trace data. The percentage of traced handguns that had moved directly (defined as within three months) from dealer to criminal use in the state jumped from 3% to 9%.[22]

These and other examples suggest that there is a direct connection between regulations on legitimate transactions and the supply chain for guns used in crime. This fact does not in itself prove that the dealers are complicit. But ATF investigations demonstrate that some dealers are in fact running criminal enterprises, supplying thousands of guns to gangs and other illicit customers. Others may simply be careless or clueless.[23]

How Are Illegal Gun Markets Different from Illegal Drug Markets?

Two differences are fundamental. First, guns, unlike drugs, are durable commodities that can remain functional for decades. The result is that every gun owner is a potential gun seller. Voluntary private transactions are common, and, in some cases, they may be a source to the underground market, as when someone sells part of his personal inventory of guns to a trafficker at a gun show. Involuntary transactions, most notably thefts from vehicles and residences, are also important.

Second, the underground market in firearms is much smaller than the market for illicit drugs. One analysis of a Chicago neighborhood compared illicit drug and gun sales. There were no more than 1,400 gun sales per year, or about one sale per year for every 30 people living in this very-high-crime neighborhood.[24] By comparison there were at least 200,000 and perhaps more than 500,000 cocaine sales in this community every year. Thus, there were more than 100 cocaine sales for every gun sale. Total revenue in this community for gun sales would be on the order of $500,000, compared to perhaps $10 million or $20 million in the market for cocaine. The drug-dealing gangs in this neighborhood did not sell guns because the extra heat from the police was not worth the meager profit to be made.

How Do American Dealers Supply Gangs in Mexico and Canada?

Gun laws in Mexico and Canada are more stringent than in the United States, and the numbers of firearms in circulation per capita are far lower in these countries. The result is that the United States is a relatively low-cost source of illegal firearms for the rest of North America. Many of the firearms used by criminal gangs in Canada, and by the drug cartels in Mexico, can be traced to US sources. The same is true for crime guns in Jamaica and elsewhere in the Caribbean.[25]

In particular, licensed dealers and gun shows near the United States–Mexico border are thought to be an important source of the assault weapons that are the guns of choice in the devastating drug-cartel wars. Overland smugglers for these weapons typically follow the same routes heading south as do the illicit drugs that are heading north. As a US ambassador to Mexico said, "Mexico would not be the center of cartel activity or be experiencing this level of violence, were the United States not the largest consumer of illicit drugs and the main suppliers of weapons to the cartels."[26]

Actually, there is considerable uncertainty about just what fraction of the weapons used in the Mexican drug wars originate in the United States. The north–south smuggling operations are not the only source. The weapons used to fight old insurgencies in Central America find their way north through Guatemala, and a surprising number of military-style weapons are diverted from the inventories of the Mexican army and police. Still, if it were possible to close down US sources, the black-market prices would increase, which might place some check on the epidemic of Mexican gang violence.

The illegal shipment of firearms into Mexico became headline news in 2011 due to an ill-advised enforcement strategy by ATF known as "gun walking." ATF was responding to the trade in assault weapons that began with straw purchases from licensed dealers in Texas and Arizona. These guns then often were smuggled across the border and used by the murderous drug cartels in Mexico. Agents surveilled suspicious purchases but did not stop them. The goal was to track the guns to their final destination and use the resulting evidence to help shut down the cartels. One of these programs, known as Operation Fast and Furious, became notorious when one of the guns that was being tracked was used to kill a US Border Patrol agent, and politicians critical of ATF exploited the situation.

How Many Guns Are Stolen Each Year?

Approximately 300,000. During the six-year period from 2010 to 2014, an annual average of 251,000 firearms were stolen in noncommercial property crimes, primarily residential burglaries.[27] Thousands more firearms are stolen annually from gun shops, other businesses, and government storage facilities. While 300,000 stolen guns is a lot, the figure has been much larger in the past. Burglary rates have greatly declined in recent decades, and the rate of firearms theft has declined in proportion. At the same time, the percentage of burglaries in which at least one gun was stolen has remained steady at around 4%.[28]

Most (63%) stolen firearms are handguns, even though the majority of firearms in private hands are long guns. It is interesting to speculate about the difference. Perhaps handguns have greater value when fenced or are less likely to be secured.

It should be noted that some gun thefts are not included in these figures, which are based on the National Crime Victimization Survey (NCVS). The NCVS does not include thefts from commercial outlets, including gun dealers (which lose about 9,000 per year to theft). In any event, the total number of guns stolen each year would easily be sufficient to supply every robbery, assault, and murder committed with a gun (about half a million per year)—even if each stolen gun were used in crime less than twice. But some evidence suggests that only a small fraction of violent crimes are committed with guns that were ever stolen. [29]

How Do Criminals Get Their Guns?

Most guns used in crime were obtained from family members or friends or from the informal "secondary" market. It is unusual for an individual to buy a firearm directly from a dealer and use it in crime.

The best source of national data on this topic is the Survey of Inmates in State and Federal Correctional Facilities, conducted from time to time by the US Department of Justice. One might ask why we should trust convicts to tell the truth about their crimes. The reason is that the respondents have nothing to gain by misrepresentation. They are guaranteed anonymity and because the crime in question has already been adjudicated. (They lost!) Furthermore, the statistical patterns from one survey to the next are quite consistent.

Here are the sources of guns listed in 2004 by inmates of state prisons who had been convicted within the past two years. They reported on the gun associated with the offense that had put them in prison this time. The tabulation is limited to male survey respondents age 18 to 40 who answered the question. Of these prisoners, 39% got their gun from a friend/family member; 33% got it off the street, from a drug dealer, or from a fence or black-market source; and 11% got it from a gun shop or pawnshop (presumably licensed). These three categories constitute nearly all the sources. The rest are minor: 1% got their gun from a gun show or flea market, 3% from the victim, and 9% from some other source.[30] Only about half of these inmates (56%) indicated that they purchased the gun with cash. Thirty percent of them said the gun was a gift or that they had "borrowed" it. Just 5% said that they had stolen it.

The national inmate surveys are limited to adults age 18 and older. Knowing how and when juvenile delinquents obtain their guns is also of importance. One interesting survey documented the sources of juvenile inmates' first guns. A surprising number found a gun in a local alley or park. Others mentioned family or friends, who typically wanted them to have a gun for self-protection.[31] The sense from this and other surveys is of youths living in dangerous neighborhoods where guns are in active circulation.

Still, it is easy to exaggerate the ease of obtaining a gun. Most assaults and robberies are not committed with guns, and most people who are arrested for violent crimes do not own a gun. When asked, a high percentage of people say that they would have difficulty in obtaining a gun or could not afford it. An ethnographic study of the underground market for guns in a high-crime area of Chicago found that some individuals, unable to find a gun on their own, hired informal "brokers" for a fee of $30 to $50. But even these brokers sometimes had trouble locating a suitable weapon for sale.[32]

6

GUN CONTROL IN AMERICA

What Are the Basics of the US System of Gun Regulation?

Gun regulations have a long history, stretching back to the colonial era. By and large, the laws have been enacted to secure the common defense, to protect individuals from harm, to assist law-enforcement officers in maintaining order, and to assert the collective values of the time.

For good or ill, American gun laws reflect the country's system of federalism, which limits the role of the national government in matters of law and order and leaves broad policymaking discretion to the states. A patchwork of laws determines who can own or carry a gun, what kinds of guns and ammunition can be bought and sold, and under what circumstances guns may (or may not) be deployed. Other laws set out the procedures that gun sellers must follow.

Table 6.1 shows the broad categories of firearms laws, together with illustrative examples that exist in one or more states and localities. We provide a more complete summary of federal and state laws later in this chapter.

Federal gun regulations, enacted in earnest beginning in the 1930s, provide a legal "floor," establishing a basic set of public-safety measures by which all Americans must abide. Generally speaking, the federal government's role is to license and oversee firearms dealers, regulate sales and transfers

Table 6.1 Categories of Gun Regulations

Target of law	Jurisdiction		
	Federal	**State**	**Local**
Ownership	Bans on purchases, possession by felons, "mental defectives," youths, other presumably high-risk groups	Handgun owner licensing, concealed weapons training, waiting periods to buy guns, safe-storage requirements	Permit to purchase a rifle or shotgun, requirement to notify police of stolen gun
Firearms	Ban on machine guns (except those registered before 1986 law), ban on armor-piercing ammunition, ban on bump stocks	Bans on assault weapons, high-capacity magazines, "unsafe" handguns	Assault weapons bans
Use	Ban on carrying guns on airplanes or in federal buildings	Licenses to carry concealed gun, "stand-your-ground" laws on self-defense, hunting laws, criminal penalties for firearms misuse	Bans on openly carrying firearms, ordinances against publicly firing a gun
Sales	Licensing and inspections of dealers, recordkeeping requirements, required background checks on sales by licensed dealers, reporting of multiple sales, bans on interstate handgun sales to private individuals	Required background checks on private sales, dealer licensing, one-handgun-per-month laws	Zoning ordinances barring gun shows on public property

across international and state lines, and keep certain categories of people from owning weapons.

States, and sometimes cities, complement and often strengthen the federal laws with measures of their own. State criminal laws make it illegal to use firearms to threaten or harm another person, except in self-defense, and often establish stricter penalties for crimes when the perpetrator uses a gun. State laws also lay out the parameters for the lawful use of weapons, such as carrying a concealed weapon for self-defense. Some states have chosen to augment federal laws by imposing tighter restrictions on the transfer and possession of weapons. Some cities and counties have passed their own firearms ordinances—though states have increasingly denied localities such lawmaking powers.

When passing laws, legislators must take care not to run afoul of state and federal constitutional provisions protecting the right to bear arms. Historically, courts have interpreted such provisions in a way that leaves legislatures broad discretion to regulate firearms. While such deference remains the rule, federal courts have begun to set broad limits on lawmakers in recent years. However, it is politics—not the courts—that serves as the greatest brake on stricter gun laws.

What Is the Second Amendment?

The Second Amendment to the Constitution was ratified, along with nine other amendments in the Bill of Rights, in 1791. The Second Amendment reads: "A well regulated Militia, being necessary to the security of a free State, the right of the people to keep and bear Arms, shall not be infringed."

To modern readers the sentence seems awkwardly constructed, helping fuel a vigorous debate among historians, legal scholars, and judges—to say nothing of activists on both sides of the gun control question—about what the amendment was intended to cover. Answering this question has required contemporary legal sleuths to draw inferences from the evidence at hand, including eighteenth-century state constitutions and other documents known to have influenced the framers' thinking; the social context and political debates of the founding period; the meaning of pivotal words, such as "militia" and "people"; and even historical norms of sentence construction.

Two dominant interpretations—and a third, hybrid interpretation—have vied for dominance. The first holds that the amendment was designed to protect the right of states to maintain militias—armed citizens mobilized for common defense (the militia theory). Another interpretation holds that the amendment was designed to protect the individual right to possess a firearm, regardless of militia service (the individual rights theory). A third, hybrid theory holds that the Second Amendment protected an individual (civic) right that was inextricably bound to a collective (civic) responsibility of bearing arms for the common defense.

In the American system, however, the Supreme Court gets to decide what the Constitution means, even though as Justice John Paul Stevens pointed out, he and his colleagues were not empaneled to be "amateur historians."[1] The court has considered the Second Amendment very rarely. The court's first three rulings (all in the latter decades of the nineteenth century) did not consider the question of whose rights the Second Amendment protected—just whether it applied to entities other than Congress. In 1939, after Congress passed a gangster-era law barring sawed-off shotguns, the court was forced to wade into the thorny question of whether the Second Amendment protected individual or collective rights. In *U.S. v. Miller*, the court found that two suspected bank robbers had no right to their sawed-off shotgun because such weapons did not bear "some reasonable relationship to the preservation or efficiency of a well regulated militia."[2] By inference, the ruling gave rise to the view that the Second Amendment protected a collective right rooted in militia service and "gave individuals no protection from ordinary gun control."[3]

For nearly 60 years, this understanding prevailed, and no federal appeals court overturned a gun control law on Second Amendment grounds. The conventional understanding of the amendment's reach changed in 2008, when the court in *District of Columbia v. Heller* invalidated the capital city's 1976 law that generally banned civilian handgun possession and required lawful firearms in the home to be trigger-locked or disassembled. The case was brought by a young, little-known libertarian lawyer against the wishes of the mighty National Rifle Association (NRA). The NRA feared that pushing the issue would be a lose–lose: If the court found no individual right to a gun, the ruling would constitute an authoritative repudiation of the organization's core beliefs, but if the court sided with pro-gun advocates, it would sap the NRA's ability to use the threat of gun confiscation to scare up money and members. The libertarian lawyer's gambit paid off. Writing for a five-to-four majority, Justice Antonin Scalia concluded that the Second Amendment indeed protected an individual right to possess a firearm for defensive purposes.

Drawing on early state constitutions, legal commentaries, and ratification debates—as well as on the contemporary writings of an ideologically diverse group of law professors and pro-gun lawyer-advocates—Justice Scalia argued that the founders had understood the Second Amendment to enshrine a preexisting right of the people to keep and bear arms for their own personal protection. The District's sweeping ban on functional guns in the home, Justice Scalia ruled, went too far. "The inherent right of self-defense has been central to the Second Amendment right," he argued. "The handgun ban amounts to a prohibition of an entire class of 'arms' that is overwhelmingly chosen by American society for that lawful purpose. The prohibition extends, moreover, to the home, where the need for defense of self, family, and property is most acute." Although he understood that some people thought gun bans would reduce violence, Justice Scalia nevertheless argued that "the enshrinement of constitutional rights necessarily takes certain policy choices off the table."[4]

Two years later, in *McDonald v. City of Chicago*, the court extended its DC ruling to decree that all-out handgun bans are unconstitutional nationwide. Whereas the court's nineteenth-century rulings had suggested that the Second Amendment was intended to constrain Congress only, the court now said that, under the Fourteenth Amendment's due process clause, states and cities likewise must respect the constitutional right to keep and bear arms as understood by the courts. In legal lingo, the protections in the Second Amendment were now "incorporated" via the Fourteenth Amendment, as most of the other amendments had been over the past century.

The *Heller* and *McDonald* rulings were controversial, even among members of the court. Writing on behalf of the four-justice minority, Justice John Paul Stevens accused the *Heller* majority of relying on a "strained and unpersuasive reading" of the Second Amendment to justify an interpretation of history rejected by most professional historians and, for more than a century, by the court itself. Embracing the traditional collective-rights perspective, Justice Stevens argued that the Second Amendment had been motivated by "an overriding concern about the potential threat to state sovereignty that a federal standing army would pose, and a desire to protect the States' militias as the means by which to guard against that danger." He took the court majority to task for having failed to produce any new evidence contradicting this long-settled view.[5]

Justice Stevens's dissent took on modern gun rights ideology. Far from guaranteeing liberty, he said, guns have a "fundamentally ambivalent relationship" to it. Indeed, he argued, the experience of other advanced democracies, which have stricter gun laws than does the United States, "undercuts the notion that an expansive right to keep and bear arms is intrinsic to ordered liberty." He rejected the notion that owning a handgun "is critical to leading a life of autonomy, dignity, or political equality." Given the toll that firearms take, and the

federalist tradition of deferring to state policy experimentation, the court had no business "meddling"[6] in local elected
officials' efforts to safeguard their communities.

The court's back-to-back rulings affirming the individual
rights view have foreclosed banning handguns in America. In
practice, however, even the most fervent gun control proponents had long ago abandoned such aspirations to pursue more
moderate, mainstream measures.

Which Gun Laws Are Unconstitutional, and Which Are Probably Okay?

Although groundbreaking and precedent setting, the *Heller*
and *McDonald* decisions were narrow in scope: They invalidated a tiny handful of unusually strict laws and appeared to
leave plenty of room for lawmakers to regulate guns. Yes, the
court said, governments cannot pass blanket bans on handguns in the home, but the right to keep and bear arms is "not
unlimited." An indeterminate number of gun laws are "pre-
sumptively lawful." Justice Scalia warned that the *Heller* ruling
should not "cast doubt on" laws that, for example, bar felons
and the mentally ill from possessing guns, ban firearms in
"sensitive spaces" such as schools and government buildings,
or mandate "conditions and qualifications" on commercial
firearm sales. He also suggested that lawmakers might restrict
weapons not in "common use" or regulate the carrying of
"dangerous or unusual" weapons.[7]

These suggestions notwithstanding, the court unleashed
what Justice Stevens would soon term a "tsunami of legal
uncertainty and thus litigation."[8] In the first eight years after
Heller, state and federal courts issued nearly 1,000 opinions
concerning the Second Amendment.[9] These cases involved
criminal defendants seeking to challenge the charges against
them and law-abiding citizens who believed that longstanding
local, state, and federal gun regulations were unconstitutional.

While many cases are still making their way through the courts, judges so far have been inclined to defer to existing laws. So, for example, courts have upheld laws barring felons and minors from owning a gun, restrictions on who may carry a concealed weapon, bans on particularly dangerous weapons, and laws requiring licensing of gun owners and registration of firearms. That said, courts have been willing on occasion to rule in favor of people challenging gun control laws not as a general principle, but rather as applied to the challenger's individual circumstances. For example, a small number of citizens have successfully petitioned to have their gun rights restored after having committed a nonviolent felony or after having been involuntarily committed to a mental institution. While favorable to these particular individuals, the rulings have not disturbed the broad applicability of the laws themselves.

In the wake of *Heller* and *McDonald*, the most significant victories for pro-gun advocates have concerned restrictions on carrying concealed weapons in public. States had been relaxing their licensing laws for decades, but until recently, Illinois and the District of Columbia had retained their bans. In *Heller* the Supreme Court left open the possibility that the Second Amendment protected the right to "carry weapons in case of confrontation."[10] In 2012, a federal appeals court adopted this logic and struck down the Illinois law against concealed guns in public. In 2014, a federal district court struck down DC's concealed-carry ban; and in 2017, federal courts invalidated a successor law letting people carry only if they could demonstrate a special need to do so. In contrast, another federal appeals court *upheld* a San Diego ordinance, similar to DC's, that required people to show "good cause" to obtain a license to carry a gun in public. In sum, the state of play on concealed carrying is as follows: States can regulate the practice within reason; absolute bans are unconstitutional; and the legality of highly restrictive laws remains up in the air. The Supreme Court has yet to weigh in on the question but is likely to do so sooner rather than later.

The Supreme Court's rulings in *Heller* and *McDonald* left lower courts to figure out which gun laws were constitutional under the new standards. Generally speaking, courts have used a two-step process. First, they decide whether the challenged law poses a burden on conduct (e.g., gun ownership) covered by the Second Amendment. If so, they next evaluate whether the government had an adequate justification for imposing the burden. That is, courts ask whether the collective interests protected by the law (for example, public safety) justify the costs to individual interests (e.g., in being free from regulation). As legal scholars Lawrence Rosenthal and Adam Winkler note, "Not all regulations restricting guns burden the right to keep and bear arms, and not all regulations that do burden the right are unconstitutional."[11]

However, neither in *Heller* nor in *McDonald* did the Supreme Court spell out for the lower courts what legal standard to use when evaluating a law's constitutionality. What counts as an adequate justification for the law? In legal parlance the court did not spell out the "level of scrutiny" that judges should bring to bear in deciding whether the collective interests outweigh those of the individuals burdened by the law. Most courts have settled on a middle-ground perspective: that gun laws must be substantially related to an important government interest. This standard lies between what gun regulation supporters would like and what pro-gun advocates would favor.

In the years following the *McDonald* ruling, the Supreme Court declined to hear dozens of Second Amendment challenges to gun regulations. But in 2019, the court agreed to consider a case against a New York City law that bars residents from taking their (licensed, unloaded, and locked) guns outside the city. Legal experts speculate that the ruling could have ramifications for gun laws beyond the quirky prohibition at hand.

How Many Gun Laws Are There?

At least since the mid-1960s, the NRA and other pro-gun advocates have claimed that there are 20,000 gun laws on the books. In the wake of the Sandy Hook shooting, NRA chief Wayne LaPierre claimed that there were 9,000 *federal* gun laws alone. These figures, especially the 20,000 number, are widely repeated in the press.

The earliest known sighting of the 20,000 statistic was at a 1965 US Senate hearing, when US Rep. John Dingell, a long-time pro-gun advocate and erstwhile NRA board member, offered it as evidence that the United States did not need more gun control. Other pro-gun advocates offered the same statistic in another hearing the same year. Nobody knows where the number came from, but it stuck. In 2013, the *Washington Post* found nearly 500 references in media reports—surely a lowball figure.[12]

In the early 2000s, scholars sought to assess the actual number of gun laws in the United States.[13] After an exhaustive search, they counted perhaps 400—only one-fiftieth the number enshrined in the conventional wisdom. To be fair, however, by then the number of gun laws had been falling as gun groups persuaded state legislatures to ban localities from enacting firearms regulations. The authors estimated that there were perhaps 300 major state laws and an additional 100 or so left in major cities. (They admitted that they could not count laws in every hamlet, but the NRA's "preemption" campaign, which quashed local laws in many states, was quickly making such research obsolete.)

Of course, how many gun laws America has depends on how we define "a law." Many state laws have multiple subparts—do we count each subpart separately? And what do we do with statutes that place marginal limits on generally permissive laws? For example, most states say it's fine to carry a gun openly, just so long as you don't brandish it. Are laws against brandishing weapons to threaten others "gun control laws"?

Incorporating the NRA's own skepticism about the 20,000 figure, the *Washington Post* concluded that the number "appears to be an ancient guesstimate that has hardened over the decades into a constantly repeated, never-questioned talking point" that has "been used for almost five decades, without much research or diligence to back it up."[14]

Regardless of the precise figure, America's gun laws do vary greatly from place to place, as described below. Depending on your perspective, this system represents either a triumph of federalism, allowing for America's geographically diverse constituencies to decide the laws that govern them, or a nightmarish landscape dotted with legal snares ready to trap law-abiding gun owners.

What Are the Key Gun Control Laws?

Federal, state, and in some cases local laws govern the transfer, possession, carrying, and use of firearms. A handful of federal laws going back to 1927 created the legal foundation by which all Americans must abide, but states and sometimes localities remain free to impose stricter regulations so long as they do so within the bounds of the federal and state constitutions.

High-profile shootings and electoral swings—both of which have happened frequently in the past two decades—can have an impact on gun laws. Regulations can change quickly as advocates win over legislatures, courts, and administrative bodies. As a result, the discussion below is necessarily general, providing a broad overview of how America regulates firearms. Check with government authorities for the most up-to-date information.

The federal government has been in the gun policy business since 1792, when Congress required able-bodied, free, white men aged 18 to 45 to equip themselves with a working firearm and ammunition. For more than a century thereafter, gun policy remained the preserve of the states. In 1919, Congress enacted a tax on gun sales to help pay for World War I. But the major federal gun laws were passed in three spurts, each driven by an uptick in firearms violence.

The first wave of federal lawmaking came in the era of Prohibition and gangster violence. In 1927, Congress banned shipments of handguns via the US Postal Service. In 1934, the National Firearms Act required registration of machine guns and sawed-off shotguns and taxed their transfer; a proposal to register handguns nationally was dropped before passage. Four years later, the Federal Firearms Act created a national licensing system for gun dealers, manufacturers, and importers and imposed (largely unenforceable) restrictions on interstate transfers. The act barred dealer sales to (and purchases by) individuals known to be felons, fugitives, under indictment, or prohibited by state law from buying guns. This early wave of lawmaking foreshadowed now-familiar dynamics: The battles pitted law enforcement and citizen groups concerned with crime against a focused set of gun owner and manufacturer interests, with the legislation (a watered-down compromise) coming after the crisis had passed.

The second wave of federal lawmaking came in 1968, a year so chaotic and painful for the nation that numerous books have been devoted to it. Urban crime had been on the rise, and national gun control proposals had been debated in Congress for five years. But with the back-to-back assassinations of the Reverend Martin Luther King Jr. in April and Senator (and presidential candidate) Robert F. Kennedy in June, Congress acted. The first bill, the Omnibus Crime Control and Safe Streets Act—which the House approved the day after Bobby Kennedy was shot—banned the shipment of handguns to individuals across state lines and prohibited people from buying handguns outside their state of residency.

Three months later, after intensive grassroots campaigning, inside maneuvering, and rhetorical bomb throwing on all sides, Congress passed the Gun Control Act of 1968 (GCA). As the foundation for today's most prominent national gun laws, the GCA protects strong-law states from states that prefer to see guns only lightly regulated. Specifically, the law extended the ban on interstate shipments of handguns to include rifles, shotguns, and ammunition; created penalties for using a gun while committing a federal crime; and imposed new rules on federally licensed gun dealers. Perhaps most importantly, the GCA expanded the categories of people to whom sales of guns would be banned (so-called prohibited purchasers, as described below). Fugitives and most felons had been covered under the 1938 law. The 1968 law barred transfers to, and possession by, people who have been "adjudicated as a mental defective" or "committed to a mental institution," as well as people who are unlawful users of, or addicts to, certain drugs. In addition, the law barred licensed dealers from transferring firearms to minors (under 21 for handguns and under 18 for long guns). Although popular accounts often portray the NRA's fierce opposition to gun laws as a relatively new phenomenon, the group's president at the time called the GCA an attempt to "foist upon an unsuspecting and aroused public" a law that would "eventually disarm the American public."[15] Meanwhile, the bill's chief sponsor, Senator Thomas Dodd (D-CT), charged that the NRA's attack on the bill amounted to "blackmail, intimidation and unscrupulous propaganda."[16]

In 1986, following NRA pressure and a conservative resurgence, Congress passed and President Reagan signed the Firearm Owners' Protection Act, which eased some federal laws but also imposed new, stricter regulations. Pro-gun folks and commercial interests were happy with provisions clarifying the definition of what constitutes a dealer "engaged in the business" of firearms sales, allowing dealers to sell at gun shows, limiting inspections of gun dealers to no more than once per year, facilitating purchases across state lines, providing protections to gun owners traveling with their weapons through strict-control states, and prohibiting the federal government from establishing a system of registration for firearms, firearm owners, or firearm transfers. Gun control advocates got a ban on private possession of machine guns, except for those weapons already registered; a requirement that federally licensed dealers report multiple firearms sales; and a clarification on the GCA's prohibitions on the possession of any type of gun by illegal immigrants, dishonorably discharged service members, and those who have renounced their US citizenship.[17]

The third wave of lawmaking came in the early 1990s, on the heels of a dramatic increase in gun-related crimes over a seven-year period. As was the case in the 1960s, the laws had been under consideration for years, awaiting the right political conditions to ease their passage. In 1993, under newly elected Democratic president Bill Clinton, Congress passed the Brady Handgun Violence Prevention Act, named after former presidential spokesman James Brady, who had been gravely wounded in the 1981 assassination attempt on his boss, Ronald Reagan. The former president delivered a pivotal endorsement of the bill. The Brady law created a way to enforce the prior restrictions on "prohibited purchasers" by requiring federally licensed gun dealers—but not private sellers—to conduct a background check on would-be buyers of handguns. The law originally required a waiting period, which ended in 1998 with the implementation of an instant "phone-in" background check system. The background check system was also extended to would-be buyers of rifles and shotguns that year. Also in the 1990s, people who had a conviction for misdemeanor domestic violence or were under a restraining order were added to the list of federally prohibited purchasers. The domestic violence misdemeanor law was fortified in 2014 (*United States v. Castleman*) and in 2016 (*Voisine v. United States*), when the US Supreme Court rejected technical challenges to its core purpose.

With gang violence in urban areas seemingly unremitting, Congress followed the Brady bill with a ban on the future production of so-called assault weapons, as well as feeding devices (magazines) that held more than 10 bullets. The 1994 law banned production of 19 specific guns and their knockoffs, as well as firearms with two or more military-style design characteristics and the capacity to accept a detachable magazine (with the last criterion not applying to shotguns). People who already owned such weapons were allowed to keep them and to transfer them to other legal buyers. Pro-gun advocates have argued that the assault weapons ban failed to reduce gun violence and that its only effect was to flip the House of Representatives to the more gun-friendly Republican Party in the 1994 midterm elections. We assess these assertions in Chapters 7 and 9. The ban expired in 2004, when Congress declined to renew it.

As of this writing, Congress had not fundamentally tightened federal gun regulations in 25 years. That said, there have been several noteworthy changes to these laws, mostly in the direction of relaxing them. After more than a dozen cities sued gun manufacturers and dealers to recover the costs of what they saw as preventable gun violence, Congress in 2005 passed the Protection of Lawful Commerce in Arms Act, which effectively doomed litigation as a gun control strategy. Although not preempting all legal action against gun dealers and manufacturers, the measure gave the industry and its trade associations broad new protections from liability for harm caused by guns. At the same time, the law offered something to gun regulation supporters: a requirement that secure storage or safety devices be distributed with new handguns sold to private individuals. After a mass shooting at Virginia Tech, pro-gun and pro-regulation forces supported Congress in passing the NICS Improvement Amendments Act of 2007, which gave states incentives to enter mental health and other records into the federal database of people barred from purchasing a gun. (NICS is the commonly used acronym for the National Instant Criminal Background Check System.) Subsequent legal changes have offered wins for both sides of the gun debate. During the Obama administration, Congress relaxed restrictions on carrying loaded guns in national parks and unloaded weapons in the luggage compartment of Amtrak trains. After a mass shooting in Las Vegas left 58 dead and hundreds wounded, the Trump administration issued a regulation banning bump stocks, devices that allow semiautomatic weapons to operate like machine guns.

Normally, questions of domestic law and order fall to states. The federal government has based its prerogative to control guns on Article 1, Section 8, of the US Constitution, which grants Congress the authority to regulate foreign and interstate commerce. The legal theory is that, because guns are distributed or otherwise flow easily across state lines, firearms sales constitute a national marketplace.

However, in two modern cases, the Supreme Court has invalidated gun control laws on the grounds that Congress exceeded its constitutional authority. In *U.S. v. Lopez* (1995), the court struck down the Gun Free School Zones Act of 1990, which generally had barred guns within 1,000 feet of school grounds. The case involved a Texas 12th-grader who had been arrested for bringing a handgun to his high school. The court ruled that Congress had no business meddling in such local matters. As Chief Justice William Rehnquist noted, "There is no indication that [the student] had recently moved in interstate commerce, and there is no requirement that his possession of the firearm have any concrete tie to interstate commerce."[18] In 1996, Congress amended the law to clarify that it applied only to guns that had moved in, or affected, interstate or foreign commerce; presumably most firearms fall into one of those categories. Congress left states and school districts the authority to license people, such as guards, to carry guns on school property.

In the second case, *Printz v. United States* (1997), the court ruled that Congress could not require state or local law-enforcement officials to conduct the background checks mandated under the Brady Act. Writing for the five-to-four majority, Justice Scalia argued that the federal mandate to state and local officials violated the principles embedded in the Tenth Amendment to the Constitution giving the states "dual sovereignty" with the federal government. In the end, the ruling had little effect. Most local law-enforcement officers were happy to comply voluntarily with the background check system. And the issue became moot in 1998, when the National Instant Criminal Background Check System came online, allowing gun dealers to run the background checks directly through the Federal Bureau of Investigation (FBI), rather than having to rely on a state or local law-enforcement agency.

Table 6.2 summarizes the major federal actions, as well as the context in which the laws were enacted.

State Laws

Although the federal government has used its power under the commerce clause to regulate firearms, state and local governments retain primary authority for maintaining law and order. Thus, most gun regulations are state laws and local ordinances. There is no definitive count of such regulations, though one estimate put it at approximately 400 significant laws.[19] The federal Bureau of Alcohol, Tobacco, Firearms and Explosives, the NRA, and the Giffords Law Center to Prevent Gun Violence do a good job keeping a record of laws in specific states, and we urge you to consult those sources for details.

Below, we briefly review the major categories of state gun laws that apply to the law-abiding population. (We exclude laws governing criminal use of firearms.)

State Right-to-Bear-Arms Provisions

Nearly all states (44 as of this writing) protect the right to bear arms in their constitutions. Early provisions often associated the right to an individual's participation in the common defense. In the modern era, some states have been explicit that the right belongs to individuals, irrespective of whether they might defend the broader public. Other states strike a balance

Table 6.2 Timeline of Federal Gun Policy

Era	Crime patterns	Federal crime policy innovations
1920s	Prohibition-related gang violence Tommy-gun era	**1919:** Congress imposes federal excise tax on handguns (10%) and long guns (11%). **1927:** Congress bans handgun shipments via US mail.
1930s	End of Prohibition in 1933 Declining violence rates	**1934: National Firearms Act** requires registration and high transfer tax on fully automatic weapons and other gangster weapons. **1938: Federal Firearms Act** requires anyone in the business of shipping and selling guns to obtain a federal license and record names of purchasers.
1960s	Crime begins steep climb in 1963 with Vietnam era & heroin epidemic Assassinations Urban riots	**1968: Gun Control Act** bans mail-order shipments except between federally licensed dealers (FFLs); strengthens licensing and recordkeeping requirements; limits purchases to in-state or neighboring-state resident; defines categories of people (felons, adjudicated "mentally defective," etc.) banned from possession; bans import of "Saturday night specials."
1970s	Violence rates peak in 1975 (heroin) and again in 1980 (powder cocaine era)	**1972:** ATF is created and located in the US Department of Treasury.
1980s	Epidemic of youth violence begins in 1984 with introduction of crack	**1986: Firearm Owners' Protection Act** eases restrictions on in-person purchases of firearms by people from out of state; limits FFL inspections by ATF; bans the maintenance of some databases on gun transfers; bars private sales to illegal immigrants, dishonorably discharged service members, citizenship renouncers; ends manufacture of National Firearms Act–regulated weapons for civilian use.

(continued)

Table 6.2 *Continued*

Era	Crime patterns	Federal crime policy innovations
1990s	Violence rates peak in early 1990s, begin to subside Mass shootings in schools	**1993: Brady Handgun Violence Prevention Act** requires licensed dealers to perform a background check on each customer before transferring a firearm. **1994: Violent Crime Control and Law Enforcement Act** bans manufacture of certain "assault" weapons and large magazines for civilian use; bars people under certain domestic-violence restraining orders from possessing firearms. **1996: Lautenberg Amendment to the GCA of 1968** bans firearm possession by those convicted of misdemeanor domestic violence.
2000s–2010s	Crime and violence continue to decline Virginia Tech shooting	**2004**: Congress allows federal assault weapons ban to expire. **2005: Protection of Lawful Commerce in Arms Act** largely immunizes firearms industry against civil suits in cases where a gun was used in crime. **2007: NICS Improvement Amendments Act** provides incentives to states to submit records of prohibited purchasers to national background check system. **2019:** Bump stock ban is enacted through regulation.

between state power and private rights. For example, the Illinois provision holds, "Subject only to the police power, the right of the individual citizen to keep and bear arms shall not be infringed."

State right-to-bear-arms provisions rarely have stood in the way of gun control laws enacted by elected officials. For example, courts ruled that an Illinois town's decision to ban handgun possession did not violate the state's right-to-keep-arms provision. (The US Supreme Court later invalidated such bans, but on Second Amendment grounds.)

Licensing and Registration of Firearms

Gun violence prevention advocates have long argued that we should treat guns like cars: require owners to be licensed and trained and the equipment to be registered with a government authority. (Note that driver licensing and car registration requirements typically do not apply when vehicles are driven only on the owner's property, which may be a relevant limit to the guns-cars analogy.) Americans historically have been supportive of gun owner licensing and, to a lesser extent, registration of firearms, but the argument has proved largely unpersuasive in the political realm.

Only about a dozen states—and a few cities, including the District of Columbia—require a license to own, or permit to purchase, a handgun. A handful of additional states also require a permit to purchase an assault weapon or other type of long gun. Only four states and a few cities require handguns to be registered, and several other states require registration of long guns, usually assault weapons as opposed to traditional hunting rifles and shotguns.

Gun groups view registration laws as a particular threat on the grounds that governments might use these lists to confiscate firearms from law-abiding owners. As a result, Congress and a handful of state legislatures have explicitly prohibited government authorities from assembling or maintaining a registry of privately held guns. In addition, records of successful background checks run through the NICS must be destroyed within 24 hours. As a result of these precautions, the most complete registry of firearm owners may be the membership databases of gun advocacy organizations.

Laws Regulating Carrying of Guns in Public

People may *openly* carry a firearm in all but a handful of states, and in the majority of states no permit is required to do so. However, the practice is rare, certainly in cities and suburbs. In recent years, open carry has become a form of political protest for gun owners unhappy with national health care reform and state and federal proposals to expand background checks for gun sales.

States regulate the carrying of *concealed* guns a bit more tightly, though the trend has been to make it easier for people to pack heat. A very conservative estimate is that 17 million people, or roughly 9% of the population 21 years or older, are licensed by a state to carry a gun concealed on their person.[20] As of this writing, every state permits private individuals to carry a concealed weapon, though stipulations vary widely. In roughly one-third of the states—a number that has grown rapidly in recent years—no firearms training, criminal or mental health background check, or government permit is required to carry a concealed weapon (these are the "permitless" or "constitutional" carry states). Another handful of states, mostly on the coasts, require background checks and training and afford law-enforcement officers discretion to deny permits ("may issue" states). About half of states lie somewhere in between, requiring applicants to submit to a background screening, undergo firearms training, and/or demonstrate a need to carry a gun and mandating that, once these requirements are met, the concealed-carry license be granted ("shall issue" states).

Assault Weapon Bans

The federal assault weapons ban ended in 2004. However, seven states maintain their own bans. In the wake of the 2012 Sandy Hook school shooting—in which a Bushmaster assault rifle was used to kill 20 first-graders and 6 educators—3 of these states (Connecticut, Maryland, and New York) expanded their laws to include more types of assault weapons. Colorado, the site of two of the most infamous mass shootings in American history, did not ban assault rifles but did ban high-capacity magazines. In response to the mass shooting at a Parkland, Florida, high school in 2018, gun-friendly Vermont enacted a package of firearms regulations, including a ban on certain high-capacity magazines.

As Chapter 5 notes, gun manufacturers are finding a market for military-style weapons adapted for civilian use—what gun makers call "modern sporting rifles." As Congress considered reinstituting the federal assault weapons ban, pro-gun advocates suggested that such bans would be unconstitutional under the Supreme Court's implied protection of firearms "in common use." Pro-gun advocates have asked courts to invalidate state bans on assault weapons on these grounds, thus far without success.

Preemption of Local Ordinances

In 1981, the suburban Chicago hamlet of Morton Grove wanted to prohibit a gun store from opening near a school. Unable to find the authority to do so under local zoning laws, the village trustees enacted a ban on the sale and possession of handguns. That move, coming on the heels of the assassination attempt on President Reagan and Chicago's freeze on handguns, sent the NRA and other pro-gun advocates into a fury. When the Seventh Circuit Court of Appeals upheld the ban the following year, the NRA's top lobbyist invoked the attack on Pearl Harbor, calling the ruling one that "will live in infamy."[21]

Although pushing local ordinances might have proved an effective strategy for strengthening firearms laws across the nation, gun control advocates were uninterested in pursuing this approach or unable to do so. On the other side, however, gun organizations saw local ordinances as a looming threat and fought back immediately with a state-by-state campaign to secure "preemption" laws. Under these laws, state legislatures barred localities from regulating the ownership, possession, transfer, manufacture, or transportation of firearms.

At the time when Morton Grove enacted its handgun ban, cities and counties in most states had some freedom to regulate guns. Only two states had comprehensive preemption laws, and five states preempted certain types of gun laws. Today, the situation is reversed: Just five states give their localities broad authority to regulate firearms.[22] Most of the other 45 states prohibit localities from imposing regulations on firearm sales and ownership. In many cases, states have refused to carve out any exceptions, even for traditionally municipal responsibilities like zoning laws. That said, it's important to remember that even under preemption regimes, localities typically are still allowed to regulate the discharge of firearms in public places.

Risk-Based Policies

Gun advocacy groups long have objected to broad gun control laws—such as those banning entire categories of firearms or requiring universal licensing of owners—on the grounds that these policies penalize law-abiding citizens who would never misuse their gun. Even people sympathetic to stricter gun laws concede that some existing policies—for example, lifetime bans on gun ownership for people with a long-ago episode of serious mental illness—could be more carefully designed. These concerns, coupled with political gridlock in the face of unacceptable levels of gun violence, have led advocates to pursue a "risk-based" approach. This approach prioritizes policies focused on narrow categories of people—stalkers and domestic abusers, for example—who have demonstrated that they pose a threat to themselves or others.

The centerpiece of the risk-based approach is the "extreme risk protection order," sometimes called a "gun violence restraining order" or "red-flag law." These novel policies provide a tool for law-enforcement officers and, usually, close family members to temporarily separate dangerous individuals from guns. Although the policy details vary by state, these laws allow police and relatives to ask a court to mandate the removal of guns from the home of individuals demonstrating an immediate threat to themselves or others and to bar these at-risk individuals from purchasing additional weapons while under the court order. The laws include provisions for the guns to be returned once a court has determined the person no longer poses a danger.

Red-flag laws have garnered bipartisan support and have spread quickly in recent years. In 2014, only two states had a version of these laws. But 5 years later, the number had reached 17 states and the District of Columbia, with legislation moving forward in many other states. Even pro-gun Republicans in Congress began entertaining the idea of encouraging these laws. Prioritizing red-flag laws reflects a larger pragmatic turn within the gun violence prevention movement, as we discuss in Chapter 11, as well as a promising policy approach, as we discuss in Chapter 12.

Which States Have the Strongest Laws, and Which Have the Weakest?

Relatively strict gun laws are concentrated in a small handful of states, mostly on the East and West Coasts. These states include California, Hawaii, and Washington on the western edge of the nation; Connecticut, Maryland, Massachusetts, New Jersey, New York, and Rhode Island, on the eastern seaboard; and Illinois in the Midwest. The states with the least stringent gun laws tend to be in the South and Southwest (Arizona, Kentucky, Louisiana, Oklahoma, and Mississippi) and in the rural West (Alaska, Idaho, the Dakotas, Kansas, Montana, Utah, and Wyoming).

Do Authorities Disarm People Who Aren't Allowed to Have a Gun?

The GCA sets the national standard on who is disqualified from possessing a firearm. That standard is reproduced, in whole or part, by the laws of many states. People who are newly indicted or convicted of a felony, or committed to a mental institution, are no longer legally entitled to possess a firearm, and it seems logical that they would be ordered to give up any in their possession. But only a handful of states (e.g., Massachusetts and Connecticut) have legislated a process by which newly disqualified people are to get rid of their firearms, with a timeline for compliance.

Of course, any disqualified person whom the police find with a gun can be prosecuted. The federal "felon in possession" law specifies a long prison term.

If I Want to Buy a Gun, What Is the Process?

We assume that you're asking about the process for buying a gun legally. The answer is, it depends on who is selling the gun—a private seller or an official gun dealer—and what state you live in.

If you are buying your gun from a private seller—your brother or a local guy selling off his private collection at a gun show—in the majority of states the process will mainly involve negotiating a good price. The seller is free to conduct the transaction so long as he doesn't have reason to believe that the law bars you from buying the gun. However, as of this writing, 20 states subject private transfers to a background check requirement. In some cases, states operationalize the background check by requiring buyers to obtain a gun permit before obtaining a firearm. Other states require a background check at the time the sale is made, at least for handguns.

If you are buying a firearm from a federally licensed dealer—your local gun store, for example—you and the dealer are subject to federal law, and the process is more tightly regulated.

In these cases, the dealer is required to perform a background check, either through the federal NICS system, operated by the FBI, or in some cases through a state "point of contact" agency.

To start the process—which is typically completed within a few minutes—you will fill out a Form 4473, though in nearly 30 states people who hold a valid state permit to own or carry firearms are exempted from the background check requirement. If you need to fill out the one-page form, you will provide your name, address, place of birth, height, weight, gender, birthdate, race and ethnicity, state of residence, country of citizenship, and (if not a citizen) alien/admission number. You also must answer 14 yes/no questions aimed at determining whether you are allowed to buy a gun. Some of the questions include the following: Have you been convicted of a felony? Are you under indictment? A fugitive from justice? Under a restraining order for harassment, stalking, or threatening your child, an intimate partner, or the partner's child? Are you in the United States illegally? Addicted to drugs? Have you been convicted of misdemeanor domestic violence? How about "adjudicated as a mental defective" or committed to a mental institution?

Once you fill out the form, the dealer fills out his part—including information on the type of firearm being sold, the location of the sale, and the number and expiration date of your driver's license or other government-issued identification. The dealer then accesses online or by phone the FBI's NICS (or "point of contact" partner in the state) and provides your basic information. The agent on the other end runs it through the system and returns a verdict: The sale can proceed, must be denied, or needs to be delayed for further checking. In "proceed" cases, the record of the check is destroyed within 24 hours. In cases of denial, the dealer can't sell you the gun (though the NICS agent does not tell him the reason). In cases of delay, the government authority has three business days to render a final decision, after which the sale can go through at the seller's discretion. This provision entered public controversy in 2015, when the delay failed to stop a white supremacist from buying the gun he used to murder nine African Americans while they worshiped at their Charleston, South Carolina, church.

Between 1998 and 2018, federal, state, and local authorities processed more than 305 million background checks on gun sales.[23] The denial rate has been roughly 1% to 1.5% in recent years.[24] Note that the number of background checks conducted each year is a poor indicator of the number of gun sales. These figures do not account for multiple sales to the same buyer, nor do they capture transfers between private individuals or sales to individuals with certain types of gun licenses in most states. In Chapter 7, we discuss the impact of NICS on violent crime, as well as suicide.

Who Is Barred from Owning a Firearm?

Federal law governs most of the rules on who may own a gun. The feds began lawmaking in this realm in 1938, when the Federal Firearms Act barred federal dealers from knowingly shipping a gun across state lines to a felon, fugitive, person under indictment, or individual barred by state law from possessing the weapon. The classes of "prohibited purchasers" have expanded since then, and the law applies to all gun sales—not merely those involving interstate shipments from dealer to buyer. Under federal law, it is illegal "for any person to sell or otherwise dispose of any firearm or ammunition to any person knowing or having reasonable cause to believe that such person" falls into one of the categories in Table 6.3.

Under federal law, licensed dealers are required to subject the would-be buyer to a background check to verify that he is eligible to buy the gun, and private sellers must not sell a gun to anyone they have reason to believe is a prohibited purchaser.

Table 6.3 Prohibited Purchasers Under Federal Law

Shorthand	Formal definition
Felons/suspects	"is under indictment for, or has been convicted in any court of, a crime punishable by imprisonment for a term exceeding one year"
Fugitives	"is a fugitive from justice"
Drug users	"is an unlawful user of or addicted to any controlled substance" as defined in Section 102 of the Controlled Substances Act
Mentally ill	"has been adjudicated as a mental defective or has been committed to any mental institution"
Undocumented	"is illegally or unlawfully in the United States"
Foreigners	"has been admitted to the United States under a nonimmigrant visa," with exceptions for those holding American hunting licenses, foreign representatives, and certain others
Dishonorably discharged	"has been discharged from the Armed Forces under dishonorable conditions"
Former citizens	"having been a citizen of the United States, has renounced his citizenship"
Domestic abusers	"is subject to a court order that restrains such person from harassing, stalking, or threatening an intimate partner of such person or child of such intimate partner or person, or engaging in other conduct that would place an intimate partner in reasonable fear of bodily injury to the partner or child" (with procedural conditions) "has been convicted in any court of a misdemeanor crime of domestic violence"

Note: See 18 USC § 922 (d), at http://www.law.cornell.edu/uscode/text/18/922.

Felons

Anyone convicted of a serious crime (punishable by more than a year in prison) is by default barred from buying a gun, even after he has paid his debt to society. But with the cooperation of Congress—and at the urging of the NRA—several states have developed procedures that allow felons to have their gun rights restored. A 2011 exposé by the *New York Times* found that in at least 11 states, restoration of gun rights was automatic for non-violent felons who had served their time, and violent felons could petition for restoration in several states.[25] Examining records from Washington State, the newspaper found that over a six-year period, more than 3,300 felons and domestic violence convicts had regained their right to own firearms, and about 13% of them had gone on to commit crimes—including murder, assault, and child rape.

Reflecting on the commonsense belief that the law surely bars criminals from buying guns, the *Times* concluded: "This gradual pulling back of what many Americans have unquestioningly assumed was a blanket prohibition has drawn relatively little public notice. Indeed, state law enforcement agencies have scant information, if any, on which felons are getting their gun rights back, let alone how many have gone on to commit new crimes."

Age Restrictions

Federal law generally controls gun possession by adults. But when it comes to minors, both the feds and the states weigh in. Federal law bars licensed dealers from transferring handguns to anyone they believe to be under 21, and it bars private purveyors from selling handguns to those under 18. In other words, unless stricter state laws apply, youths aged 18 to 20 can buy handguns but just not from the local gun store or other licensed dealer. (This distinction becomes important below.) Federal law also bars licensed dealers from selling long guns to those under 18, but the law does not apply to private sellers.

Within these constraints, states are free to make the laws around kids and guns. With respect to handguns, nine states and the District of Columbia bar anyone under 21 from possessing such weapons. With respect to long guns, about half of the states have chosen to fill the federal gap by defining a minimum age (usually 18) for purchasing or possessing these weapons. A handful of additional states make exceptions for kids who gain the consent of their parents. In 2012, a federal circuit court panel ruled against the NRA's constitutional challenge to the longstanding ban on federally licensed dealers' sales of handguns to those under 21; the Supreme Court declined to review the case. The 2018 shooting at a Parkland, Florida, high school, in which 17 students and educators died at the hands of a 19-year-old gunman, prompted changes. Florida raised its minimum age to buy firearms to 21, and the major sporting goods retailer Dick's ceased selling guns to anyone under that age (a change that Walmart had made three years earlier).

Who Enforces Gun Control Laws?

Local police, county sheriffs, and state law-enforcement authorities do most of the work, though federal authorities play certain designated roles.

The principal federal agency enforcing gun laws is the Bureau of Alcohol, Tobacco, Firearms and Explosives (known by its old acronym, ATF). ATF traces its roots to America's earliest years as the agency charged with collecting alcohol taxes. It got jurisdiction over firearms in 1942, an expanded portfolio after enactment of the GCA in 1968, and independent bureau status within the Treasury Department in 1972. In 2003, the ATF moved to the Justice Department as part of Congress's reorganization of the federal security apparatus following the 9/11 terrorist attacks. With respect to guns, ATF is charged with assisting local and state law enforcement with criminal investigations, including by tracing firearms used in crime to their original seller, licensing and inspecting federal firearms dealers, and making technical judgments about weapons banned from importation.

The other key federal law-enforcement agency is the FBI, which operates NICS and processes mandated background checks on firearms sales going through licensed dealers and in some states through private sellers as well. The FBI also investigates, and US attorney offices prosecute, federal crimes involving guns.

You will also see federal agencies involved in special joint operations, including Project Safe Neighborhoods, through which the federal government provides resources to local and state law-enforcement agencies to combat gang violence. In high-visibility or especially complicated cases—for example, the DC-area sniper shootings in 2002 or the Boston Marathon shooting and bombing in 2013—federal authorities will play a prominent role alongside their state and local counterparts.

What Are the Challenges of Enforcing Gun Laws?

While gun violence prevention advocates seek stricter gun laws, gun organizations typically implore the authorities to just "enforce the laws we already have." On occasion the two groups have found common ground and supported programs to do just that, but mostly the two sides talk past each other. Historically, law-enforcement agencies have quietly complained that they needed gun violence prevention groups to show up and fight for them when they have come under political attack by pro-gun forces. Meanwhile, pro-gun advocates have talked out of both sides of their mouths—saying all the right things about the value of enforcement while at the same time actively undermining it.

As the federal agency primarily responsible for enforcing federal gun laws, ATF operates, in the words of gun violence prevention advocates, "blindfolded, and with one hand tied behind the back."[26] These constraints come in many forms: legal restrictions placed on ATF's ability to fulfill its mission efficiently, vulnerability to uneven political support from the White House, the absence of pressure groups willing to offer support, and a lack of money to perform its tasks.

Behind these problems lie the NRA and other pro-gun interests, which have devoted decades to vilifying and attempting to undermine ATF. Most accounts trace the animosity to 1971, shortly after ATF had acquired expanded responsibilities under the GCA. That year, ATF agents raided the home of a suburban Washington NRA member and gun collector; when the man rushed out in response to his wife's screams, an agent shot him in the head. The event became a cause célèbre and helped to transform the NRA into the hardline organization that we recognize today.

In the late 1970s and early 1980s, gun advocacy organizations stepped up their attacks. Pressure from gun groups prevented ATF from collecting firearms turned in through a private gun buyback program, hastened the retirement of the agency's director, produced withering congressional oversight hearings purporting to show widespread malfeasance within ATF, and persuaded Congress to hit the agency with a budget cut.

In a famous incident in 1995, the NRA sent a mass fundraising mailing that called federal agents "jack-booted government thugs" and accused federal agents of wearing "Nazi bucket helmets and black storm trooper uniforms."[27] The letter drew a firestorm of criticism several weeks later, when antigovernment militia sympathizers blew up the Oklahoma City federal building, killing 168 people. The NRA's letter led lifetime member and former president George H. W. Bush to publicly resign from the group.

Distrust of federal firearms enforcement agencies has led to enactment of several important laws limiting these agencies' ability to use data to investigate gun trafficking and other crimes. As noted above, Congress has barred the federal government from saving records of successful background checks, leading critics to charge that it's virtually impossible to detect patterns in "straw purchasing," in which a legal buyer goes from store to store buying up weapons for confederates who are barred from owning them.

Congress also has placed restrictions on the use of data gathered by ATF when it traces guns used in crime. Often when local, state, or federal authorities recover a firearm at a crime scene, they ask the ATF to run a trace, which consists of the agent's calling the manufacturer with the serial number and asking for the name of the dealer to whom the gun was first shipped. If that dealer is still in business, ATF then calls the dealer and requests that he search through sales records to identify the initial buyer. If the dealer is out of business, however, the ATF has the records—millions of them arrive each year—and must search them manually. Since 1979, Congress has barred ATF from computerizing these records.

In 2004 Congress passed the so-called Tiahrt Amendments, sponsored by then-representative Todd Tiahrt (R-KS). These amendments barred ATF from disclosing to the public any data, either detailed or aggregated, on its traces of crime guns. The amendments also restricted law-enforcement officers' access only to trace data pertaining to a specific investigation or prosecution within their own jurisdiction. Under pressure from mayors and police chiefs, Congress has since loosened these restrictions, for example by allowing ATF to issue aggregate gun-trace reports and allowing local and state police broader access to the data.

Also in 2004, Congress barred the ATF from requiring federally licensed firearms dealers to keep an inventory of their weapons—standard practice in virtually every business. Such inventories would help agents identify "missing" guns that may have been sold illegally. Congress also barred trace data from being used as evidence in civil proceedings.

In congressional hearings after the Sandy Hook school shootings, pro-gun advocates—including senators—were openly critical of the US Department of Justice for not vigorously prosecuting felons who had attempted to illegally purchase a weapon. Federal authorities argued that they had to focus their limited resources on the bad guys who had already committed a crime with their gun, not those whom the system had stopped from obtaining one. Still, it is remarkable that there were only 12 federal prosecutions stemming from 112,000 federal denials in 2017.[28]

How Do US Laws Compare to Those in Other Countries?

Most nations—certainly advanced industrialized democracies—have gun laws considerably stricter than those in the United States. The US system starts with the premise that citizens should be allowed to own guns unless there is a compelling reason to bar citizens from doing so, while other nations begin with the opposite premise—ownership should be severely restricted or banned unless there is good reason to allow it.

A comprehensive comparative analysis of gun laws in the world's nearly 200 nations is well beyond what we have room for here. But Table 6.4 offers a broad overview of national gun laws in other Anglo nations, in nations often discussed in gun policy debates, and in a sample of the world's economic powerhouses. Note that the laws are complicated, and the table provides a simplified view.

Of course, the table merely provides a snapshot of the laws. Enforcement of national gun laws inevitably will vary, as will the degree to which citizens obey them. While the United States has a far higher gun violence rate than do many peer nations that regulate firearms more strictly, the rate in the United States is lower, often significantly, than in developing countries with tougher gun laws, such as the Central American nations.

Why Aren't Guns Treated Like Cars, Toys, or Cigarettes?

Politics mostly.

Gun control advocates have argued for close to 50 years that the government should treat firearms like any other potentially dangerous consumer product. If we require drivers to get training and a government-issued license and to register their cars with a government agency, why not impose similar rules

Table 6.4 Gun Regulation Around the Globe: A Sampler

	Firearms banned for civilian ownership?	Owner license required for nonprohibited guns?	Requirements for gun owner license?	Must demonstrate need to own?
Australia	Automatic, semiautomatic firearms, certain shotguns, short-barreled handguns	Yes	Background check; character reference in some circumstances; training course	Yes; hunting, sports, collecting, occupational needs constitute valid reasons; personal protection does not
Brazil	Automatic firearms, handguns (with narrow exceptions)	Yes	Background check; training course	Yes; hunting, sports, protection constitute valid reasons
Canada	Automatic firearms (pre-1978), short-barrel handguns, certain modified firearms	Yes	Background check; character reference; training course; notification of spouse/partner or next of kin	No, except in case of restricted weapons
China	All firearms, with narrow exceptions for hunters, herdsmen, government-sponsored sports	Limited licenses to carry for sports, hunting, wildlife protection	Private ownership generally banned	Need limited to hunting, herding, government-sponsored sports

Germany	Automatic weapons	Yes	Background check; training course	Yes; hunting, sports, collecting, protection are valid reasons
Israel	n/a	Yes	Background check; must reapply and requalify every three years	Yes; hunting, sports, self-protection are valid reasons
Japan	Automatic and semiautomatic weapons, handguns except for accomplished sports shooters	Yes	Background check; training; must reapply and requalify every three years	Yes; hunting, sports (with permission) constitute valid reasons
New Zealand	Semiautomatic rifles and large-capacity magazines	Yes	Background check; character reference; training course; notification of spouse/partner or next of kin	Yes, for handguns; self-defense not a valid reason
Switzerland	Automatic weapons	Yes, dealer sales only; primarily for handguns	Background check; license limits number of purchases; training for concealed-carry license only	No

(Continued)

Table 6.4 *Continued*

	Firearms banned for civilian ownership?	Owner license required for nonprohibited guns?	Requirements for gun owner license?	Must demonstrate need to own?
United Kingdom	Handguns, semiautomatic assault weapons, automatic weapons	Yes	Background check; character reference	Yes; hunting, sports, collecting constitute valid reasons
United States	Machine guns (except those registered before 1986 law), sawed-off long guns	No, except in a few states	No national license, but background check required for sales by all dealers nationwide and by private sellers in about 40% of states	No

Source: GunPolicy.org; http://www.loc.gov/law/help/firearms-control/switzerland.php; https://www.loc.gov/law/help/firearms-control/china.php.

on gun owners? If we regulate toy guns, why not real guns? If we can heavily tax cigarettes and hold tobacco companies responsible for the harm their products cause, why can't we do the same for guns and gun manufacturers? In some cases advocates made headway with these arguments, only to be stopped in their tracks by lawmakers and the gun lobby.

Cars

Let's start with the automobile analogy. It is apt as far as it goes: Both cars and guns are commonplace and have productive uses, but both can cause harm in untrained, reckless, or criminal hands. Extending registration and licensing to firearms and their users was a top priority of gun control advocates from the 1970s through the 1990s but met with furious resistance from gun groups. It is worth noting that the proposed requirements for guns and gun owners would have gone further than the analogous regulations for cars and drivers, which do not need to be registered or licensed when operating only on private property. Pro-gun advocates argued, successfully, that if the government had a central record of gun owners and firearms, it would provide a road map for confiscation and hasten the demise of a free American society.

Gun control advocates never came close to seeing national licensing of gun owners or registration of everyday firearms. (In 1934, the National Firearms Act required owners to register their existing stocks of machine guns.) Indeed, for four decades ATF's appropriations legislation has barred the agency from maintaining or centralizing gun purchase records. The 1986 Firearm Owners' Protection Act specifically prohibits a national gun registry. Licensing and registration, particularly of assault weapons, exist in a handful of states. However, not even the most "antigun" jurisdictions, including New York City, have used these registries to confiscate firearms.[29] The one narrow exception is California, where authorities have begun a program to retrieve guns from owners who have committed a felony or otherwise become disqualified from owning a firearm.

As licensing and registration have proved politically radioactive, gun violence prevention advocates have sought to translate other lessons from the experience of automobile safety, considered a major success story in using public health methods to solve public problems. The public health perspective—developed by physician-researchers, epidemiologists, and some economists—maintains that people will inevitably behave carelessly, so we might be better off finding ways to prevent or mitigate the harm they cause by altering their environment and "idiot-proofing" (our words) the products they use.

Consider product design. Until the 1950s, society treated deaths and injuries in car crashes as the inevitable result of reckless driving—"Cars don't kill people, people kill people." However, physician-researchers began making the case that many lives could be saved if cars were better designed, an argument later popularized by the consumer advocate Ralph Nader in his groundbreaking exposé *Unsafe at Any Speed* (1965). In the 1980s, physicians and public health experts applied these lessons to guns. If seat belts can save lives, what about safety mechanisms that prevent a gun from firing when a bullet is unknowingly left in the chamber? If we have child safety seats, why not childproof guns? Similar analogies extend from the driving environment to the gun-owning environment. If speed limits can reduce deaths, what about laws mandating safe storage of guns in the home?

Advocates have made some headway with such proposals. For example, at least 7 states and DC regulate handgun design to keep cheaply made and unreliable "junk guns" out of the marketplace; 10 states and the federal government require dealers to sell locking devices on handguns intended for private use; and more than half of states have laws imposing criminal liability on gun owners who leave their firearms accessible to children. Companies are developing "smart gun"

technology that would prevent anyone other than an authorized user from firing the weapon (see Chapter 1). However,
dealers are reluctant to carry these firearms for fear that gun
organizations will call for a store boycott. These advocates
worry that if such next-generation firearms become widely
available, states will require that all guns be smart guns.

After the Sandy Hook school shooting, media commentators and lawyers began to discuss whether gun owners, like car
owners, should have to buy liability insurance. Although the
proposal sounds intriguing to many, there are problems with
the gun–car parallel. Drivers need insurance only if they drive
their car off their property; many guns remain in the home—
and accidental misuse may be covered by some homeowners'
policies. Insurance also doesn't cover criminal activity, and it's
unclear whether insurers would want to provide coverage for
noncriminal incidents outside the home. That said, the proposal remains to be fully explored.

Toys

Gun regulation groups often ask questions along these lines: If
your kid visits a friend's house, which of these do you want
to be sure has been regulated for safety: the teddy bear, the
toy gun, or the real handgun? The question is intended to be
rhetorical, dramatizing a little-known law that prohibits the
nation's product-safety watchdog from regulating firearms
and ammunition.

The storyline by now is familiar. In the 1970s, gun control
advocates sought stricter controls on handguns. Getting nowhere in Congress, these advocates turned to the newly formed
Consumer Product Safety Commission, which is charged with
devising and enforcing safety standards for thousands of
commonly used items, such as paint, lawnmowers, pajamas,
household chemicals, and, yes, teddy bears and toy guns.
When Congress created the commission in 1972, then-Rep.
John Dingell (D-MI), who had been an NRA board member,

slipped into the legislation a provision barring the new agency from regulating guns. The commission interpreted this prohibition to extend to ammunition as well.

However, in 1974 a group of Chicago gun control advocates found a loophole—the commission was also charged with enforcing a separate law, the Hazardous Substances Act, which made no mention of bullets. Thus began the group's "Ban the Bullets" campaign. The commission balked at the effort; but a federal court ordered hearings, and gun groups mobilized. More than 37,000 letters poured in—all but about 100 of which opposed the commission's proposal to regulate ammunition. Congress quickly ended the matter by passing legislation excluding ammunition from the commission's jurisdiction.

In 2000, the Massachusetts attorney general made headlines by using the commonwealth's consumer protection law to promulgate regulations, still in effect, barring sales of cheaply made handguns (so-called Saturday night specials) and requiring new handguns sold in the state to include tamperproof serial numbers, childproof triggers, and safety devices.

Today gun violence prevention advocates still occasionally try consumer protection approaches. Rep. Debbie Dingell (D-MI), the widow and congressional successor of Rep. John Dingell, introduced legislation in 2018 to allow the Consumer Product Safety Commission to regulate in the domain of firearm safety—authority that his legislation had foreclosed in the 1970s.[30] Likewise, bills are regularly introduced in Congress to spur the development of personalized handguns (those that only an authorized user can fire).

Cigarettes

Seeing strong parallels between harm caused by cigarettes and harm caused by firearms, gun violence prevention advocates have long looked to the antismoking movement for inspiration. While efforts by state regulators and private advocacy groups have dramatically changed laws and social norms around smoking in just a few decades, gun violence prevention advocates have enjoyed less success.

Consider some of the parallel strategies.

Taxation. A principle long enshrined in both law and economic theory holds that it's socially desirable to tax products and practices that impose costs on society, what economists call "negative externalities." Lawmakers also impose "sin taxes" to discourage private behavior that society deems morally objectionable.

The individual dangers and social costs of smoking having long been established, antitobacco advocates have secured significant increases in cigarette excise taxes imposed by many cities and states, as well as by the federal government. The federal government has taxed firearms since 1919, at a level that currently stands at 10% of the manufacturer's price for handguns and 11% for long guns. But lawmakers and gun violence prevention advocates have not until very recently embraced taxation as a strategy.[31] In 2013, Cook County (Chicago and environs) imposed a new $25 tax on guns, and lawmakers in several states have introduced measures to tax guns, ammunition, or both. The intent is to use the new revenue to cover the costs of gun violence prevention programs.

Place-based restrictions. Thirty years ago, it was common to find people smoking in offices, in restaurants, even on airplanes. Today, smoking is banned in virtually every enclosed public space. With respect to firearms, the trend has gone in the other direction. Laws on carrying guns in open public spaces have been relaxed or eliminated in most states. And gun groups have secured provisions allowing firearms in bars and on public university campuses. In 2010, President Obama signed legislation permitting loaded guns in national parks.

Litigation. Antismoking advocates, including state attorneys general, have enjoyed some of their biggest successes in the courtroom. In the 1990s, states sued Big Tobacco for deceptive and fraudulent marketing, targeting children in their campaigns, and hiding the harm caused by their products. These lawsuits resulted in a series of settlements totaling nearly $250 billion and the release of voluminous evidence documenting underhanded industry practices. The federal government also successfully sued the tobacco companies for conspiring to conceal the health risks of smoking and for illegally marketing cigarettes to kids.

In the 1990s and early 2000s, cities, advocacy groups, and gun violence victims pursued a similar litigation strategy against gun manufacturers and dealers. In some of these cases, the plaintiffs sued firearms manufacturers for negligently marketing their products in a way that they knew, or should have known, would be especially attractive to criminals. Gun manufacturers were also sued for failing to design guns with features to prevent accidental shootings. In yet other cases, gun dealers were sued for flooding the market with firearms in violation of "public nuisance" laws and for selling their wares to suspicious buyers in violation of laws against negligent distribution. New York City famously sued out-of-state gun dealers for providing guns that ended up in the "Iron Pipeline," the colloquial name for the I-95 highway corridor along which guns are trafficked from dealers in the South to criminal enterprises in the North. (Laying the groundwork for these cases, police sting operations had caught dealers selling to "customers" who were sending strong signals that they were buying the gun illegally.)

In all these lawsuits, the claim was *not* that gun makers and dealers should be held to account because their products were designed to kill—and often do. Rather, the legal theory was that manufacturers and dealers should be held liable (and thus forced to pay up) when they could have foreseen the misuse of their products *and* taken reasonable care to prevent it. The goal was to compensate those bearing the costs of gun violence—either individuals or governments—and to change corporate conduct to reduce future harm.

Gun industry representatives and pro-gun groups vigorously fought these lawsuits, both in court and through the legislative process. These advocates argued that whatever happens down the line with a gun, the industry is "remote" from the crime, and its hands therefore are clean. Advocates also argued that cities are not entitled to recover the costs of gun violence from private entities. Legalese aside, gun industry representatives saw the lawsuits as nothing but an abuse of the legal system—a sneaky way of securing public policy goals that served no purpose except to bankrupt lawful businesses.

Whatever the particulars of the legal claim, these cases did not deliver the victories for which cities, victims, and gun regulation advocates had hoped. Courts dismissed most cases outright, and those that succeeded initially were almost universally overturned on appeal.

In cases brought against out-of-state sellers, New York City was able to secure settlement agreements aimed at curbing gun trafficking. But at the national level, the big breakthrough settlement—the proverbial "game changer"—fell apart. The story will sound familiar by now. Manufacturer Smith & Wesson reached an agreement with the Clinton administration and various cities to take steps to curb careless distribution and sales, but the company had to abandon the pact after a crippling boycott and the departure of the company's chief executive officer.

By 2005, 33 states had enacted laws barring antigun litigation, and that year the federal government sealed the deal nationally by enacting the Protection of Lawful Commerce in Arms Act, which barred future lawsuits against dealers and manufacturers except when they had negligently or knowingly violated firearms laws. The law allowed suits over firearm defects but only when the gun had been "used as intended or in a reasonably foreseeable manner" and not in crime. The so-called immunity law also required the dismissal of pending cases. In anticipation of signing the bill, President George W. Bush said it would "further our efforts to stem frivolous lawsuits, which cause a logjam in America's courts, harm America's small businesses, and benefit a handful of lawyers at the expense of victims and consumers."[32] With passage of the NRA-backed law, individuals and localities especially affected by gun violence largely stopped turning to the courts for help.

That said, after the mass shooting at Sandy Hook Elementary School in 2012, families of nine of the victims sued the gun manufacturers, distributors, and dealers associated with the tragedy. The Connecticut Supreme Court ruled that state and federal law precluded most of the families' claims. But the judges decided that one of their arguments deserved its day in court: that the manufacturer had marketed a military-style weapon to civilians for illegal uses. Depending on the outcome, this closely watched case has the potential to open a new front in gun litigation.

To answer the question we posed—why aren't guns treated like any other consumer product?—the answer is mostly rooted in politics. No other consumer product has been championed by a lobby as politically powerful *at the grassroots* as the pro-gun lobby. To be sure, business is powerful: Automakers, tobacco companies, and other manufacturing interests are often able to get their way in Washington and in state capitals. But these interests don't have the same passionate voter base that the gun lobby does, a base that keeps lawmakers in a state of electoral vigilance. What's more, many Americans associate guns with deeply personal and democratic values to a degree not enjoyed by cars, toys, and cigarettes. When values and emotions are at stake, policy change based on dry cost/benefit calculations or technocratic approaches becomes politically challenging. Finally, of course, there is the Constitution. Since 2008, the Second Amendment has been interpreted to protect ownership of a gun for self-protection; there is no right to cars, cigarettes, or toys.

What Are Stand-Your-Ground Laws?

Stand-your-ground laws are policy innovations at the state level that give you the right to defend yourself with deadly force if you have reason to feel threatened.

American law has long allowed people to use deadly force to defend themselves at home. This principle is enshrined in the Castle Doctrine, which refers to the seventeenth-century English legal precept that "a man's home is his castle." But the law historically has not extended such a broad right of self-defense outside the home. There, most states traditionally imposed a "duty to retreat": If you think you can get out of a bad situation, you should try. Stand-your-ground laws in essence remove this obligation.

Since 2005, 30 states have adopted such provisions. Now, people who use force when they feel threatened generally are entitled to immunity from criminal prosecution and civil liability. In effect, these laws confer police powers on private citizens, without the training and accountability procedures to which police are subject.

Florida was the first state to pass a stand-your-ground law. It came into public focus in 2012, when a self-styled neighborhood watchman followed a 17-year-old high school student, Trayvon Martin, in the gated community where he was visiting his father. After an altercation, the watchman, George Zimmerman, shot and killed the unarmed teenager. The local police initially released Zimmerman, but after a broad public outcry, he was charged and tried for Martin's death. More than a year later, a jury acquitted Zimmerman of second-degree murder and of manslaughter, provoking national controversy. Though Zimmerman did not invoke the stand-your-ground law, the trial focused on possible interactions between him and the victim, and the judge's instructions to the jury echoed the statute's language: "If George Zimmerman was not engaged in an unlawful activity, and was attacked in any place where he had a right to be, he had no duty to retreat and had the right to stand his ground and meet force with force, including deadly force if he reasonably believed that it was necessary to do so to prevent death or great bodily harm to himself or another."[33]

It is interesting to speculate about what would have transpired if Trayvon Martin had killed Zimmerman. In that scenario, Martin might well have invoked the stand-your-ground law on the basis that he was not engaged in an unlawful activity, was attacked by Zimmerman in a place where he had a right to be, and reasonably believed that deadly force was necessary to defend himself. This counterfactual illustrates an important point: that stand-your-ground laws—dubbed "Shoot First" by critics—make it easier to get away with what would heretofore have been considered criminal homicide. Because legal presumptions favor defendants, the prosecution has the burden of disproving the survivor's story. Casting doubt on the survivor is difficult if he has killed the only witness.

The NRA promotes stand-your-ground laws using arguments that resonate with many Americans worried that police cannot defend them. Proponents argue that these laws, in conjunction with laws facilitating the carrying of concealed weapons, make criminals think twice about attempting a carjacking or a rape (or even a bar fight) because they know that the intended victim has the legal right to shoot them.

However, the best empirical work casts doubt on the public benefits of stand-your-ground laws. At least three peer-reviewed studies have concluded that these laws are associated with a substantial increase in gun homicide rates, even after accounting for other factors.[34] One of these studies also finds an increase in gun-related hospitalizations.[35] Likewise, the research provides no reason to believe that stand-your-ground laws deter crime, such as assault or robbery.[36] And, indeed, a closer look at how these laws operate suggests that they may perpetuate racial bias. Police are more likely to rule a homicide justified when a white person kills a black person than in the reverse case.[37] And courts are more likely to acquit the killer when the victim is a person of color rather than a white person.[38]

In evaluating the costs of stand-your-ground laws, it is impossible to ignore the interaction between permissive policies and the prevalence of guns. In the 2016–2018 timeframe, Florida was issuing about 350,000 to 400,000 concealed-carry permits per year, up roughly 60% to 85% in population-adjusted terms since the year before the 2005 stand-your-ground law was passed.[39] Proponents might see these trends as enhancing public safety by creating a well-armed civilian police force. But police are required to have training in handling weapons and dealing with threats, and they are subject to internal rules as well as legal restraints whenever they discharge a weapon. As Miami's former chief of police explains: "Trying to control shootings by members of a well-trained and disciplined police department is a daunting enough task. Laws like 'stand your ground' give citizens unfettered power and discretion with no accountability. It is a recipe for disaster."[40]

In a 2012 investigation, the *Tampa Bay Times* documented nearly 200 cases in which defendants asserted stand-your-ground claims.[41] This defense worked to get cases dismissed 70% of the time and is now used in hundreds of cases per year. In nearly a third of the cases, explained the *Times*, "defendants initiated the fight, shot an unarmed person or pursued their victim—and still went free." Judges appeared unsure about the boundaries of the doctrine, and outcomes in courts were highly inconsistent. Such uncertainties gave defense attorneys a strong incentive to invoke stand-your-ground claims in most cases of violent crime. The extra procedural protections that stand-your-ground laws afford turn out to be a burden on the prosecution.

In short, research suggests that stand-your-ground laws have encouraged the use of deadly force and had a disparate impact on people of color. These laws have opened the door to a more dangerous world where everyone feels pressure to carry a gun—and if you feel threatened, to shoot first and tell your story later.

7

EFFECTIVENESS
OF FIREARMS POLICY

With So Many Guns Out There, Is There Any Point to Gun Control?

Yes. The evidence suggests that certain regulations have been effective in reducing gun use in crime. And even in the United States, guns are not as readily available as some commentators have claimed.

While there are enough firearms in circulation for every adult to have one, only one in four adults actually does own a firearm. Most violent crime is committed not with guns, but rather with knives, clubs, and bare fists. Even for robbery, a crime where a gun is a very useful tool, the perpetrator is more likely to use a less intimidating weapon. One explanation: Most offenders lack ready access to a gun.

Those who argue that offenders will do whatever is necessary to obtain their guns may have in mind some violent gang members or career criminals. But even if such people are successful in obtaining the firearms they want, that does not necessarily extend to the "amateurs"—the much larger group of people who get into bar fights, abuse their intimate partners, sell drugs occasionally, and so forth.

As Chapter 3 discussed, most criminals who do become armed obtain their guns from friends, family members, or street sources, rather than from legitimate retail dealers. These informal transactions are likely easier to arrange in

Mississippi, where 60% of households have at least one gun, than in Massachusetts, where just 13% of households do. Various studies have found a close statistical link between the prevalence of gun ownership and the illegal use of guns. For example, across the 200 largest urban counties, gun carrying by teenage males is highly correlated with the prevalence of gun ownership, as is the percentage of robberies committed with a gun.[1] At the state or county level, an increase in guns is closely followed by an increase in the gun homicide rate.[2]

The old bumper sticker says, "When guns are outlawed, only outlaws will have guns." Perhaps a more accurate statement is "When guns are scarce, outlaws will use less lethal weapons"—with the result that fewer victims will die.

Other evidence indicates a close link between the prevalence of gun ownership and the use of firearms in attempted suicides. In fact, the percentage of suicides committed with a gun is highly correlated with the percentage of gun-owning households—so highly that the weapon mix in suicide serves as an accurate proxy for the prevalence of gun ownership in the population.[3] Thus the weapon selected to attempt suicide appears to be greatly influenced by what is readily at hand. A firearm in the home becomes a risk to its occupants who may (at least occasionally) consider suicide. And when a firearm is used rather than razor blades or pills, the chance of death is greatly elevated. (Chapter 3 develops this point more fully.)

Given that availability influences the mix of weapons in crime and suicide, regulations that make it more difficult for high-risk people to obtain firearms may curtail misuse and save lives. But what sorts of regulations are effective in reducing availability to dangerous people? A logical place to start is with regulations that reduce the overall prevalence of guns. In the United States this approach has been used selectively, usually for particular types of firearms (machine guns, assault weapons, and in a few jurisdictions handguns). But other strategies have been more widely adopted.

One strategy is what might be called "partial prohibition"—banning gun possession by people who are identified as high risk (teenagers, convicted felons, substance abusers). Partial prohibitions are primarily enforced through regulations on transactions: restrictions on gun shipments, background checks for buyers, mandated waiting periods before delivery of a gun, license or permit requirements for buyers, and so forth.

A second strategy is to restrict certain uses of guns that are conducive to criminal use. An important distinction is between keeping a gun at home and carrying it in public. State and local regulations have traditionally restricted carrying a concealed gun in public and banned guns from schools, bars, airports, government buildings, and other venues. Police in violence-plagued cities have attempted to "keep guns off the street" by making gun carrying a primary focus of patrol activities. But in recent years such "place and manner" regulations have been repealed in many states.

A third strategy is to induce offenders to give up their guns by increasing the likelihood or severity of punishment for crimes committed with a gun. Many state codes specify sentencing enhancements for crimes committed with a gun. And the likelihood of arrest may be increased if police are in a position to use ballistic evidence to solve gun crimes. The ultimate goal is to make guns a liability to the criminal so that he will choose to desist from crime, or at least use some other type of weapon. Note that in this approach the firearms regulations are a complement to effective law enforcement. For example, legal restrictions on carrying concealed weapons facilitate police efforts to prevent gang members from launching attacks in public places. And solving gun crimes through ballistics investigations is greatly facilitated if regulations require that records be kept of firearm transactions and that owners be licensed.

Regulations and laws are never 100% effective. The question is whether they are effective enough to justify the cost. It seems that in the gun control arena, everyone has an opinion about what works, but scientific evidence is often lacking. This chapter summarizes some of the relevant research. What we would like ideally is direct evidence that a regulation affected the rate of homicide or suicide. Unfortunately, such evidence is not always available or is hotly contested.[4]

Do Restrictions on Military-Style Firearms Reduce Gun Violence?

The federal assault weapons ban was implemented in 1994 and ended in 2004, when Congress allowed it to expire. There is no compelling evidence that it saved lives.[5] A more stringent or longer-lasting ban might well have been more effective.

The law banned the introduction of new assault weapons into commerce. The law also banned new large-capacity magazines, ones that could accommodate more than 10 rounds of ammunition. The assault weapons ban was directed at semiautomatic firearms that incorporated design features from infantry weapons that are of little use in hunting, target shooting, or other traditional civilian uses. Such firearms are in fact rarely used in routine criminal violence. The ban on large-capacity magazines (LCMs) had greater potential to make a real difference; such magazines, which hold 30, 50, or even 100 rounds of ammunition, allow the shooter to fire many times without pausing to reload. That is a real advantage to rampage shooters bent on killing as many people as possible.

Since the end of the ban on assault weapons in 2004, millions of AR-15–style rifles have been sold to civilians. The AR-15 is modeled on the standard M16 and M4 infantry rifles, but without the option of firing multiple rounds with a single pull of the trigger. Some of the most notorious mass shootings in recent years have involved this weapon, including those at Virginia Tech, Las Vegas, San Bernardino, Newtown, and Parkland.[6]

The details of the 1994 ban undercut its effectiveness. Assault weapons and LCMs already manufactured were "grandfathered," so they could continue to be possessed or exchanged. By 1994, there were around 25 million LCMs and additional millions available for legal import from Europe. Eventually the ban on newly produced LCMs would have reduced their availability, but 10 years was not enough to dry up the available supply. We can hope to learn more in the future from the experience of the handful of states that currently ban assault weapons and LCMs.

It is interesting to compare the 1994 assault weapons ban with another federal initiative from 60 years earlier, the National Firearms Act (NFA). As explained in the previous chapter, the NFA was intended to end the use of the gangster weapons that became notorious during the Roaring Twenties. But rather than an outright ban on Thompson submachine guns and the like, the law required that owners register them with the federal government. The NFA was also intended to shut down the secondhand market in these weapons by imposing a $200 tax on any transaction, an amount equivalent to thousands of today's dollars. Unfortunately, there are no good statistics on the use of fully automatic weapons prior to the NFA, and hence it's impossible to estimate the extent to which the NFA suppressed criminal use. By 2017 there were 630,000 machine guns registered under the NFA, so they are definitely available to collectors and at shooting ranges and the like. But they are rarely used in crime these days. Of the crime guns submitted for tracing by law-enforcement agencies, only 4 in 1,000 were machine guns.[7] Thus a type of weapon that would likely appeal to modern-day gangsters, as it did to Al Capone, is rarely used in crime, a plausible "win" for federal regulation.

The Las Vegas massacre in 2017 (58 killed and 422 wounded) was perpetrated by a lone shooter equipped with AR-15–style rifles that had been modified using a device called a bump stock. This device in effect converted the semiautomatic rifle into an automatic, firing multiple rounds with a single pull of the trigger. The Trump administration banned bump stocks in April 2019 on the grounds that they violated the NFA. It remains to be seen whether this new ban will prove effective.

What Did We Learn from Local Handgun Bans?

Two cities play a distinctive role in the history of gun control: Washington, DC, and Chicago. They were the only large cities to attempt to ban handgun acquisition in modern times—in 1976 and 1982, respectively. And their bans became the basis for the two recent rulings of the US Supreme Court on the Second Amendment, having the effect of establishing a right of the public to keep a handgun in the home for self-defense (*District of Columbia v. Heller* in 2008) and extending that ruling to prohibit state and local handgun bans nationwide (*McDonald v. Chicago* in 2010). But the fact that the bans were ultimately ruled unconstitutional does not answer the interesting question of whether they were effective when in force.

Evaluating these bans requires a comparison between observed gun violence while they were in effect with an estimate of the volume of gun violence that *would have* occurred in the counterfactual condition of no ban. What we actually observe in Washington is an initial drop in gun violence in the late 1970s, after the ban took effect, followed by a devastating increase during the late 1980s, when the city was dubbed the nation's "murder capital." Thankfully that epidemic of violence, associated with the introduction of crack cocaine to the city, has long since passed, and murder rates are relatively low now. A similar epidemic occurred in Chicago, and for that matter in every large city in the nation. Estimating the counterfactual is very difficult in such volatile circumstances. Could lethal violence rates during the crack epidemic have climbed still higher in Chicago and Washington in the absence of the handgun bans? Perhaps, but it is impossible to say with any confidence. All too evident is that dangerous gang members and drug dealers have been able to arm themselves despite the bans.

Further doubts about the bans' efficacy are raised by the fact that the general prevalence of gun ownership in these cities appears to have been little affected by the bans.[8] Tracking our preferred proxy for gun ownership rates (the percentage of suicides with guns), we see no evidence of an unusual decline following the implementation of either ban. Our tentative conclusion is that the bans were largely ineffective, not only in reducing gun use by criminals, but also in reducing handgun ownership by ordinary people.

One reasonable explanation is that these cities are not islands. Chicago residents could purchase handguns legally at any number of gun shops located just outside the city limit, and while it was technically illegal for them to then bring the guns back to their homes, that restriction was tough to enforce. Similarly, DC residents live close to gun shops and gun shows located in the Virginia and Maryland suburbs, where DC residents could readily obtain a gun—perhaps with the help of a friend who lived in one of these states.

The apparent failure of these local bans tells us very little about what would happen in a jurisdiction that could better enforce an imposed ban. For evidence on that score we might turn to the experience of Great Britain, which had stringent regulations of handguns in place and then banned them outright in 1998 following the massacre of schoolchildren in Dunblane, Scotland.[9] Needless to say, Great Britain *is* an island. Since the ban went into effect, the prevalence of gun ownership has stayed at a very low level. As usual, weapon choice in suicide provides a guide to the prevalence of gun ownership: In the United Kingdom, suicides by gun remain at about 2% of all suicides—compared with around 50% in the United States. And the United Kingdom suffers only about two or three dozen gun homicides each year.

This experience suggests yet another version of that "When guns are outlawed, only outlaws will have guns" bumper sticker. The experience with Great Britain tells us that "when guns are *effectively* outlawed, then almost no one will have guns."

Do Gun Buybacks Reduce Gun Violence?

Government agencies, churches, and nonprofit groups sponsor occasional gun buyback programs in an attempt to dry up local availability. Typically, these sporadic, days-long programs offer cash or goods in exchange for guns. The evidence suggests that these approaches are not effective at reducing gun violence. Unsurprisingly, people are inclined to turn in guns that are no longer useful—they are broken or have become redundant, given all the other guns owned by the individual. And these programs can even have perverse effects: If the reward is in the form of cash, there is always a possibility that the cash will be used to buy a replacement firearm.

It should be noted that while occasional, temporary buybacks have little apparent effect on gun crime, logic suggests that the consequence of a permanent buyback program may be stronger. For example, the New York Police Department (NYPD) runs a Cash for Guns program that pays $200 for a working gun. Unlike a temporary buyback plan, the NYPD's offer would logically be expected to shape the underground market in guns, setting a minimum price at which illegal transactions occur. For a cash-strapped youth looking to buy a gun, that minimum price may serve as a substantial barrier.

Discussions of gun buybacks often turn to Australia's experience. Australia's 1997 buyback of semiautomatic rifles—a program inspired by the rampage shooting in Port Arthur, Tasmania—appears to have been very successful. A fundamental difference between the Australian buyback and buybacks in the United States is that Australia was offering to buy guns that were no longer legal and hence subject to confiscation.[10] Thus, Australian owners could not exploit the buyback to exchange their old gun for a new one, nor was the buyback limited to owners who had no further use for the weapon. Ultimately, more than 1 million firearms were sent to the smelter—something like one-third of the entire stock of firearms in Australia. There is strong evidence that the great

Australian buyback reduced gun homicide and ended rampage shootings, which had been a regular occurrence prior to the ban.[11] Needless to say, such a program would not be politically feasible in the United States.

What Measures Are Effective in Reducing Gun Trafficking?

The Gun Control Act of 1968 (GCA) was designed to regulate gun commerce to prevent the gun market in states with weak laws from undercutting the regulations in states with stronger laws. Only federally licensed dealers can receive interstate firearms shipments, and they are barred from selling handguns to anyone from out of state. Private sales have the same restriction.

The GCA has provided the more regulated states some protection from the laxer states, but it does not achieve 100% compliance. There is a well-established pattern whereby firearms sold in lax states flow to those with stringent regulations.[12] New York City Mayor Michael Bloomberg was particularly outspoken about the illicit flow of guns, and justifiably so given that some 90% of all crime guns in the city came from out of state. While New York City has been highly successful in reducing gun violence since its peak in the early 1990s, the city could have done still more if its efforts had not been undercut by the Iron Pipeline of illicit shipments from Virginia, the Carolinas, Georgia, and Florida. Bloomberg sued more than 20 dealers in 2006 and won settlements with a number of them, requiring that they change their sales practices.

A couple of specific case studies help document the economics of interstate gun flows—and establish the importance of regulation in influencing these flows. First is the federal Brady Act, which since 1994 has required licensed dealers to conduct background checks on would-be buyers. The background check requirement makes it more difficult for felons and other disqualified people to "lie and buy" from dealers. Some states had their own background check requirements in place before the federal requirement went into effect. One of these states was Illinois, and prior to 1994, its background check requirement was undermined by lax practices in other states. In fact, many guns that ended up in the hands of Chicago criminals were first sold by dealers in the Deep South. Those states became less attractive as sources to gun traffickers with the advent of the federal background check requirement. Overnight the percentage of new Chicago crime guns that originated in the states that were required by the Brady Act to adopt background checks dropped from around 35% to just 14%. Thus the Midwestern version of the Iron Pipeline was reined in by this modest federal requirement.[13] (It should be said that Mississippi remains a major illicit "exporter" of guns to other states, the most prolific source on a per capita basis in the nation, but still is more restrained than in the pre-Brady era.)

A second case study is of a state that relaxed its regulations. In August 2007 Missouri rescinded its longstanding requirement that all handgun buyers obtain a pistol permit from the local sheriff. Without the requirement private sales became unregulated, and sales by dealers no longer required the sheriff's approval. One result was an abrupt reduction in the percentage of crime guns originating out of state; the repeal of the pistol permit law made it easier for felons to buy guns from local sources. Similarly, there was a sharp increase in the percentage of crime guns that flowed quickly from a licensed dealer into crime. In 2006, 3.2% of guns recovered by the police had been sold by a dealer within the prior three months. By 2008, just after the permit requirement was rescinded, that figure had tripled to 9.4%. It appears that some scofflaw dealers in Missouri took advantage of deregulation to sell directly to criminals or their straw purchasers—still illegal transactions, but with the sheriff out of the picture, harder to regulate.[14]

The clear conclusion is that laws matter. State and federal regulations influence how quickly or easily firearms flow from legitimate sales to criminal use.[15]

Do Prosecutions of Felons for Possession of Firearms Deter Gun Crime?

One noteworthy approach to deterring illicit carrying and use has been to threaten people who have been convicted of a felony with federal prosecution if they are arrested in possession of a gun. Since federal law specifies longer prison sentences for "felons in possession" than do state laws, federalizing such cases might well have a deterrent effect on this high-risk group. A federal program called Project Safe Neighborhoods was implemented during the late 1990s to encourage federal–local cooperation in prosecuting such cases.

"Felon in possession" laws are an example of "focused" or "targeted" deterrence. People who have already been convicted of a felony constitute a high-risk group compared to the general public. The prominence of the federal prosecution strategy owed much to the publicity given to Project Exile in Richmond, Virginia. This partnership between local prosecutors and the US attorney was implemented in 1997, after which a number of ex-cons arrested for firearms possession were referred for federal prosecution and received hefty prison sentences. The deterrent effect of this program was widely credited for the subsequent drop in murder rates, although a careful look at the timing of the drop in gun murders suggests that claim is dubious at best.[16]

On the other hand, an evaluation of Project Safe Neighborhoods in Chicago found evidence of an initial deterrent effect in two high-violence neighborhoods. A key element of this effort was to personalize the threat of long prison sentences for felons in possession by use of notification sessions with small groups of convicts. It appears that the program became less effective over time, perhaps due to a dilution of effort.[17]

Has the Federal Background Check Law Reduced Gun Violence?

The Brady Handgun Violence Prevention Act, implemented in 1994, is the most significant federal gun control law enacted in the past half-century. Under the law, more than 300 million background checks have been processed on gun buyers since 1998. Yet, early evidence suggests that the law had little effect on homicide rates, at least in the first few years. The likely explanation is that its regulations did not cover the kinds of transactions by which most criminals become armed.

James Brady, press secretary to President Reagan, was shot during an assassination attempt in March 1981. Together with his wife, Sarah, Brady became a leader of the gun control movement, and through Handgun Control Inc. worked for seven years to achieve passage of the bill that bore his name. The first set of provisions, implemented in February 1994, required licensed dealers to conduct a background check on would-be buyers and wait five business days before transferring a handgun to a customer. Only 32 states were directly affected by these provisions because the other 18 states and the District of Columbia already met the minimum requirements of the act. In effect these provisions created what social scientists call a "natural experiment," with 32 states in the "change" or "treatment" condition and the 18 no-change states serving as "controls." After the Brady Act was implemented, economists Jens Ludwig and Philip Cook utilized this experiment-like setting to estimate the causal effect of the Brady Act on certain outcomes. Their article in the *Journal of the American Medical Association* found that average homicide rates in the treatment states and the control states followed almost exactly the same trajectories before 1994. Following implementation of the act, homicide rates declined, but equally so in the two groups of states. There was no added advantage in the newly regulated states.[18]

Since the Brady Act provisions were limited to regulating sales by licensed dealers, the informal transactions by which almost all criminals get their guns were not directly affected. It is plausible that a more comprehensive law would have been more effective.

Does Closing the "Private Sale Loophole" Reduce Gun Crime?

Federally licensed firearm dealers, retail stores, and individuals whose regular business includes selling guns are required to conduct a background check to ensure that the would-be buyer is not a felon or otherwise barred from owning a firearm. The primary system for conducting these checks is the National Instant Criminal Background Check System (NICS). Mandated by the Brady Act and launched by the Federal Bureau of Investigation (FBI) on November 30, 1998, NICS is used by dealers to quickly determine a customer's eligibility to buy a gun. The query goes through either a state agency or the FBI, which maintains or has access to databases on criminal records, fugitives, illegal aliens, and those disqualified due to severe mental illness. Since initiation in 1998, NICS checks have blocked more than 3 million transactions. The denial rate has been roughly 1.5% in recent years.

There is a loophole in this system, which is really more like a gaping barn door: Transactions that do not involve a licensed dealer are unregulated in most states. In all but 20 states and the District of Columbia, private citizens can sell, loan, or give a firearm to anyone else, no questions asked, so long as the provider does not knowingly transfer a gun to someone prohibited from owning one. In most cases violent offenders get their guns through private transactions.

An obvious solution is to extend the background check requirement to private transactions. Ten states impose this requirement on all firearms sales or transfers at the point when they occur, and two others have this "point of sale" mandate just for handgun transactions. A number of other states impose the background check indirectly by requiring buyers to have a permit or license, which itself requires a check. For example, since 1921 North Carolina has stipulated that before acquiring a handgun the buyer must get a permit from the local sheriff. California's regulation takes a somewhat different approach, requiring (since 1991) that all transactions be channeled through a licensed dealer, who is responsible for conducting the background check.

Following the Sandy Hook school massacre in 2012, a vigorous campaign by gun violence prevention advocates, along with President Obama and Vice President Biden, sought to persuade Congress to create a universal background check requirement, closing the private sale loophole nationwide. As of this writing, the effort had been unsuccessful, despite the overwhelming support of the American public.

A universal background check requirement would by no means eradicate gun crime. But such a federal law might reduce gun violence simply because some dangerous people—those disqualified from gun ownership—would find it more difficult to obtain a gun quickly or to exploit differences in state gun regulations. The benefits of this law could be counted in terms of lives saved in street crime, domestic violence, and suicides. Just how many lives would be saved would depend on how well the law was enforced.

But is a universal background check enforceable? California's system is complemented by a requirement that handguns be registered to their owner, which is useful in holding owners accountable when they decide to sell a handgun. Even without a registration requirement, a universal background check system could be enforced in a variety of ways, including law-enforcement oversight of gun shows and internet sales and undercover "buy and bust" operations by the police. Whether the California universal background check system has been successful in reducing gun violence has not been established.

Another approach for making the background check requirement more reliable is to improve the databases kept by the FBI. In recognition of this problem Congress established the National Criminal History Improvement Program

(NCHIP) to provide grants and technical assistance to the states to improve the quality and immediate accessibility of criminal history records and related information. This federal investment resulted in a large increase in the criminal records accessible for background checks, thereby increasing the chance that a disqualified person would be identified as such through the NICS process. NCHIP has continued to provide modest funding for improving records and was supplemented in 2007 by a new program focused on helping states to incorporate mental health records into the NICS system. About half the states have recently changed their laws to authorize and require submission of mental health records to the FBI's database. Millions of additional records have been filed, although there are still large gaps.[19]

How Effective Are Laws in Reducing Gun Use in Domestic Violence?

In 1993, the year before Congress passed the Violence Against Women Act (VAWA), the FBI counted about 1,400 homicides of adults by family members, either a man killing a woman (996 cases) or a woman killing a man (381 cases). Most of these murders were by firearm (62%), and many were the culmination of a history of domestic violence. Research by Jacqueline Campbell and her associates has demonstrated that chronic domestic violence is five times more likely to result in death if a gun is available in the home.[20] Thus a plausible approach to reducing intimate partner homicide is to remove guns from violent households. With that in mind, Congress in 1994 adopted a ban on firearms possession by anyone under a restraining order for posing a threat to his or her intimate partner or child or to a partner's child. In 1996 the ban was extended to anyone with a misdemeanor conviction for violence against an intimate partner (the Lautenberg Amendment). During the same decade a number of states adopted parallel statutes that in some cases went beyond the federal laws, for example by extending gun possession bans to people under temporary (not just permanent) restraining orders. A number of these states permit or require police to remove firearms from the scene when they are called on a domestic violence case.

State laws that ban gun possession by those under a restraining order appears to have been somewhat effective in reducing intimate partner homicide, with a best estimate of an 8% reduction.[21] The Lautenberg Amendment (banning possession by those with a misdemeanor conviction for domestic violence) also saves lives. A persuasive evaluation, conducted by Professor Kerri Raissian, took advantage of the natural experiment created by the staggered rollout of this federal law. Although the Lautenberg Amendment is federal, it did not immediately become law in states with criminal codes that did not distinguish between domestic violence and common assault. That issue was litigated in each of the federal circuits, with rulings extending over the course of 13 years.[22] Eight of the federal circuit courts (and then the US Supreme Court) ultimately ruled that the federal law applied in states using assault statutes to prosecute domestic violence. Raissian found that the law was particularly effective in reducing killings of female intimate partners. The gun murder rate for this group was reduced by 17%, estimated quite precisely, and with no indication of an increase in non-gun murders.

Should People Convicted of Violent Misdemeanors Have Guns?

While there is broad consensus that violent criminals should not be allowed to possess firearms, determining where to draw the line is controversial. Federal law enumerates disqualifying characteristics, of which the most important in practice is felony conviction. Yet a study of adult murder defendants in Chicago found that only 43% of them had a felony conviction on their record.[23]

A natural next step would be to disqualify those convicted of violent crimes at the misdemeanor level. Compared with those with a clean record, gun buyers with a misdemeanor conviction for assault and battery, say, or for brandishing a weapon have a greatly elevated risk of subsequent violence. With that in mind, California (and some other states) legislated a ban on gun possession for those with a violent misdemeanor on their record. (The disqualification extends for 10 years from time of conviction.) A study by Garen Wintemute and colleagues compared would-be gun buyers before and after the ban went into effect in 1991. Before implementation of this restriction, this group was allowed to complete the transaction, whereas after they were disqualified. Wintemute found that after the ban went into effect, those with a misdemeanor violence record were less likely to reoffend than were their counterparts before the ban.[24]

Are there other types of crime that should disqualify people from gun ownership? The GCA specifies that anyone who is an illegal user of a controlled substance (such as cocaine, heroin, or marijuana) is disqualified. Taken literally, this condition would disqualify more people than any of the other disqualifying criteria, since 1 in 10 adults is a current user of illicit substances. But in practice drug use is not a factor in screening gun buyers. To make the drug criterion operational, it would be helpful to make the law more specific, and that raises the question: Should it be enough to have a recent conviction for illicit drug possession? And what about a failed drug test for employment? Or the use of marijuana, banned by federal law but permitted (at least with a doctor's recommendation) in two-thirds of the states?

Another possibility would be to disqualify habitual alcohol abusers from possession (or at least from concealed carrying). To make that dimension operational, individuals who have accumulated several driving-under-the-influence convictions could be disqualified for a period of time. Most states have a weaker restriction that bans gun possession while under the influence.

Should Criminals Be Banned for Life from Owning Guns?

A felony conviction and several other disqualifying conditions in the GCA bar firearms possession for life unless gun rights are restored. It was the Reagan-era Firearm Owners' Protection Act (1986) that opened the door to restoration of gun rights. Today a number of states restore rights automatically for nonviolent felons after they finish their sentences or soon thereafter. Even violent felons may petition the court to have their firearms rights restored, and the process for doing so is often perfunctory, with many documented instances of serious crimes committed by ex-cons after restoration of rights.[25]

It would make sense to approach this issue scientifically. Criminologists have long known that the likelihood of reoffending for ex-convicts declines over time. Similar to cancer survivors, the longer a convicted criminal maintains a clean record, the greater the chances that he will remain clean. Given enough years, it is possible to say that the ex-con is no more likely to be arrested than the average member of the community. In an actuarial sense, that is the point of "redemption"—a striking term coined by the dean of criminologists, Alfred Blumstein, and his associate Kiminori Nakamura.[26] In their research on the subject, they identified the point of redemption at around 11 to 15 years for violent offenders, slightly less for drug or property offenders. Thus, there is a scientific basis for considering convicted felons who have lived in the community for 15 years without an arrest to be good bets for restoration of gun rights.

The same issue arises with severe mental illness, which, like criminal careers or drug abuse, is not necessarily a permanent condition.

What Are Sound Strategies for Handling Mental Illness and Firearms?

The shooter in the Virginia Tech rampage of 2007 had been diagnosed with and treated for severe mental illness, but the record was not in the background check system used by gun dealers. As a result, he was able to pass a NICS check and arm himself with the weapons he used to kill 32 people. The mental health aspects of this horrendous event were prominent in the political aftermath. As one result, Congress enacted a program to fund state-level efforts to improve the compilation and reporting of data on people disqualified due to severe mental illness. Virginia, Connecticut, and several other states have improved their reporting, but in many states reporting is still woefully incomplete. (The money comes with strings attached—states are required to adopt a procedure for restoring gun rights to those who are disqualified due to mental illness.)

The GCA bans gun possession by those who have been "adjudicated as a mental defective." That archaic terminology has been operationalized to include four categories of people whom a court has ruled to be severely mentally ill: incompetent to stand trial; not guilty by reason of insanity; involuntarily committed to a mental institution; or subject to a conservatorship.

Connecticut provides a case study of the possibilities and limitations of the mental health disqualification. In 2007, Connecticut began compiling data on people who were disqualified due to severe mental illness and reporting to NICS. A careful study of administrative records over eight years in Connecticut found more than 23,000 cases in which someone was hospitalized for severe mental illness—schizophrenia, bipolar disorder, or major depression. As a whole, this group was at high risk of violence—39% were convicted of a violent crime during the eight years. But of this group, just 7% were disqualified as a result of their mental illness, since all the rest were voluntary self-commitments. The mental health disqualification had no statistical effect on the likelihood of their committing a violent crime prior to 2007, but after 2007, when Connecticut began submitting data to NICS, it was quite effective.[27]

Thus, for those mentally ill people whose only disqualification for gun possession is involuntary commitment, state reporting of records to NICS can make a real difference in forestalling violence. Nonetheless, the federal disqualification is of very limited scope, missing the great majority of people whose mental illness makes them a threat to themselves or others.

An alternative approach is to focus on dangerousness rather than mental illness per se. Many episodes during which someone poses an imminent threat to himself or others are the result of temporary mental states associated with trauma, emotional stress, illness, a drug reaction, transitory psychosis, or a variety of other causes. If the court puts an individual under a restraining order, it should prompt an inquiry into whether the person is armed and if so, lead to an appropriate intervention. In many cases, even before a court order is issued, there may be a need for a quick response to save lives. A typical scenario is that people contact the police to report family members or neighbors who are threatening to kill themselves or threatening others. If a gun is involved, removing that gun should be a high priority—but the authority to do so has been limited in the past. Things are changing.

Connecticut created the first "extreme risk protection order" (ERPO) in 1999 after a workplace shooting. Indiana passed a similar law in 2005. In 2014, California created Gun Violence Restraining Orders after the Isla Vista shooting, in which a young man killed 6 people, 3 by gun, and injured 13. Before the rampage, the perpetrator's parents had pleaded with local police to confiscate his weapons, to no avail. By 2019, 14 more states and the District of Columbia had adopted some version of a "red-flag law," and legislatures in many of the remaining states were considering the possibility.[28]

The implementation of these policies has been highly variable across states and even counties. In Connecticut, which has the longest experience with a red-flag law, a majority of orders have been issued in response to a suicide threat rather than threats to others. There is some credible evidence that it is saving lives, with about 1 suicide averted for every 10 orders issued.[29]

Do Sentencing Enhancements Reduce Gun Use in Violent Crime?

About half of the states have legislation that stipulates a longer sentence for someone who is convicted of assault or robbery with a gun than with a less lethal weapon. These sentencing enhancements, most of which were adopted in the 1970s and 1980s, were intended to reduce firearm use in violence; criminals would be induced either to desist from violence or to substitute another weapon. Economist David Abrams of the University of Pennsylvania Law School found that the introduction of enhancements in several states reduced gun robberies by an average of 5%, with no effect on non-gun robberies.[30]

Which Police Tactics Are Effective in Reducing Gun Violence?

The police are in a position to curtail gun violence and its precursors, including illegal carrying in public places. A variety of tactics that focus enforcement on guns appear worthwhile.

The best known of the focused-deterrence strategies to reduce illicit gun use is Boston's Operation Ceasefire.[31] Beginning in 1995, an interagency working group composed of Harvard University researchers, members of the Boston Police Department, and other criminal justice agencies conducted research and analysis on Boston's youth violence problem and launched a carefully designed program to reduce youth

violence. Their research showed that the problem of youth violence in Boston was concentrated among a small number of
serially offending gang-involved youths. The key intervention
was for the police to make gang members believe that gun use
by any one member of the gang would result in a crackdown
on all members. (Most of them were vulnerable to more stringent enforcement since they had outstanding warrants, traffic
tickets, or other legal problems.) The intent was for each gang
to have an incentive to discourage gunplay by its members.

A key element of the strategy was the delivery of a personalized message to a small target audience regarding what kind
of behavior would provoke a law-enforcement response. This
"retail deterrence" message was delivered by talking to gang
members on the street, handing out fliers in the hot-spot areas
explaining the enforcement actions, and organizing forums between violent gang members and members of the interagency
working group. The youth-homicide rate plunged in Boston
following the intervention. Evaluation efforts have focused on
whether Ceasefire should get the credit for this sharp reduction. Several replications of this general approach have been
evaluated, with generally positive results.[32]

A second type of proactive policing against gun violence is
through preventive patrol activities. Over the past 25 years,
police departments have become increasingly systematic
about mapping crime. Crime is highly concentrated in particular neighborhoods or even specific blocks. Concentrating
police activities in the high-crime areas ("hot spots") can be
an efficient use of available police personnel. While one could
imagine this tactic would simply push crime into other neighborhoods, such displacement rarely happens in practice—and
in some cases neighboring areas appear to benefit. Evidence
in support of this approach includes randomized field experiments, beginning with the Minneapolis Hot Spots Patrol
Experiment in 1988.[33] The effects on serious crime are well
established—more police, less crime and violence.[34]

Police have targeted the specific problem of gun violence by patrol activities directed at getting guns off the street, using "reasonable suspicion" stops as a primary tactic. This sort of targeted policing became religion for New York City's Police Department, which at peak in 2011 conducted almost 700,000 stops of individuals on the street to question and frisk for weapons. While the yield with respect to confiscated guns was low, police officials claimed (and it is reasonable to believe) that this tactic had a deterrent effect on illicit carrying and gun use in crime. Several experiments with hot-spots patrol targeted specifically on reducing gun carrying have shown promising results.[35]

Of course, this policy placed a considerable strain on police–community relations and has been successfully challenged in court due to apparent racial profiling in selecting targets, as well as possible violations of the constitutional standard for a police stop. As a result, the police departments in New York, Chicago, Los Angeles, and other cities have greatly reduced the use of stop, question, and frisk tactics. William Bratton, whose innovative policies as chief of the New York Police Department have been given much of the credit for the extraordinary crime drop in that city over the last generation, has recently developed an alternative approach dubbed "precision policing" that is much more selective in engaging with suspect individuals.[36]

A final note. The potential effectiveness of targeted patrols against illicit carrying depends on the regulatory environment. If carrying a concealed gun is not restricted by law (as is true in an increasing number of states), then the goal of "getting guns off the street" may be unattainable.

How Effective Are Hunting Regulations on Firearms Safety?

Hunters handle and occasionally discharge lethal weapons. The risk of injury was brought to the public's attention in 2006, when Vice President Dick Cheney shot Harry Whittington, a 78-year-old Texas attorney, while they were on a quail hunt. Because it appeared at the time that Whittington was not seriously injured, the event was good for some laughs in some quarters. Of course, some of us remember Tom Lehrer singing "The Hunting Song" with the lyric "I went and shot the maximum the game laws would allow, two game wardens, seven hunters, and a cow." But hunter safety is in fact serious business.

Licensing requirements for hunters are intended to reduce accidents by ensuring that hunters know the regulations on hunting and know how to handle their weapon safely. These requirements are imposed by states and, as with concealed-carry permits, tend to differ widely among states. Typical requirements include enrolling in a hunter education course for 10 hours, passing a written test, and completing a "field day," which may include a live-fire exercise and even a marksmanship requirement. In some cases, the requirements for a hunting license are a good deal more stringent than the requirements for carrying a concealed handgun. Vermont and Wyoming, for example, have *no* requirements for carrying concealed, but do require that hunters enroll in a training course and be licensed. One might ask why competence in handling a firearm is more important in the fields and forests than on the city streets. As Congressman Mike Thompson, a hunter, observed: "Federal law prohibits me from having more than three shells in my shotgun when I'm duck hunting. So federal law provides more protection for the ducks than it does for citizens."[37]

In any event, the number of hunting accidents has declined over time, and fatal accidents are quite rare. In New York State, for example, the steady decline in gun accidents far outpaced the general decline in hunting. The number of accidental shootings while hunting averaged 137 in the 1960s and just 30 in the 2000s. In 2018 there were 13 accidental hunting-related shootings state-wide, 3 of them fatal. Two of those three were self-inflicted.

If it is true that training requirements have enhanced hunter safety over the last few decades, that fact would surely be relevant to the consideration of appropriate requirements for other uses of firearms.

8

GUNS AND GUN CONTROL IN HISTORY

Is There a Uniquely American Gun Culture?

Yes. We know of no other country where firearms are as plentiful and as inextricably linked to individual identity and popular values as they are in the United States. Citizens of other nations possess and use guns, to be sure, and some of these gun owners associate their firearms with personal meaning. But no country imbues private possession with larger social, historical, and political significance to the extent that the United States does. If a gun culture rivaling America's existed somewhere, we are confident that someone would have noticed.

It's hard to describe what a "gun culture" looks like in practice, but we like the political scientist Robert Spitzer's definition:

> the long-term sentimental attachment of many Americans to the gun, founded on the presence and proliferation of guns since the earliest days of the country; the connection between personal weapons ownership and the country's early struggle for survival and independence followed by the country's frontier experience; and the cultural mythology that has grown up about the gun in both frontier and modern life, as reflected in books, movies, folklore, and other forms of popular expression.[1]

In a famous 1970 essay, "America as a Gun Culture," the historian Richard Hofstadter defined the culture a bit more darkly. The United States, he said, is

> the only industrial nation in which the possession of rifles, shotguns, and handguns is lawfully prevalent among large numbers of its population. It is the only such nation that has been impelled in recent years to agonize at length about its own disposition toward violence and to set up a commission to examine it, the only nation so attached to the supposed "right" to bear arms that its laws abet assassins, professional criminals, berserk murderers, and political terrorists at the expense of the orderly population.[2]

American gun culture is really several overlapping subcultures, as Spitzer observes. One subculture is oriented around hunting and other shooting sports. As we noted in Chapter 1, gun-oriented recreation is prevalent, especially in rural areas, where it often is a core feature of family life. For boys in particular, the gift of a first gun traditionally has served as a rite of passage, though this practice is fading amid urbanization and the decline of hunting.

A second subculture, what Spitzer calls the "militia/frontier ethos," remains prominent in American society and politics and is often what we think of when we hear the term "gun culture." The militia/frontier subculture takes its inspiration from American history and the mythology that has developed around it. In this perspective, citizen militias of privately armed men won American independence from tyrannical King George, and rugged rifle-toting settlers finished the job of nation building by conquering the frontier. Brave individualists made America, and they did so with firearms. Historians accept this account up to a point, but as we discuss below, they also find considerable hype and oversimplification in the retelling. But no matter. To those who view guns as pivotal to American greatness, the lessons of history are ignored at the nation's peril. Relatively unfettered access to firearms is equally relevant today as it was in 1776, for guns allow everyday citizens to serve, so the narrative goes, as a vigilant counterpoise to creeping tyranny.

This traditional, even patriotic perspective has morphed into two distinct ideologies about guns. One is centered on the idea that individuals must use guns to take care of themselves because the state cannot protect them. This perspective is evident in interviews with modern gun owners and in survey findings that protection is the dominant reason for owning a firearm. A second ideology, the "insurrectionist" perspective, holds that widespread gun ownership is necessary because at any moment individuals may need to take up arms against the government. Fringe elements have embraced this perspective—witness recent standoffs between armed "sovereign citizens" and local sheriffs caught in the middle of federal land-use disputes. But insurrectionist ideology echoes within some mainstream pro-gun organizations. It seems that in the twenty-first century, the old militia/frontier subculture has birthed a *sub*-subculture of armed men and women who believe that private violence, or the threat thereof, may be a necessary solution to the problems of government.

Although the notion of American gun culture resonates with people across the ideological spectrum, scholars struggle with what the term "culture" means in practice and how to measure it. One common understanding is that culture encompasses symbols, stories, rituals, and worldviews that everyday citizens draw on to engage in politics.

Symbols

When Americans want to win a political argument, they are wont to invoke the Constitution and the rights it protects. These rights have practical legal import as well as symbolic value. For pro-gun advocates, the Second Amendment's "right to keep and bear arms" has long served as a rhetorical anchor, one strengthened by Supreme Court rulings in 2008 and 2010. The Constitution is a powerful tool: Even though most Americans favor gun control, more than 4 in 10 people nevertheless believe that laws limiting gun ownership infringe on the right to bear arms.[3]

Stories

History texts, popular fiction, movies, and marketers lionize guns and have done so for more than 150 years. From iconic tales of musket-bearing minutemen at Lexington and Concord, to Buffalo Bill Cody's fabulously successful Wild West shows, to Laura Ingalls Wilder's bestselling *Little House* children's series, to postwar John Wayne Westerns, to immigrant tales such as *The Godfather* and *The Sopranos*—guns figure prominently in the story of America. The storytelling about American history may contribute as much as history itself to the creation of the American gun culture.

Rituals

Family life and rites of passage, particularly in rural areas, often revolve around shooting sports. Hunting season signifies not just a time of year but also an opportunity to strengthen one's ties to family and community traditions. Studies have found that hunting typically begins at a young age and that kids are initiated by members of the immediate family. Although hunting is declining in America, schools in some rural areas still close on the first day of hunting season. Even decades ago, the parental practice of acculturating kids to guns caused alarm in some quarters. In a definitive account of homicide in the United States, a sociologist in the 1930s noted that sales of toy revolvers was booming, leading children to "lurk in ambush and in sport hold up pedestrians" and to kill "song birds and household pets, meanwhile endangering the lives of bystanders and becoming accustomed to the reckless use of firearms."[4]

Worldviews

Advocacy groups skillfully link guns to American values of liberty and equality, an association that simply does not resonate to the same extent in other democracies. The National Rifle Association (NRA) refers to the Second Amendment right to keep and bear arms as "America's first freedom" because in the organization's view the Second Amendment protects all the other freedoms. The NRA's major donors are inducted into the "Ring of Freedom." Its annual conventions are festooned with flags and other cultural symbols. It refers to itself as "America's longest-standing civil rights organization." Studies have found that attitudes toward guns reflect larger worldviews about individual versus collective responsibility. Even after accounting for gun ownership and other factors, people with a dim view of government's role in solving problems are more likely to have a pro-gun perspective than are people more favorable to government.[5]

A variant on the "gun culture" argument concerns the belief that violence, particularly involving guns, solves problems. This theme has come up mostly in the context of the American South, where observers going back to Charles Dickens have suggested that citizens seem to be unusually quick to draw their weapons, particularly where questions of honor are concerned. Honor culture is probably a contributing factor to American gun violence, though not the overriding one.

Guns are central to the American experience, but they don't define it. While on average Americans are probably more tolerant of guns in public life than are citizens of other advanced democracies, many Americans are also troubled by the sentimental attachment to firearms and wish that stricter gun laws were in place. What most people think of as the American "gun culture"—passionate, highly politically engaged gun owners who believe that firearms do more good than harm and that most law-abiding people should own them—is actually a relatively small subculture of, at most, 5% of the adult population.[6] But this figure translates into upward of 10 million people willing to email and call their elected officials and show up at their town hall meetings.

Where Does the Gun Culture Come From?

The gun culture has its roots in lived experience magnified by mass marketing, media, and interest groups.

The historical antecedents are true enough. From the earliest settlements, guns have had important practical functions. As the historians Lee Kennett and James Anderson have observed, "Survival dictated that old social distinctions of arms ownership give way to the practical necessities of creating a new colony."[7] Virginia moved early on to require all men to be armed, and citizen militias formed in the 1620s in response to conflicts with Native Americans. Laws encouraged men to hunt to sharpen their marksmanship skills.

The American Revolution owed its success in part to civic-minded men—the militia—who took up arms against a despot and then served as reinforcements for the Continental Army. Anywhere from 175,000 to 500,000 men served in the militia during this period. As Kennett and Anderson note, "The militiaman symbolized the nation—crude, unorganized, undisciplined, but ready to protect his rights."[8]

Moving westward in the post-Revolutionary period, American frontiersmen required firearms to hunt, ward off threatening wildlife, vanquish Native Americans, and shoot cattle rustlers and pugnacious troublemakers in mining camps and other untamed surroundings. In areas with little if any organized law enforcement, private individuals relied on themselves. Prominent citizens often had to band together in vigilante groups to chase down outlaws holding up stagecoaches, banks, railroads, and mine offices, while gun-slinging sheriffs, such as the legendary Bat Masterson, tried to keep law and order in town.

The federal government and firearms makers encouraged the arming of the frontier. Congress legalized the firearms trade with Native Americans in 1834 and used rifles as inducements for them to move westward in the 1840s.[9] The US government began handing out surplus guns to settlers in 1849.[10] In the middle decades of the nineteenth century, the marketing genius Samuel Colt created a line of affordable firearms and promoted them with "a system of myths, symbols, stagecraft, and distribution that has been mimicked by generations of industrial mass marketers and has rarely been improved upon."[11] Celebrity spokesmen were key: Colt deployed the famous artist and adventurer George Catlin, as well as Mexican American War heroes and political luminaries, to vouch for his wares.[12]

In his history of the Winchester rifle, Harold Williamson has suggested that "firearms, the axe, and the plow were the three cornerstones upon which the pioneer Americans built this nation. Of the three, firearms were the most dramatic and appealed most to popular imagination."[13] However, historians have argued that the heroic militiaman and his gun were far less effective than children's stories would have us believe, and the frontier far less of a firearms free-for-all than we think. For historical embellishment of guns and their place in American history, we can thank entrepreneurial fiction writers, moviemakers, showmen, political advocates, and even gun makers.

Children's textbooks portray the "minutemen" and other colonial musket-bearers as a ragtag force that, through quintessentially American grit and ingenuity, beat back a well-disciplined, more heavily armed British army. In reality, the Continental Congress quickly realized that citizen militias were not up to the task of fighting a prolonged war and created a standing army under the command of George Washington, a Virginia militia leader. Although the militia had achieved notable victories, Washington's complaints about the militia reflected the general belief that citizen-soldiers could not re-place a professional army. Without considerable help from European allies, most notably the French, the American Revolution might have turned out differently.

The narrative of the frontier gun culture, while surely containing more than a grain of truth, also owes a great deal to popular entertainment. Historians looking at homicide statistics have found that even places synonymous with Wild West violence had relatively few murders—the cattle town of Dodge City, Kansas, for example, averaged 1.5 per year.[14] As the historian Robert Dykstra notes, anyone "looking for true mayhem and big body counts should forget Little Bighorn, forget Wild Bill and Wyatt Earp, forget Dodge City. Instead, consider the lethal character of simply working on the railroad."[15]

True, the cattle towns and mining camps of the Old West had some legendary gunslingers and their own brand of justice, to say nothing of more firearms violence than the average prairie community of upstanding farmers and shopkeepers. But the popular image of the gun-soaked West owes much to mythologizing that began after the Civil War, when dime novels proliferated and Buffalo Bill Cody's legendary Wild West show traveled the country for decades dramatizing buffalo hunts, Indian battles, and Annie Oakley's marksmanship. As the cultural historian Richard Slotkin has observed, the show "was the most important commercial vehicle for the fabrication and transmission of the Myth of the Frontier."[16]

By the dawn of the twentieth century, the frontier narrative had taken on new life on screen. One of the earliest motion pictures, *The Great Train Robbery* (1903), featured Western banditry. In the middle decades, the award-winning director John Ford popularized the Western and brought the ultimate cowboy-actor John Wayne to stardom in *Stagecoach* (1939) and kept him there with *The Searchers* (1956) and *The Man Who Shot Liberty Valance* (1962). Clint Eastwood continued the glorification of the historic West with films such as *The Good, the Bad, and the Ugly* (1966), *The Outlaw Josie Wales* (1976), and *Unforgiven*

(1992). Not to be upstaged, television fueled America's insatiable appetite for hero gunslingers in shows such as *The Wild Wild West, The Lone Ranger, Gunsmoke, The Rifleman, Wagon Train, Rawhide*, and *Bonanza*, which were replayed in syndication long after their initial runs.

Gun advocacy groups have embraced this cultural iconography and made it relevant to a modern, urbanized, industrialized America. Listen to the NRA's then-president, Charlton Heston—an actor whose oeuvre was ironically nearly devoid of Westerns—addressing the association's 2000 annual convention:

> When freedom shivers in the cold shadow of true peril, it's always the patriots who first hear the call. When loss of liberty is looming, as it is now, the siren sounds first in the hearts of freedom's vanguard. The smoke in the air of our Concord bridges and Pearl Harbors is always smelled first by the farmers, who come from their simple homes to find the fire and fight—because they know that sacred stuff resides in that wooden stock and blued steel, something that gives the most common man the most uncommon of freedoms. When ordinary hands can possess such an extraordinary instrument, that symbolizes the full measure of human dignity and liberty.

Heston ended the speech by hoisting a vintage rifle above his head and leveling a warning to presumptive Democratic presidential nominee Al Gore and other "divisive forces that would take freedom away." They would get his gun, he suggested, only by prying it "from my cold dead hands!"[17]

Scholars have a different explanation for the staying power, even resurgence, of American gun culture. One account holds that it represents conservative white men's reaction to liberalism—an attempt to recapture "frontier masculinity" amid threats to status and identity posed by the "nanny state,"

feminism, and multiculturalism.[18] Another account holds that
the lionization of firearms is a reaction not to an overweening
state, but rather to a state that has failed to protect its citizens.[19]
The NRA and other pro-gun rights groups work both angles,
mocking mothers and liberal "gun grabbers" who seek stricter
firearms laws and portraying America as a land in which violent criminals are free to savage communities and anarchy is
only one terrorist attack or natural disaster away. Indeed, a recent study argues that the NRA has been as responsible as anything for American gun culture. The organization has used its
magazines and training programs to cultivate, politicize, and
spread a civic identity rooted in gun ownership and then mobilized members around threats to this identity.[20] One in four
gun owners says that being a gun owner is central to his or
her identity, a number that rises with the number of firearms
owned.[21] The NRA has solidified gun owners' common bond
by connecting their social identity to broader political forces,
including the nationalistic populism that has become the centerpiece of the modern Republican Party.[22]

Was There Gun Control in Frontier America?

Yes—and in fact gun control goes back to the America's
earliest days.

In the Revolutionary era, citizen militias were responsible for the common defense, and the states had an interest
in ensuring that citizen-soldiers were well prepared, which
meant well regulated. State laws dictated who belonged to
the militia—typically able-bodied white males in their prime
years—and outlined the requirements of militia service. These
requirements typically included maintaining private arms and
turning out for periodic "musters" in which weapons were inspected and recorded on public rolls—what the legal historian
Adam Winkler terms "an early version of gun registration."[23]
And colonial governments conducted door-to-door inventories of privately owned weapons. When the Revolution

arrived, colonial governments confiscated private weapons for use in the war effort.

In 1792 the new Congress adopted the Uniform Militia Act, requiring all free, able-bodied white male citizens under 45 to muster with a local militia and equip themselves "with a good musket or firelock." As Winkler notes, guns were private property with a public purpose.[24] States and localities regulated the storage of gunpowder, prohibited the discharge of firearms in towns and cities, and in some cases prohibited militiamen from traveling to muster with a loaded weapon.

In the early nineteenth century, states inaugurated new forms of gun control in the form of bans on carrying concealed weapons in public and on firing guns in certain places—so-called place and manner restrictions. Kentucky and Louisiana banned the concealed carrying of firearms in 1813, and many states and territories followed throughout the century. One goal of these laws was to curtail the practice of dueling, in which gentlemen challenged to a shootout those who had offended their honor. These laws also were enacted to prevent impulsive acts of revenge. Judges upheld the bans. A Louisiana court, for example, supported the state's prerogative to curb citizens' use of concealed weapons on the grounds that they facilitated "secret advantages and unmanly assassinations."[25] Outside of the South, states concerned about the proliferation of conceal-able guns passed laws against traveling armed unless the individual had reason to fear imminent danger.

Even in the "Wild West," laws generally banned the carrying of weapons, except by law-enforcement officers. Rather than leaving each man to his own, "Frontier towns handled guns the way a Boston restaurant today handles overcoats in winter," Winkler notes. "New arrivals were required to turn in their guns to authorities in exchange for something like a metal token. Certain places required people to check their guns at one of the major entry points to town or leave their weapons with their horses at the livery stables."[26]

Early gun laws presaged the modern gun debate. In the "right hands," firearms were instruments of civic value; in the "wrong hands," they were instruments of unnecessary death. It was up to lawmakers and judges to decide how best to preserve the good while preventing the bad.

Is Gun Control About Protecting Elites Against Everyone Else?

Yes, no, and maybe. Throughout history, firearms regulations have been enacted in response to threats to public order. In some cases, the self-appointed guardians of the public order have targeted specific groups, either explicitly in the language of the law or effectively in its design and implementation. The laws have evolved over time, and their intent is often subject to inference and interpretation.

Consider African Americans. In the early period, even in the South, free African Americans were allowed to possess firearms and, in some states, to serve in the militia. Some laws carved out restrictions. In 1680, for example, Virginia banned both slaves and free African Americans from carrying weapons. One legal scholar argues that the Second Amendment may have been intended, at least in part, to reassure the South that it could maintain militias to put down slave revolts.[27]

In the antebellum period, amid slave revolts and threats thereof, Southern states began clamping down on the rights of free African Americans, including the right to possess firearms, and in some cases began regulating slaves' use of guns, previously the province of the slaveholder. In the three decades leading up to the Civil War, Delaware required free blacks to obtain a license to carry a gun; Maryland and Virginia prohibited the practice altogether; and Georgia and Mississippi prohibited both carrying and owning.[28] Florida authorized white citizen patrols to confiscate guns from black homes.[29] Several states incorporated right-to-bear-arms provisions in their state constitutions but limited that protection to free white men. Free blacks were targeted because "they served as a bad example to slaves and because they might instigate or participate in a rebellion by their slave brethren."[30] Meanwhile, Louisiana, Mississippi, South Carolina, and Texas passed laws aimed at restricting or barring slaves' handling of guns.[31]

It is important to note that these clearly racially motivated laws were separate from other laws passed during the antebellum era that addressed the problem of concealed weapons.

After the Civil War, freedmen were at the center of policy debates over guns. The Confederate states passed "Black Codes," including laws barring freedmen from carrying guns, but those laws were soon rendered unconstitutional by the Fourteenth Amendment, ratified in 1868. With full citizenship and equal protection for African Americans now enshrined in the US Constitution, states wishing to control freedmen's access to firearms would have had to try stealthier strategies. Modern gun advocates argue that states did so by banning the carrying or sales of the small, cheaply made pistols affordable to poor blacks; by exempting from gun restrictions service weapons that, in practice, were owned by white Confederate veterans; or by charging business taxes that would have made guns unaffordable to freedmen. States also empowered white citizen groups, including the Ku Klux Klan (KKK), by selectively enforcing gun laws and, in at least one state, exempting "special deputies" from the ban on pistol sales.[32] African Americans seeking protection in the Second Amendment found none, for in 1875 the Supreme Court ruled in *U.S. v. Cruikshank* that the amendment applied only to acts of Congress, not vigilante groups or other usurpers of gun rights.

At the same time, during Reconstruction Republicans recruited freedmen to join citizen militias, which had once been restricted to whites. These militias not only served as a counterbalance to groups such as the KKK but also provided a way of organizing African Americans for citizenship.[33]

In the late nineteenth and early twentieth centuries, some observers believe, gun regulation was part of a larger effort to control "dangerous classes," which would have been imagined to include not only African Americans but also immigrants from southern and eastern Europe, labor organizers, and agrarian reformers. The nation's first handgun licensing law, enacted in New York in 1911, was part of a broader Progressive movement led by business and social elites, along with good-government reformers, in response to urban social disorder. The so-called Sullivan Law was a direct reaction to lawbreaking by Italian mobs and Chinese gangs—which at the time posed a legitimate public safety problem. The law had been preceded by lesser efforts to regulate firearms in these communities, including canceling concealed pistol permits in Italian neighborhoods of New York City and barring non-citizens from having guns in public places. But the Sullivan Law had other precipitating factors: the shooting of the New York City mayor and a prominent author; extensive newspaper coverage of family violence; and, most obviously, a 50% jump in gun homicides in the prior year.

While legal historians find consensus about the racial and ethnic roots of many gun laws enacted through the early part of the twentieth century, there is less agreement about efforts in the modern era. No doubt some gun laws have been enforced in a discriminatory fashion. For example, gun advocates have long complained that New York City issued handgun permits "only to the very wealthy, the politically powerful and the socially elite" and to those who guard their interests.[34] For many decades, North Carolina's handgun permit law left it up to local sheriffs to determine whether the applicant was of "good moral character," an invitation for abuse in a state with a history of racial strife. In 1956, after his house was bombed, the Reverend Martin Luther King Jr. applied for a permit to carry a concealed weapon, but the Montgomery, Alabama, police chief used his discretion to deny the application.

In the 1960s, the Black Panther Party for Self-Defense, a radical wing of the civil rights movement, decided it was time to embrace firearms as tools of defiance and political empowerment. In much-publicized acts of political theater, the

Panthers strapped on fully loaded firearms and marched on the California State Capitol, in one case entering the assembly chamber during a legislative debate. A newspaper report at the time recounted, "It was one of the most amazing incidents in legislative history—a tumultuous, traveling group of grim-faced, silent young men with guns roaming the Capitol surrounded by reporters, television cameramen, stunned state police and watched by incredulous groups of visiting school children."[35] Shortly thereafter, the state enacted a law banning the carrying of loaded guns in public, adding a special provision that made the law effective immediately.[36]

On the other hand, the impetus for, and the design and implementation of, modern gun laws make it hard to support charges of racism. The 1968 Gun Control Act was spurred by the back-to-back assassinations of Sen. Robert Kennedy and the Reverend Martin Luther King Jr. The first effort to regulate assault weapons, in 1989, came in response to a shooting of immigrant schoolchildren by a white assailant. Federal laws requiring licensed firearms dealers to run background checks on would-be buyers (1993) and banning certain types of assault weapons (1994) followed an epidemic of gun crime concentrated in urban neighborhoods, but the laws were designed and enforced without disparate racial impact and enjoyed support from civil rights organizations. Early efforts to expand background checks to private gun sales (for example, in Colorado and Oregon) came in response to shootings at predominantly white schools by white students. Recent state-level gun reforms have come in response to mass shootings in schools.

The history of guns and race is complicated, emotionally fraught, poorly documented, and subject to widely varying interpretations. Debates over guns and gun laws, particularly in earlier centuries, have been lost to history, and no doubt the individual and collective motives behind these laws were varied and often obfuscated. From what we do know, however, it's clear that gun ownership and gun regulation have been central to American efforts to maintain social order.

How Have Laws Governing Carrying and Self-Defense Changed?

It has become easier to carry guns legally in public and, as we note in Chapter 6, to defend oneself without fearing jail time. Ironically, states that in the nineteenth century were strict on gun regulation are now among the most lenient.

Beginning in the early nineteenth century, many states passed laws banning the carrying of concealed handguns outside the home. The first in this category was Kentucky, in 1813, and by the late 1930s, 20 states had such bans.[37] Constitutional challenges were not uncommon, but courts nearly always upheld the laws.[38] Historically, legislatures and courts observed what amounted to a two-tiered system: Guns kept for public purposes, namely collective defense through militia service, enjoyed the highest level of constitutional protections (they could not be sold to pay taxes owed, for example), while those intended for private purposes, such as hunting or self-defense, were subject to state powers to promote public safety and health.

Bans or strong restrictions on carrying concealed firearms were adopted in every region of the nation. But real questions remain about whether citizens followed these laws and whether police enforced them. A 1925 book on America's homicide problem quotes a South Carolina attorney general lamenting that the "deplorable custom" of pistol carrying had turned the state into "an armed camp in time of peace."[39] He remarked that "our young men and boys, black and white, rich and poor, seem to think that their outfit is not complete without a pistol," and that guns were routinely carried "at public meetings, on the streets, at social gatherings, even at dances, even at daily labor, and following the plough, and I add also even at church and prayer meeting."[40]

By the 1920s and 1930s, the laggard states had started to take concealed handguns seriously. "The trend of pistol legislation in the last ten to fifteen years has been toward stricter regulation," a legal commentator noted in 1938. "More and more it has been recognized that the possession of a pistol that can easily be concealed in the pocket furnishes a temptation which many young hoodlums are impotent to resist."[41] As he wrote, nearly every state that didn't bar carrying outright had passed a law requiring those who wished to carry a gun to obtain a permit from the local police chief or judge. By the late 1930s, 26 states had enacted licensing provisions. The NRA supported the licensing laws at the time, but in the latter decades of the twentieth century, the organization would mount a full-bore campaign against them on the grounds that they were unjustly restrictive, even discriminatory. Legal experts had the opposite concern—that these laws were lax and easily evaded.

Thus, for most of American history, concealed carrying of guns was either prohibited or strictly regulated in all but one or two states. This all changed in the 1980s and 1990s, when the NRA made liberalization of these laws a top priority. States that had banned concealed carry began to legalize it. States that strictly regulated the practice by giving law enforcement discretion over who received a permit (the "may issue" system) switched to the looser "shall issue" system, in which law enforcement must grant a permit to anyone meeting basic legal requirements, such as not having been convicted of a felony, not abusing drugs or alcohol, and being of sound mental health. Today, all states allow concealed carry. Most states that require a license have adopted the "shall issue" standard, and one-third of states have abandoned concealed-carry licensing requirements entirely (a standard that gun groups call "constitutional carry").

The campaign to liberalize the laws that began in Florida in 1987 has been one of the NRA's biggest policy successes. Before 1977, only about one-fifth of states treated concealed carrying favorably (eight states had the pro-gun "shall issue" system, and one state did not require a license). By 2019, more than four-fifths of the states had adopted gun-friendly policies.

In just one generation, lawmakers across the states have fundamentally upended public policy on packing heat. It's hard to think of such a sweeping change in law that has received so little public notice. Having largely succeeded in changing the concealed handgun laws, the NRA is now working to ensure that carriers licensed in one state may legally carry in another. The ultimate goal is to secure a federal reciprocity law that would bind all states.

Did Hitler's Gun Control Laws Cause the Holocaust?

If gun advocates have one refrain, it is that firearms regulation will lead to gun confiscation, which will lead to tyranny. Exhibit A: Nazi Germany. Hitler disarmed the Jews, and then he murdered 6 million of them in one of history's greatest abominations. To gun advocates, the Holocaust has become a gruesome warning about the hidden threat behind even seemingly mild firearms control. As one pro-gun lawyer put it, "The record establishes that a well-meaning liberal republic would enact a gun control act that would later be highly useful to a dictatorship. . . . This dictatorship could, generally, disarm the people of the nation it governed and then disarm those of every nation it conquered."[42]

Because the putative linkage between gun control and tyranny, even genocide, rests largely on one historical case, it's important to get the history right. As one might expect, the story of Hitler, gun control, and the Holocaust contains core truths while drawing inferences that are at best debatable.

Although historians have written volumes about the Nazi period, they have paid little or no attention to the role of gun laws in facilitating Hitler's rise and reign—a fact that is either a terrible oversight or a telling omission. Instead, the argument that gun control facilitated Nazi terror emerged from the contemporary writings of American pro-gun lawyers and activists.

Scholars and activists on the other side have answered with their own analysis. Remarkably, the two sides agree on the basic historical narrative, but they disagree on the inferences we should draw from the case.

The first point of agreement is that Germany was in the process of relaxing its strict gun laws before Hitler came to power in 1933, and, with critical exceptions, he continued that trend. At the end of World War I, the parliament of the Weimar Republic banned gun possession and required that citizens surrender existing guns and ammunition. These laws remained in effect until 1928, when parliament eased the ban by allowing certain people to own, transfer, carry, and manufacture guns so long as they obtained a permit. To acquire a gun, regular citizens had to be of "undoubted reliability"; government and railway officials, as well as certain community leaders, were exempt from the permit requirement. The 1928 law also created a licensing system for manufacturing and sales. In 1938, Hitler further relaxed the law, removing rifles and shotguns from the permitting system and lowering the legal ownership age to 18. The law also exempted more groups from the permit system, including hunting license holders, additional government workers, and, importantly, Nazi Party members. As one legal scholar concluded, "The Nazis were relatively more pro-gun than the predecessor Weimar Republic."[43]

However, the liberalization of gun laws did not apply to Germany's Jews. Hitler's 1938 law barred them from manufacturing guns or ammunition, although it did not explicitly ban them from obtaining a license to acquire or carry a firearm. After the law had been enacted, but before the implementing regulations had been formulated, a 17-year-old German Jewish refugee shot a German embassy worker in Paris. This event precipitated an immediate ban on Jews' acquiring, possessing, and carrying firearms, ammunition, or "cutting or stabbing weapons." Jews were ordered to surrender their weapons or be sent to a concentration camp for 20 years. During the infamous Kristallnacht, Nazi "wrecking crews" conducted massive raids on Jewish homes and businesses to search for weapons and arrest their owners. Thousands of homes, businesses, and synagogues were ransacked and destroyed. The mass extermination of Jews began not long thereafter.[44]

So what are we to make of the connection between gun control and the Holocaust? And is the case relevant to firearms policymaking in the contemporary United States or other established democracies?

To pro-gun scholars, the lesson is clear. When democracies require people to register their weapons, the government unwittingly creates a handy road map that can be appropriated by future dictators to guide them in disarming "enemies of the state" and thereby consolidating power. In his history of Weimar and Nazi gun laws, lawyer Stephen Halbrook presents evidence, for example, that local officials acting on the orders of Interior Minister Hermann Göring scrutinized firearms license lists to revoke permits of Jews and other political opponents. He speculates that these lists also may have been used to disarm or even arrest Jewish gun owners. But to Halbrook and other pro-gun advocates, a larger lesson emerges from the Nazi era: that humanity is well served when nations have "an armed populace with a political culture of hallowed constitutional and natural rights that they are motivated to fight for."[45]

To those more sympathetic to gun control, the idea that regulation leads to genocide seems farfetched, both in its particulars and as a larger cautionary tale. In the case of Nazi Germany, these critics argue, there is no way that a small, despised minority ever could have been a match for Hitler's well-armed storm troopers, police, and regular army, particularly in the absence of armed Gentiles willing to fight alongside the Jews. Even before the anti-Jewish gun control regulations, Hitler had suspended constitutional liberties, including freedom of speech and association; appropriated democratically organized shooting clubs; expanded search-and-seizure powers; ransacked the homes and offices of political enemies, including Jews; and used force to engineer the dissolution of parliament—facts that pro-gun writers don't dispute. Indeed, no direct evidence has been presented that the Nazis used a gun registry as a road map for raids on Jewish homes, which were often concentrated in Jewish quarters anyway and thus easily identified for mass sweeps.[46] In a context in which democracy had long since ceased to exist, "A right to keep and bear arms would have been as meaningless as other suppressed rights in the Third Reich."[47] If anything, one might argue that holes in gun laws helped Hitler to build up his private army, as Nazi Party members were exempt from the later permitting system.

The larger question is whether it's useful to invoke the Nazi experience as a cautionary tale for gun policy today. How you answer that question probably depends on whether you are fundamentally optimistic or pessimistic about democracy specifically and the human condition generally. Optimists can point out that modern states have longer liberal traditions and sturdier institutions for checking and sharing power than did the weak Weimar Republic, which lacked such popular norms and was beset from the start by internal strife and unable to stave off armed factions. Optimists can also note that roughly a dozen US states, to say nothing of many industrialized nations, have maintained gun registration or owner licensing, often for decades, while remaining thriving democracies. On the other hand, pessimists can point to countless state-sponsored atrocities as evidence that evil can erupt anywhere in our time—witness Bosnia or Rwanda. Given the alternative, it behooves freedom-loving individuals never to let their guard down.

Of course, there is a third possibility, satisfying to no one, which is that a well-armed and vigilant citizenry is unlikely to be any match for a well-trained and far more heavily armed military. Given advances in the technology of modern warfare, this observation may be even truer now than in the 1930s.

9

PUBLIC OPINION, POLITICAL PARTIES, AND GUNS

Do Americans Want Stricter Gun Laws?

Public opinion experts have long observed that the United States has a gun control paradox: Most Americans favor all sorts of firearms regulations—sometimes overwhelmingly so—yet these regulations are not enacted into law. Four decades ago, one scholar noted that "it is difficult to imagine any other issue on which Congress has been less responsive to public sentiment for a longer period of time," a frustration that many Americans voice today.[1] Most answers to the paradox revolve around different levels of political mobilization: Gun owners are highly organized at all levels of government, and they make their voices heard, including at the ballot box. Conversely, gun regulation supporters are less well organized and, in some renditions, less focused and less intense. We believe that the organizational explanations are correct, and we address them later in this book. At the same time, opinion polls are a piece of the puzzle.

Do Americans support gun control laws? If you look at national opinion polls, the headline is yes. But degrees of support vary widely by policy question, as well as by gender, race, gun ownership status, and, especially, political party. And sometimes the poll findings are contradictory, indicating that most

Americans probably do not understand the current state of gun regulation as well as they might think.

Broadly speaking, support for gun control declined from the early 1990s through 2010 and then stabilized or began to rise again. Two long-running survey questions provide a broadly similar picture. The Gallup Organization has tracked whether people want stricter gun laws, the status quo, or looser gun laws. Most Americans, about 90%, support keeping existing laws or strengthening them. That said, the fraction supporting stricter gun laws has risen by about 15 percentage points between 2010 and 2019, to about 6 in 10 Americans.[2] In another series, the Pew Research Center has tracked whether Americans generally prefer protecting gun rights or controlling gun ownership. America was firmly in the pro-control camp until about 2010, when the country became evenly divided on the question. As of 2019, the pro-control side may be gaining a tiny bit of ground.[3]

These general survey questions tell us about Americans' basic orientation in the gun debate. However, surveys that ask about specific types of commonly debated regulations tend to find high levels of support for gun control. Specific proposals that are not currently on the books nationwide, such as requiring all gun buyers to undergo a background check, enjoy commanding levels of support. Other proposals that the majority of Americans would like to see enacted include creating a federal database to track gun sales and banning assault weapons and high-capacity ammunition magazines.[4] In general, Americans are far more supportive of laws narrowly aimed at criminals and other dangerous people than of proposals targeting guns and ammo that "good guys" might want.

One proposal that has never enjoyed majority support (except in one possibly anomalous poll in 1959) is a ban on civilian handgun possession—which was a goal of gun reformers in the 1970s. In recent polls, fewer than 30% of Americans have supported such a provision.[5] And, as we have noted, the Supreme Court has ruled that blanket handgun bans are unconstitutional.

While America's mood toward gun control in general has shifted over time, support for specific, modest policy proposals has remained about the same, or even strengthened. For example, in the 1990s and early 2000s, roughly 80% of Americans favored background checks on private gun sales; polls in the 2010s have put that number at 85% to 90% or more. The fraction supporting a ban on high-capacity magazines (generally defined as feeding devices holding more than 10 to 15 bullets) is about the same in the 2010s —in the 55% to 67% range in most polls—as it was in 1999 (67%). Most Americans seem to be fine with gun control and will continue to support reasonable regulation as long as they don't "hear" echoes of gun bans in the pollster's question.

Digging deeper into the polling data reveals some curious contradictions in Americans' attitudes toward guns. On the one hand, solid majorities favor specific firearm regulations not currently on the books nationally or in most states, implying support for stricter gun laws. On the other hand, when asked the general question of whether they support stricter gun laws, far lower numbers say yes. Reading the polls, you would be forgiven for scratching your head: Americans want stricter gun laws . . . and they don't? One explanation for these contradictory findings is that Americans don't know what gun laws are currently on the books. Another possibility is that the gun lobby's narrative has sunk in and Americans are more likely now to equate "gun laws" with "gun bans." There is evidence for both interpretations.

It is a truism of American politics that most people don't know much about the policies governing them. People are busy with jobs and families and are content to leave the lawmaking to the people the voters elect. Firearms regulation is no exception. Take a recent experiment in which pollsters identified people who believe the government should enforce the gun laws already on the books before passing new laws—the standard position of the National Rifle Association (NRA). The pollsters then asked these people whether federal law currently requires background checks on private sales, including at gun shows. Nearly half got the answer wrong, and a tenth admitted they didn't know the rules. Large numbers also didn't know that assault weapons were legal in most states or that people on the government's terrorist watch list can buy guns. As the pollsters concluded, "About 6 out of 10 people who believe we just need to do a better job of enforcing existing laws don't realize that those laws are far weaker than they think."[6]

Ignorance of the laws can lead to nonsensical positions. For example, in a 2012 poll 44% of Americans backed banning semiautomatic guns—a figure that seems quite high given that these guns constitute most firearms sold today and few Americans believe in banning mainstream weapons. Another poll found that more people backed a ban on semiautomatic weapons than on assault weapons—the opposite of what one would expect. We suspect that many survey respondents mistakenly thought semiautomatics were machine guns.

Looming beneath these muddled poll findings, of course, is the question of trust in government. Pollsters have long known that if questions imply a government role in gun control (which of course government would have), support for the proposal declines. An experiment by Gallup illustrated the dynamic: When asked whether they would vote for a law expanding background checks, 83% said yes; when asked whether the US Senate should have passed such a measure, support dropped nearly 20 points. People who opposed the Senate measure cited a violation of the Second Amendment as their chief reason.[7]

Who Supports Gun Control, and Who Supports Gun Rights?

Not surprisingly, subgroups of Americans hold different, often fundamentally contrary views on gun policy.

One of the most interesting developments over the past two decades has been the growing partisan divide, which has become especially wide in recent years. The gap between Democrats and Republicans has reached a remarkable 60 percentage points on one bellwether gun control question, far greater than differences marked by race, gender, and geography, or even the presence of a gun in the home.[8] Indeed, if you want to know someone's party affiliation, the best question to ask (besides "Who did you vote for in the last election?") is "Do you own a gun?"[9]

In the early 1990s, strong majorities of Democrats, independents, and even Republicans believed that America needed stricter gun laws. Now only Democrats subscribe to that view. While their support has been declining, the partisan gap has been mostly driven by Republicans, whose support for the general idea of gun control has plunged by more than half since the early 1990s. The party gap persists on specific policy questions—such as whether we should ban assault weapons—and is even more pronounced on questions of whether gun reforms would be effective (the view of most Democrats, but not Republicans) or whether gun control gives undue power to the government (the view of most Republicans and independents, but not most Democrats).

Views toward gun control also vary with individual characteristics that closely track political beliefs. So, for example, people of color are more likely than whites to support gun control (with a gap of about 30 points), women are more supportive than men (with a gap of about 15 points), and Easterners and Westerners are more sympathetic than are people from the South and Midwest (with a gap of roughly 5 to 15 points). Requiring background checks of all would-be gun buyers is one proposal supported by majorities of Republicans, Southerners, Westerners, and gun owners—all groups traditionally hostile to gun regulation.[10]

Gun owners are more likely to oppose new gun laws than are nonowners, but this difference is mostly driven by the overwhelming opposition of *Republican* gun owners.[11] Again, psychology (identifying with a party) seems to be more important than circumstance (owning a firearm). Nevertheless, even gun owners—and NRA-member households—voice majority support for one prominent gun control proposal, to expand the background check system to private sales.[12] Other gun reforms, such as bans on military-style weapons or high-capacity magazines, are more divisive within gun-owning households, with NRA-member households considerably more skeptical than those without an NRA member.[13]

However, lots of the personal characteristics associated with support for gun laws are also associated with one another—for example, women and Democrats tend to favor gun control, but women are also more likely than men to vote Democratic. These statistical correlations mean that it's hard to tell what's shaping public opinion and what's merely incidental. To sort out the separate effects of different factors, scholars use a statistical technique called regression analysis.

The results of regression analyses can depend on the particular techniques used and the variables included in the model. That said, various models using different sources of data have produced a consistent set of findings over the years. The characteristics that typically predict a person's support for stricter gun laws include identifying as a Democrat, being female, being a person of color, having more education, hailing from the Northeast, and not owning a gun. Each of these factors is statistically meaningful in its own right, independent of the others. Of all these factors, political party identification matters more than any other, including gun ownership itself. Put another way, political affiliation explains a lot of the opinion gaps we see between whites and nonwhites, men and women, and even between gun owners and nonowners.[14]

Why Are Guns and Gun Control So Emotional for Many People?

Because they touch on everything we hold dear: our lives and the lives of our family members and friends, our property, and our civic values. The deep emotions surrounding firearms may be a particularly American phenomenon, but it is a powerful one nonetheless.

Do High-Profile Shootings Shift Public Opinion on Gun Policy?

Sometimes—but not by much, and the effects usually don't last long.

At any given time, guns and gun violence are a back-burner issue for most Americans, far below government performance, the economy, and health care. Most people have settled views on the question. So when we are looking for a shift in opinion—on this issue or any other hot-button topic—we would not expect to see much of one, even in the presence of traumatic events.

Two polling organizations—Gallup and Pew—have regularly asked broad questions that gauge people's feelings about the gun issue in general. In several cases, the surveys have been fortuitously timed to capture opinion shortly before—and shortly after—mass shootings.

Gallup's survey—which asks whether laws governing firearms sales should be more strict, less strict, or kept as they are—appeared to register measurable yet modest bumps in the "more strict" direction after the shootings at Columbine High School shooting (April 1999), Virginia Tech (April 2007), the Tucson shopping center (January 2011), the Sandy Hook school (December 2012), the Las Vegas music festival (October 2017), and Marjory Stoneman Douglas High School (February 2018). However, these bumps—which we cannot definitively link to the shootings—were followed by retreats in support for stricter gun laws in the months after each incident.

Pew's survey—which asks people whether they prioritize protecting gun rights or controlling gun ownership—showed significant declines in pro-control sentiment between the early 1990s and the early 2010s before leveling off for several years after the Sandy Hook shooting. Since 2016, the survey has found consistent, though very modest, growth in pro-regulation sentiment. Although Pew's data, like Gallup's, show little to no movement in response to any particular mass shooting, the sheer cumulation of tragedies may be starting to change the equation. While too early to tell, Americans may be starting to think anew about stronger firearm laws as a desirable approach to gun violence.

These generalizations require a huge caveat. Beneath these broad national statistics lie deep differences of opinion among Americans that even mass shootings cannot bridge. Consider a recent study. The study's authors figured that if mass shootings change people's minds about gun control, we would see the largest opinion shifts among people who live close to an incident. But the study found that living near a mass shooting had no discernible effect on gun control attitudes, on average.[15] This finding seemed to support the view that mass shootings are momentary tragedies that don't change anything. However, when the authors dug deeper into their data, they discovered that these "non-effects" might actually be offsetting effects. Mass shootings might slightly boost Democrats' support for gun regulation while slightly decreasing support among Republicans. The study bolstered the view that how Americans think about guns depends on their politics.

Where Do Republicans and Democrats Stand on Gun Control?

By and large, Democrats favor stricter gun laws, while Republicans favor either keeping the laws the same or relaxing them. The party divide on gun issues has grown stronger over time among both lawmakers and everyday citizens.

Not until 1968 did the two major parties first include positions on gun control in their platforms. The Republicans balanced competing concerns of controlling "indiscriminate
availability" of guns with "safeguarding" gun rights for law-
abiding citizens. The Democrats supported "passage and enforcement of effective" gun control laws. Thereafter, the party
positions began to diverge.

Beginning in the 1970s, Republican platforms increasingly
emphasized support for the Second Amendment and the right
of self-defense, as well as opposition to certain gun laws.[16]
This reflects the rise of the "new right" forces within the GOP
and their emphasis on cultural "wedge" issues.[17] As we discuss in Chapter 10, recent decades have witnessed growing
institutional ties among conservative movement groups, the
Republican Party, and the NRA.

Meanwhile, the Democrats called for various new gun laws,
including a ban on cheap pistols (1972, 1976); a waiting period
on handgun purchases and a ban on assault weapons (1994);
mandatory gun locks, gun owner licensing, and background
checks on private sales (2000); and the continuation or renewal
of the assault weapons ban and, again, expanded background
checks (2004, 2008). In the 2004 campaign, fearful of the gun
lobby—which had been widely credited (or blamed) with
helping to defeat Al Gore in the 2000 presidential election—
the Democrats began including language supporting Second
Amendment rights.[18] This language stayed in place until 2016,
when the party shifted to a more nuanced message that "we
can respect the rights of responsible gun owners" while also
enacting stricter gun laws.[19]

The party positions on guns reflect each party's
base: Republicans are strongest in the South and in rural
areas, where gun ownership is widespread and reflective of
strong traditions of individualism and distrust of government.
Democrats are strongest in urban areas and among women
and people of color, who either lack a broad gun-owning tradition or see the dangers of gun violence up close. Within each

party there are exceptions—Democratic voters who are fervent gun rights supporters, and Republican voters who are comfortable with stricter controls. But among elected officials, votes on gun legislation almost always fall along party lines. Several months after the Sandy Hook shooting, for example, the US Senate voted down a background check measure with nearly all Democrats voting in favor and nearly all Republicans voting against. The handful of Democrats who voted against the bill came from rural states with strong gun lobbies, while the handful of Republicans who voted for the bill represented ideological moderates or had to worry about suburban voters. In February 2019, the US House approved a similar background check bill, and the pattern was predictably similar: an almost entirely party-line vote, except for a handful of moderate Republicans in support and a couple of rural Democrats opposed.

Does Support for Gun Control Cost Candidates Their Elections?

After the July 2012 massacre at a suburban Denver movie theater, Colorado's legislature passed, and the governor signed, a package of new gun control laws. Within three months, angry gun owners had gathered enough signatures to force recall elections for two Democrats who had supported the legislation. Three months later, the lawmakers were out of a job. A third Democratic lawmaker resigned in the midst of a recall effort.

To many people the events in Colorado underscored the conventional political wisdom that casting a pro-gun control vote virtually ensures political defeat. For years, candidates outside urban areas have feared earning an "F" on the NRA's vaunted scorecard and drawing a primary challenge from an opponent supported by gun lobby dollars. But the electoral politics of guns started changing in the early 2010s. The two major parties, Democrats and Republicans, have staked out clear positions on either side of the debate, and their voters have lined up accordingly. In practice, the self-sorting of gun rights people into the Republican Party and gun control people into the Democratic Party means that candidates can feel confident running on the issue without worrying about alienating their base. Unlike in years past, Democratic candidates usually don't need to worry about pro-gun men (who are now mostly Republicans), and Republican candidates usually don't have to worry about pro-control women (who are now mostly Democrats or independents). As voters increasingly agree with their party's position on guns, candidates are finding that they can take strong stands without fear of reprisal. Republicans got there first, but increasingly Democrats are discovering that the gun issue is a winning one, not only in urban strongholds, but also in swing suburban districts.

Democrats' willingness to run on gun control marks a dramatic reversal after two decades of ambivalence, even silence. The Democrats' drubbing in the 1994 congressional midterms cast a long shadow. Although the NRA's Wayne LaPierre and Bill Clinton don't see eye to eye on much, they agree that gun control decided this pivotal election and flipped the House of Representatives to the Republicans. The argument is that the NRA, its members, and gun owners generally were angered by two federal gun laws—the Brady background check bill (1993) and the federal assault weapons ban (1994)—passed in the 103rd Congress.

Social scientists decided to test Clinton's hypothesis by looking at how a newly invigorated GOP, led by firebrand Georgia congressman Newt Gingrich, picked up more than 50 seats and retook control of the House of Representatives after four decades in the minority. These same social scientists also looked at 1996, in which Congress members were again up for election. The thrust of their findings: Even after accounting for local idiosyncrasies and broader political trends, having the support of the NRA probably helped, but only in 1994 and only if the candidate was a Republican challenger. On average, the NRA endorsement provided a two-percentage-point boost to these candidates. Having lots of NRA members active in the district also helped challengers generally, but again only in 1994. In 1996, the NRA had no statistically discernible impact.[20]

The liberal journalist Paul Waldman also attempted to answer the $64,000 question of whether the NRA swung the House of Representatives to Republican control in the 1994 election. He noted that, if an NRA endorsement boosted Republican challengers by two points, it could have decided, at most, a dozen especially close races. However, even if the NRA had stayed out of the races, and all had gone to the Democrats, the GOP still would have won control of the House. In short, the NRA may have helped elect a few new Republicans, but it didn't deliver the House to the GOP.

Exhibit B for the proposition that gun votes swing elections is Al Gore. If he had won his home state of Tennessee in the 2000 presidential election, as the Clinton–Gore ticket had in 1996, he would have become the 43rd US president—and the term "hanging chads" never would have entered the lexicon. Instead, he lost Tennessee. Was the defeat due to gun owners angered by gun laws enacted in the first Clinton administration and threatened by further regulations proposed after school shootings in the run-up to the 2000 election? No scholar has a definitive answer, but a reasonable interpretation is that gun rights may have been a part of a constellation of intertwined cultural issues moving Southern whites away from the Democrats.[21]

Which brings us back to the growing party divide. Whereas Barack Obama had avoided talking about guns in his two presidential campaigns (2008 and 2012), Hillary Clinton made gun regulation a marquee issue in her 2016 bid. She criticized the Supreme Court's reasoning in the landmark gun rights case *District of Columbia v. Heller*; campaigned with women who had lost children to gun violence; and said she would not only seek stricter gun regulations but also try to reverse a law favorable to the firearms industry. As we discuss in Chapter 11, gun violence prevention groups, which traditionally had not spent much on elections, began to make state and federal campaigns a priority. Much of the spending came from new organizations that had formed after the Sandy Hook school shooting. These groups had tested the electoral waters in swing states such as Virginia and learned that moderate Democrats could win elections on the promise of supporting stricter gun laws. For Democrats, gun control was no longer taboo.

Of course, Hillary Clinton did not prevail in the 2016 election (though she did win the popular vote). The victor, gun-owning businessman and reality television star Donald Trump, courted the NRA and enjoyed more than $30 million in NRA campaign spending on his behalf.[22] The NRA's spending on all 2016 races topped $54 million, dwarfing the $3 million outlay of all major gun violence prevention groups combined.[23] Clinton lost several historically "blue" states that have both large urban centers and strong rural gun cultures. She also faced challenges having little to do with her stance on guns. She was seeking to transcend a decades-long life as a political lightning rod, succeed a two-term incumbent of the same party, and become America's first woman president—all at once.

What does 2016 tell us about the role of gun policy in elections? It tells us that gun organizations continue to have a significant spending edge (which, by the way, is true beyond elections). It tells us that elections seldom come down to one issue, even an issue as politically salient as guns. And it tells us that the cultural divide in America is real. Although gradual demographic changes may change the role of guns in American politics, for the time being the issue is likely to remain a critical divide. Candidates and voters might agree on proposals such as universal background checks. But the gun debate has come to reflect Americans' competing worldviews, as well as differences over public policy. These divides are likely to remain as long as the two-party system reflects and reinforces Americans' geographic and lifestyle differences.

10

THE GUN RIGHTS MOVEMENT

What Is the Gun Rights Movement?

The gun rights movement consists of several hundred local, state, and national organizations that seek to promote a positive view of firearms in public life and to prevent and remove restrictions on gun ownership and use. Generally speaking, you can think of the gun movement as being an interlocking set of actors:

National and state membership organizations that do a substantial amount of policy advocacy, whether lobbying, mobilizing individuals for direct action, or communicating with the media. Prominent examples include the National Rifle Association (NRA) and the Virginia Citizens Defense League.

Think tanks and researchers who conduct studies on policy issues and sponsor lawsuits to overturn gun control laws. Prominent think tanks include the Independence Institute and the Second Amendment Foundation, and key advocate-lawyers include David Kopel and Stephen Halbrook.

Gun safety and training organizations, sport-shooting associations, and gun shops whose primary mission is not political but which bring gun aficionados together to reinforce worldviews and communicate about policy and politics.

Gun manufacturers, distributors, and retailers, which are represented by the National Shooting Sports Foundation, based in Newtown, Connecticut. Compared to many other big businesses, such as defense and health care, the gun industry per se is not an especially significant political player, leading critics to contend that the NRA does the industry's bidding or that the industry is beholden to the NRA.

Political action committees, such as the National Rifle Association of America Political Victory Fund and the Gun Owners of America Political Victory Fund, that raise money to finance candidates for public office.

Unaffiliated activists, including libertarian sheriffs and private individuals who challenge gun laws. For example, several hundred sheriffs have vowed not to enforce any federal gun laws that they consider unconstitutional.

The NRA, founded in 1871, is the oldest and dominant organization in the gun rights movement. Headquartered in a Washington, DC, suburb, the NRA also enjoys the head seat at the table when major firearms legislation is under consideration and is the go-to organization for reporters seeking comment on all matters relating to gun policy. The organization claims 5.5 million members, but a more reliable estimate is about 4 million; either way, it is one of the largest pressure groups in the country.[1] It recently has taken to calling itself "America's longest-standing civil rights organization."

What we call the NRA is actually three organizations: a political advocacy organization of several million members; a charitable foundation that develops gun safety education programs and provides grants to hundreds of gun clubs and ranges around the country; and a political action committee (PAC), which gives money to candidates. The largest of these three is the membership association, the NRA, which had expenditures of $330 million in 2017. The NRA Foundation spent only about one-seventh as much—$44 million. The PAC, known as the NRA Political Victory Fund, spent about $19 million in the 2018 election cycle.

The NRA has multiple missions: to "protect and defend the US Constitution"; "to promote public safety, law and order, and national defense"; "to train law enforcement agencies and civilians in marksmanship"; and "to promote shooting sports and hunting."[2] That the political mission comes first is no accident. Although founded to improve civilian marksmanship in the wake of Union troops' lackluster performance in the Civil War, the NRA has become increasingly concerned with politics, particularly after gun control rose on the congressional agenda in the 1960s. At the group's 1977 national convention, a hardline faction took control of the board, and its willingness to work with lawmakers on gun reform—however mild—dissipated.

Even if the NRA is the best-known gun rights advocacy group, the movement is much broader. Other national gun groups are smaller, but they fill niches that the large organization does not and sometimes serve as a burr in its saddle. Gun Owners of America is proud to be called "the only no compromise gun lobby," a not-so-subtle dig at the NRA, and makes a lot of noise in lawmakers' offices when gun control legislation is on the agenda.[3] The National Association for Gun Rights likewise calls itself a "no compromise" grassroots organization and prioritizes the right to carry concealed weapons without a license.[4] The Citizens Committee for the Right to Keep and Bear Arms, which calls itself "the common sense gun lobby," and its allied organization, the Second Amendment Foundation, engage in public education, advocacy, and litigation.[5]

Gun owner organizations exist in every state. Many originated as rifle and pistol associations in the latter decades of the nineteenth century and the first decades of the twentieth to promote the shooting sports. Beginning in the 1990s, however, more explicitly political grassroots groups have sprung up in at least 40 states. These groups often herald their "no compromise" stance toward gun policy and evoke American values ("citizens defense," constitutional rights) in their names. These groups see guns not simply as tools of recreation or defense, but as integral to a free and orderly society. In that vein, many newer groups arose to advocate for unfettered carrying of guns in public and popular acceptance of the same.

Around the fringes of the gun rights movement is the patriot movement. Motivated by different threats—taxes, secularism, multiculturalism, globalization, gun control—"patriot," militia, and "sovereign citizen" groups agree on one thing: The federal government has run afoul of the Constitution, and at any moment citizens may need to lead an armed insurrection to restore the system that God and the founders intended. Mainstream gun advocacy groups have an uneasy relationship with the patriot movement. The two movements' philosophy and rhetoric can sound similar, but gun advocacy groups work within the system of laws to achieve their ends and risk undermining their legitimacy if they associate too closely with actors on the fringe. Gun violence prevention advocates have warned, however, of the increasingly strident antigovernment, insurrectionist positions voiced by representatives of mainstream gun rights advocacy groups.

Why Is the Gun Lobby So Strong?

In surveys of Washington political insiders, the NRA routinely ranks as one of the most powerful interest groups. In public opinion polls going back at least three decades, steady majorities of the public, around 50% to 60%, have viewed the NRA favorably, though Republicans are far more likely to feel that way than are Democrats.[6] After the Sandy Hook school shooting, a Democratic congressional staffer, speaking to a reporter on condition of anonymity, bemoaned, "We do absolutely anything they [the NRA] ask and we NEVER cross them . . . Pandering to the NRA is probably the worst part of my job."[7] However, there is some evidence that the organization's seeming invincibility may be diminishing.

The main source of the NRA's power is its committed membership base of somewhere around 4 million gun owners. In the American system, with its many points of political access and relatively weak political parties, dedicated citizen groups pushing very specific ideas often prevail, especially when their opposition is spread out and unorganized. What's more, in an era in which membership has come to mean little more than sending a check to Washington, the NRA and allied gun rights advocacy groups stand out in their ability to generate true grassroots engagement—getting members to show up at lawmakers' town hall meetings, contact elected officials, write letters to the editor, harass opponents, and cast their votes based on a candidate's gun rights positions. In recent decades, the NRA has become stronger as it has forged a strong alliance with the Republican Party. The NRA provides tens of millions of dollars in each election cycle to promote GOP candidates and includes Republican operatives on its board of directors. It also helped lay the groundwork for Donald Trump's political rise. Combining white American nostalgia, disdain for coastal elites, and hyper-vigilance against perceived threats to social order, the NRA primed conservatives for a modern brand of reactionary populism and gave force to candidate Trump's pledge to "make America great again."[8]

If the gun lobby's success is due to its members' engagement and symbiotic relationship with one of the main political parties, how does the lobby pull it off? And why have opponents had difficulty ginning up an equal and opposite force to neutralize the pro-gun side? The answer is that gun organizations have certain built-in advantages that leaders have leveraged with strategies that are especially well suited to succeeding in American politics.

The first key to the gun lobby's success is its structure: With national, state, and local organizations, it can apply pressure on lawmakers at all three levels of government. When legislation comes up in Congress, the national lobbyists are on the scene. NRA-affiliated sportsmen's organizations and independent political groups do the same in state capitols, augmenting lobbying with grassroots activities such as protests. Finally, in most localities there are gun shows, gun shops, shooting ranges, and other venues where individuals can meet and share information. Although few states allow cities or counties to do much by way of gun control, locally rooted activists are available should the need arise. Gun groups also are positioned to apply pressure across the three branches of government, with lobbyists working on the legislative branch, lawyers taking gun rights cases to court, and technical experts and lobbyists weighing in on regulations promulgated by the executive branch. In short, the gun lobby succeeds in part because its structure mirrors that of government.

The second key to gun groups' power is the mix of incentives that they can offer to potential members.[9] Here the gun lobby has a distinct advantage over its opponents. First, it can offer tangible things of value that people will join the organization just to receive—in the NRA's case, items such as magazines with useful information and discounts on everything from hotels to hearing aids (though many companies, including Delta Airlines and the major car rental companies, ended these benefits after the shooting at Marjory Stoneman Douglas High School in Parkland, Florida, in 2018). Once you have joined the NRA, you may be eligible for a cut-rate membership at your local gun club. Beyond tangible incentives, the NRA and other gun groups also can offer social incentives to join, such as marksmanship awards, leadership opportunities, and the sense of connection that comes from shared experiences. Gun rights advocacy groups benefit from the social side of the shooting sports by recruiting members at shooting clubs, gun shows, and even firearm shops.

A third membership inducement that groups can offer is the sense of meaning and satisfaction people get when they work for a cause they hold dear. Gun groups have leveraged people's need to be part of something larger than themselves by connecting gun ownership and use to widely held understandings of American history and values. The political scientist Matthew Lacombe has shown how the NRA for decades has carefully crafted a gun owner identity that can be mobilized for politics.[10] Although the American belief system contains contradictions—for example, between individualism and populism—pro-gun advocates have sampled and combined core American values to promote the idea that guns contribute to the public good.

With all these incentives to offer, the NRA has attracted a lot of members, and the income that comes from member dues—some $128 million in 2017—finances a panoply of programs that enhance the association's political clout. These programs include developing and disseminating authoritative research and talking points for lawmakers, orchestrating grassroots and inside-the-Beltway lobbying, communicating with members, and influencing elections.[11]

Although the gun lobby is suspicious, even contemptuous, of the federal government, one longtime scholar of gun politics has observed that "the NRA probably owes its existence to its long-term, intimate association with government subsidies and other forms of support."[12] Throughout the twentieth century, the US government's civilian marksmanship program directly subsidized the NRA and its state affiliates. The War Department and its successor, the Department of Defense, provided guns and ammunition to rifle clubs, supported rifle range operations and instruction, and sold military surplus weapons at rock-bottom prices. Until 1979, one had to be an NRA member to buy the surplus guns, meaning that the government was providing a tangible incentive for gun aficionados to join. As an internal NRA report concluded in 1971, the association's "phenomenal growth . . . to more than one million members was made possible primarily by the Defense Department."[13] Even today, the federal government provides special concessions that help the NRA, including permission to build target ranges on federal land, which is not subject to local zoning laws.

After a century and a half, the NRA has built up a widely recognized brand, an organizational infrastructure with affiliates and training programs around the country, and an army of politically engaged citizens. At the same time, the organization has become embroiled in controversies surrounding unusual ties to Russian nationals, large budget deficits, and questionable outlays to vendors and top officials. The NRA has denied any wrongdoing and, as of this writing, has not been charged with any illegality. Although the NRA retains broad public support, at least among Republicans, polls suggest that growing numbers of people have begun to question its clout. After the Sandy Hook shooting, for example, 39% thought the NRA had too much influence over gun policy, but five years later, that number had risen to 44%, including nearly one-third of gun owners.[14]

It is worth bearing in mind that "the NRA" is not synonymous with "the gun rights movement." While the NRA is the oldest and best-known pro-gun advocacy organization, it has competitors on its right flank at both the national and state levels. These organizations are arguably as important as the NRA in driving grassroots citizen activism. Gun groups are at their strongest in threatening political environments—for example, when Democrats win major elections or when mass shootings put gun control on the agenda. Political opportunities for gun violence prevention groups ironically give gun rights advocacy groups a boost in donations and political engagement.

Do Pro-Gun People Care More Deeply About Gun Policy Than Pro-Regulation People?

For decades social scientists have pointed to the "gun control paradox," which in its simplified form holds that "most people want stronger gun laws but rarely get them." Gun rights advocacy groups would object to that framing—see our discussion in the section "How Many Gun Laws Are There?" in Chapter 6—but the paradox contains a timeless truth. If the polls are to be believed, national gun laws are weaker than most Americans would like them to be. At the state level, laws and public opinion are better aligned, but popular proposals, such as background checks on all sales, nevertheless can languish.

The traditional resolution to the gun control paradox concerns intensity. Yes, people support gun control, but they don't feel that strongly about it. If they do feel strongly, they also care about a lot of other issues and aren't prepared to make gun regulation the focus of their activism or the deciding factor in their vote. In contrast, the argument goes, gun rights supporters are passionate single-issue voters who will stop at nothing to prevent passage of stronger gun laws. Although combined into a single narrative, these are two different propositions. In our opinion there is strong evidence for the latter (that gun rights advocates care a lot) and mixed evidence for the former (that gun reform advocates don't care all that much).

As noted above, gun groups have some natural organizing advantages allowing them to develop a strong sense of collective civic identity among gun owners and to project their voice into politics. As we discuss in the next chapter, gun control supporters historically have faced more challenges in finding one another, creating politically powerful shared identities, and overcoming barriers to enacting social regulation of any form. Given these organizational disparities, then, it's not surprising that surveys find pro-gun people participate more around the gun issue than do their opponents. But there's less evidence that pro-gun people care more—or, to be more precise, that gun regulation supporters don't care much. Some of the perceived intensity gap is about differences in organization and in perceived ability to effect change.

Two recent surveys illustrate the point. In the week after the Sandy Hook shooting, the Pew Research Center gauged people's feelings about whether it's more important to protect gun owners' rights or to control ownership. Among respondents who prioritized gun control, 42% felt strongly about the matter, compared to 37% of those who prioritized protecting gun rights.[15] Several months later, Pew sought to figure out how many people are truly single-issue gun voters. In that poll, 41% of gun rights supporters claimed to be single-issue voters, meaning they would refuse to support a candidate who disagreed with them on gun policy but agreed with them on other issues. On the gun control side, the comparable figure was 31%.[16] Adjusting for the fact that there are more gun control supporters in the population, we find—as did a similar study three decades before—that the number of single-issue voters on each side is more balanced than the conventional wisdom would suggest (20% of the population claims to vote on a pro-gun basis, compared to 16% on a pro-control basis).

The more significant gap is not in intensity, but in action. In a 1978 poll, scholars Howard Schuman and Stanley Presser found that compared to pro-control supporters, gun rights proponents were three times as likely to have taken some political action on the issue, such as writing a letter or giving money.[17] Even when correcting for the fact that there were more pro-control supporters, nearly two-thirds of all letter writers and donors were from the pro-gun rights side. A 2013 poll reached a similar conclusion: Gun rights supporters were four times as likely as gun control supporters ever to have given money to an organization active on gun policy and considerably more likely to have contacted a public official, expressed an opinion on a social networking site, or signed a petition on the gun issue.[18] By 2017, the action gap had narrowed considerably, but gun rights supporters remained more likely than gun regulation advocates to contact lawmakers and contribute money to a gun-related organization.[19] We conclude, as did other scholars four decades ago, that America has "an efficient lobby against gun control legislation, which is able to activate adherents whenever necessary."[20] However, as we discuss in Chapter 11, organizations seeking to reform gun laws are quickly catching up.

Although polls are a blunt instrument for measuring political engagement, the findings are broadly consistent over time: It's not intensity per se that favors the gun rights movement, but rather its ability to translate passion into action. Perhaps more importantly, lawmakers' votes and election outcomes are often decided at the margins, meaning that a few especially loud, focused activist efforts can have outsized influence not detectable in national polls. One of the interesting findings from a 2013 Pew survey is that single-issue gun voting seems to be concentrated among conservative Republicans.[21] As the GOP has moved rightward, moderate Republicans and even establishment conservatives increasingly must fear a primary election challenge. In such circumstances, particularly engaged constituency groups have disproportionate influence, given that they may determine the outcome of low-turnout primary elections. Elected officials know that gun owners, who may see each other regularly and keep abreast of ongoing developments, will be a consistent presence and for that reason must be taken into account even when gun policy is not in the headlines.

How Has the NRA Shaped Gun Control Policy?

Profoundly, and its influence stems in large part from its structure. The national media focuses on the NRA's hold over Congress, but the group's influence is as strong at the state level, where many recent successes have occurred.

As of mid-2019, the NRA had not lost a decisive battle over federal gun control legislation in a quarter-century. In 1994 Congress passed and President Clinton signed legislation banning the future manufacture of certain types of assault weapons and high-capacity magazines for civilian use, but gun policy enacted thereafter was friendly to gun rights. In the mid-1990s, the NRA worked its congressional connections to effectively halt government-sponsored research on the public health consequences of firearms. In 2005, the organization secured a federal law that largely immunized gun makers, distributors, and dealers from a broad range of lawsuits, thereby undermining one of the gun regulation lobby's most promising strategies. In 2007, after the Virginia Tech tragedy, Congress passed a law to help states enter records of prohibited purchasers into the national background check system. Although some gun advocacy groups balked, the NRA shaped the legislation and extracted numerous concessions to make it a "win for American gun owners."[22] In 2009, gun groups won passage of legislation lifting the ban on loaded guns in national parks. In addition to this string of victories, the NRA and its allies staved off congressional proposals to reinstate the assault weapons ban and to require background checks on most private gun sales. Although the NRA did not get all that it wanted—for example, a federal law that would force states to accept each other's concealed weapons permits—the organization was successful at preventing further gun restrictions.

At the state level, the NRA, its affiliates, and independent gun rights advocacy groups have worked methodically on a series of issue campaigns to deregulate firearms. We touched on several of these campaigns in Chapter 6. They include securing preemption laws in most states, thereby limiting or eliminating the authority of local governments to regulate firearms; passing state laws barring lawsuits against the gun industry before Congress did so nationally; easing or eliminating licensing requirements to carry concealed weapons; protecting shooting ranges from lawsuits or other actions brought by annoyed neighbors; removing restrictions on guns in bars, on campuses, and in other public spaces; and securing reciprocity laws that allow concealed-carry license holders to holster their guns in other states.

These campaigns owe their success to a combination of smart strategy, the disproportionate representation of rural interests in many state legislatures, the ease with which gun owners can be located and organized for political action, and historically weak opposition at the state level. The upshot of these efforts is that guns have a more prominent place in public life today than they did 50 or 100 years ago.

Does the NRA Represent the Firearms Industry?

The question is a matter of interpretation, but as a practical matter the answer may not matter much.

The NRA has long prided itself on being an authentic grassroots membership organization focused on firearms training and recreation. NRA tax filings show that membership dues have made up between 41% and 50% of the organization's revenues over the past decade—by far the single largest source of income. Until recently, the website for its youth safety program stated that the NRA "is not affiliated with any firearm or ammunition manufacturers or with any businesses that deal in guns and ammunition."[23]

However, in recent years, gun violence prevention advocates and liberal journalists have challenged that statement. Their evidence:

In 1999, when the gun industry was facing lawsuits from cities and victims, the NRA's then-president, Charlton Heston, told gun industry executives at their large annual trade show, "Your fight has become our fight." The NRA then made its top legislative priority passage of a federal law immunizing the gun industry; the measure was enacted in 2005. Such intervention was necessary, observers note, because the gun industry's official trade association, the National Shooting Sports Foundation, had nowhere near the NRA's political muscle.

After enactment of the federal law granting legal protections to the gun industry, the NRA introduced a corporate giving program that has reaped rewards from gun and ammunition manufacturers and dealers. Between 2005 and 2013, according to one report, the gun industry contributed somewhere between $19 million and $60 million through the NRA's "Ring of Freedom" corporate sponsorship program.[24] Some gun makers allow customers to "round up" their gun purchase to the nearest dollar, with the extra money—several million dollars in recent years—going to the NRA's political advocacy arm.

Several gun industry executives serve on the NRA's 76-member board of directors. But it's important to note that they are not plentiful. For example, the most recent board whose members were publicly identifiable as of this writing (2017) included only a small handful of industry people, including the NRA's then-president Pete Brownell.

Having the NRA take the lead on the political front serves the gun industry's bottom-line interests. Most obviously, the industry benefits when gun advocacy groups generate fear of firearm confiscation and gun owners respond by stocking up. Profits are higher when the industry doesn't have to spend money on political fights and when fewer regulations are in place. What's more, the widely respected NRA can insulate the industry from political heat when its products are misused—say, in a school massacre.

If you are persuaded by this evidence, the question is, what does it mean? To NRA critics, it means the organization will take positions primarily to shore up corporate profits, even if those positions are at odds with mainstream gun owners' views. Here is Mark Kelly, who became a gun violence prevention activist after the shooting of his wife, Rep. Gabrielle Giffords (D-AZ), writing an op-ed coinciding with the NRA's 2013 convention in Houston: "The NRA leadership's top priority is to make sure the corporations that make guns and ammunition continue to turn huge profits. Their top priority isn't you, the NRA member."[25]

But it's not clear that the views of the industry are really more extreme than the views of the NRA's base; in fact, the opposite is probably true. And the larger suggestion—that the

NRA is working for the gun industry—has its skeptics. If anything, say insiders, the NRA runs the show and the industry goes along because it fears the NRA's wrath and because their interests are largely aligned anyway. It is perhaps telling that the NRA's 2017 board included five times as many political figures as gun industry people.

Rather than being a tool of the industry, the NRA is more like its front group. Gun makers and dealers didn't have a lobbyist until 1989, and their organizations keep a low profile compared to activist gun groups. In the 1990s, when gun manufacturers attempted to compromise with the Clinton administration, the NRA penalized them for stepping out of line. Since then, the industry has been content to continue supporting the NRA financially—by advertising in its magazines, contributing to its corporate fundraising program, and selling NRA memberships in gun shops—while deferring to the association on the handling of policy questions and political controversies. As reporter Paul Barrett, author of a book on the Glock company, wrote, "The companies that make and market firearms might prefer a softer tone, but they rarely complain publicly about NRA fear mongering because it's good for business."[26]

For gun violence prevention groups, however, there may be strategic reasons to play up NRA–industry ties. As longtime gun control advocate Josh Sugarmann noted, "I think it's much easier for policymakers to defend the NRA when they're perceived as efforts on behalf of gun owners. That equation changes dramatically when they're seen as defending the gun industry."[27]

11

THE GUN VIOLENCE PREVENTION MOVEMENT

What Is the Gun Violence Prevention Movement?

Like the gun rights movement, the gun violence prevention movement includes national, state, and local organizations. Some are single-issue organizations, spending all their time on gun violence prevention, while others are multi-issue allies from the women's, religious, people-of-color, and other communities. And like the gun rights movement, gun violence prevention groups use an array of educational, lobbying, and electoral strategies to advance their cause.

However, historically the gun violence prevention movement (sometimes called the gun safety movement or the gun control movement) has lacked the energized grassroots membership, state infrastructure, and steady financial resources that gun rights advocacy groups enjoy. A 2006 scholarly history argued that by any reasonable standard there was no real gun control movement in America—it was a "missing movement."[1] But during the next dozen years, the United States experienced regular mass shootings—including most of the deadliest massacres in history. In response, Americans began organizing, establishing membership organizations, incorporating new constituencies, and bringing in lots of money. As 2020 approached, the gun control movement was no longer missing.

Although social movements are important in US policy-making, they are not always necessary. Unlike civil rights laws, for example, gun regulations often have been enacted without pressure from below. In the 1930s, when Congress enacted restrictions on machine guns and created a federal licensing scheme for dealers, the key player was the US attorney general, though women's groups testified and mobilized their members in favor of these landmark laws. The major gun control laws of the late 1960s, including the Gun Control Act of 1968, were the handiwork of key Congress members and President Johnson, though a short-lived Emergency Committee for Gun Control generated thousands of letters from concerned citizens in support of the bill.

The institutional gun control lobby really began to form amid the handgun-crime wave of the early 1970s. Between 1974 and 1976, six state gun control groups and five national organizations were established, including two that would go on to lead the movement in the decades to come: the National Council to Control Handguns (later renamed Handgun Control Inc. and now called Brady United) and the National Coalition to Ban Handguns (now called the Coalition to Stop Gun Violence). The Brady group is a membership association that traditionally has relied primarily on contributions from the public that tend to flow most heavily in response to high-profile acts of gun violence; the Coalition was founded by the Methodist Church as an association of women's, labor, and religious groups and today also includes individual members.

The gun control universe expanded during the gun violence epidemic of the 1980s and 1990s. The Violence Policy Center was founded in 1988 to conduct research useful to gun control advocates. During the 1990s, often in response to incidents involving children, 46 state groups were formed to pursue educational and legislative strategies to reduce gun violence.[2] Generally, these groups had small budgets, tiny staffs (if any), and little clout in state capitols. After a spate of school shootings in the late 1990s, women formed the Million Mom March to develop a grassroots base for gun control advocacy. The women later became part of the Brady Campaign to Prevent Gun Violence (now Brady United). However, the resources of the gun control lobby in these years never came close to those of the National Rifle Association (NRA). One study estimated that the combined membership of state and national gun control groups in the early 2000s was no more than 7% of the NRA's membership.[3] The combined revenues of the Coalition and the Brady Campaign (and their respective educational arms) likewise totaled about 7% of the NRA's revenues at that time.[4]

These longtime gun regulation advocacy groups are still far smaller than the NRA, but in the 2000s, they were joined by a 600-pound gorilla: Michael Bloomberg, whose personal wealth in 2019 was estimated at $55 billion[5] and who has made gun reform a key priority both as mayor of New York City from 2002 to 2014 and as a philanthropist. In 2006, Mayor Bloomberg, along with then-mayor Thomas Menino of Boston, founded Mayors Against Illegal Guns (MAIG), a research and political advocacy organization that included some 1,000 city leaders. In 2013, MAIG merged with a grassroots group of mother-activists to form Everytown for Gun Safety, and Mayor Bloomberg pledged $50 million to the gun reform cause. With his support, along with that of everyday donors, Everytown became the dominant player in the gun violence prevention movement, with nearly three times the budget of all other national gun violence prevention groups combined.

Paralleling Bloomberg's efforts are those of Gabrielle Giffords, the Arizona congresswoman who was shot in the head and nearly killed at a constituent event outside a Tucson grocery store in 2011. Along with her husband, the former astronaut Mark Kelly, Giffords founded Americans for Responsible Solutions, a political action committee and a lobbying group, after the Sandy Hook school shooting. The organization absorbed a public education organization, the Law Center to Prevent Gun Violence, in 2016. The following year, the three sister organizations became known as Giffords, Giffords PAC, and Giffords Law Center. As longtime gun owners and self-identified Second Amendment supporters, Giffords and Kelly lobby, appear in the media, and sponsor television ads in favor of stricter national gun laws.

In addition to the emergence of well-staffed and generously funded national organizations, three other recent developments may help the gun violence prevention movement continue to level the playing field against its better-funded, better-organized opponents.[6]

The first development is the diversification of voices within the movement. As of 2019, longstanding national and state groups had been joined by organizations trying to amplify the public voice of specific constituencies affected by gun violence. Some constituencies, notably people of color, are involved because they suffer disproportionately from gun violence on a daily basis. Other constituencies have organized in response to a particular mass shooting: family members and survivors (Virginia Tech, 2007; the Aurora theater, 2012), mothers (Sandy Hook Elementary School, 2012), LGBTQ people (Pulse nightclub, 2016), and young people (Marjory Stoneman Douglas High School, 2018). The organizations constituting the contemporary gun violence prevention movement benefit from far greater resources, organizing tools, and strategic direction compared to advocates during the gun violence epidemic and school shootings of the 1990s.

The second, and related, development strengthening the gun violence prevention movement is the decision to engage family members and survivors as full-time lobbyists, media spokespeople, and grassroots organizers. Although victims and family members had always played a key role at the local and state levels—often they were the founders and volunteers fueling scrappy little gun violence prevention groups—these people generally did not maintain a high-profile presence on the national stage. Some notable exceptions included Sarah Brady, whose husband, James, was severely wounded in the 1981 assassination attempt on President Reagan; Tom Mauser, whose son, Daniel, was killed in the 1999 Columbine High School shootings; and Mary Leigh Blek, a Southern California activist whose son was murdered and who became chair of the Million Mom March organization. With the mass shooting at Virginia Tech, the number of survivors and family members advocating for stricter gun laws increased. The Virginia Tech families were key to passage of the 2007 federal legislation to improve the national background check system, and many have continued to be active on other gun reform measures at both the state and national levels. Parents of children killed at the Sandy Hook school created an organization to support training and education programs for students and school personnel that allow them to identify students at risk of violence before it occurs.

The Virginia Tech families also created a model for organizing family members and survivors after mass shootings, and others have followed suit. Survivors of the 2011 Tucson shooting, which gravely wounded Giffords and killed six others, organized and helped inspire the creation of a 2,000-member national network within Everytown for Gun Safety, the largest gun violence prevention organization. The 2012 massacre at an Aurora, Colorado, theater, which killed 12 and injured dozens more, led two grieving parents, Sandy and Lonnie Phillips, to create a mutual support organization, Survivors Empowered. The couple sold most of their possessions, bought an RV, and now travel to sites of mass shootings to support those affected. Beyond these networks, individual survivors and family members have taken on prominent roles in long-established national gun violence prevention groups and helped to create new ones, such as March for Our Lives (arising from the Marjory Stoneman Douglas shooting in 2018); the Pride Fund (Pulse nightclub, 2016); and Giffords, Sandy Hook Promise, Newtown Action, and Moms Demand Action for Gun Sense in America (Sandy Hook school, 2012).

A third way that gun regulation advocates have begun to level the playing field is through their decision to get seriously involved in electoral politics. In earlier decades, gun control groups focused on pressuring lawmakers from the outside; now they are also seeking to influence who becomes a lawmaker in the first place. In some cases, gun violence survivors and activists are running for office themselves. The father of an Aurora theater victim now sits in the Colorado state House, and the mother of an African American teen shot for playing loud music picked up a congressional seat in suburban Atlanta. More than a dozen members of the Moms Demand Action gun violence prevention group won elections at all levels of government in 2018.

Gun regulation advocates also are spending big money to support sympathetic candidates and defeat their opponents. Such expenditures were almost nonexistent two decades ago. Bloomberg led the way, using his Independence USA PAC to unseat NRA-friendly legislators and support candidates vowing to advocate for stricter gun laws (among other causes). Giffords PAC, which raises money from both small and large donors, is another important player. It spent $18 million in the 2018 election cycle, with a focus on the gun issue. In the 2018 election cycle, these two PACs spent more than four times what the NRA's PAC, the Political Victory Fund, spent ($19 million).[7] When it comes to direct contributions to candidates, gun regulation groups dwarfed the NRA.

However, the NRA still has a decisive advantage in all-important independent expenditures—the money that organizations use to support or oppose candidates without working with or through specific campaigns. In the 2016 election cycle, according to data compiled by the Center for Responsive Politics, the NRA provided more than twice as much ($35 million) in independent expenditures as the Bloomberg and Giffords PACs combined (roughly $16 million).

Bottom line: The NRA still dominates electoral spending. But gun violence prevention organizations have become formidable foes in the regulated world of direct candidate contributions and to a lesser extent in independent expenditures.

Money is important in determining which candidates are viable and successful, as well as in shaping lawmakers' priorities once elected, so these developments may end up mattering for gun policy. That said, the importance of money shouldn't be overstated. Gun rights advocacy organizations have influenced politics not so much because of their money, but because of their members' activism.

Is the Gun Violence Prevention Movement Relatively Weak?

Although gun violence prevention groups have had some notable victories, including enactment of a federal background check law in 1993 and of modest reforms in some states, the movement historically has struggled to raise the money and mobilize the sustained, grassroots engagement enjoyed by the gun rights movement. This asymmetry may be the real gun control paradox: Americans favor stronger gun laws but historically have not mobilized very noticeably to achieve that goal. Although the dynamics are changing, the gun violence prevention movement faces some built-in obstacles.[8]

One set of challenges is inherent in the issue itself. As we noted earlier, an axiom of politics holds that it's easier to block legislative proposals than to get them passed. While opponents simply have to agree that they don't like a proposal, supporters of new policies have to agree on what they would like done. Historically, gun control leaders have disagreed among themselves, sometimes bitterly, over which policy option would be most effective, while the gun rights movement has been unified around the notion that having fewer gun laws is better than having more. The general public—whose consent gun regulation advocates presumably must court—also has lacked consensus on how best to prevent firearms violence: Should we put more police in schools? Spend more on mental health screening and treatment? Reduce the depiction of violence in the media? Ban assault weapons? Polls suggest there is no single, overwhelmingly supported approach.

Recently, something like a consensus has begun to form, within the gun violence prevention movement and the general public, about the priority of expanding background checks to most or all gun sales, plugging holes in gun laws pertaining to domestic abusers and stalkers, and passing laws to allow temporary removal of guns from people at an elevated risk of misusing them. Agreement on a basic policy agenda has strengthened the movement.

A second challenge is that gun control belongs to a broader category of social regulatory policies, which restrict individual liberties in the interest of the public good. To people whose behavior is regulated by these policies, they have moralizing overtones, with the government telling individuals how to live their lives. In a political culture that prizes personal autonomy, such regulations are often difficult to enact. This challenge is compounded in the realm of gun control, which has been successfully branded as a threat to American values.

Gun regulation advocacy groups also face the challenge of promoting what economists call a public good—in this case, a society free of gun violence. Because people benefit from a public good regardless of whether they helped to achieve it, they have a tendency to withhold their time and money and "free ride" on the contributions of others. One way to overcome this problem is to offer incentives for people to join, as we discussed in Chapter 10. While gun rights advocacy groups can offer all sorts of incentives for members—glossy magazines, opportunities to have fun at the firing range, the feeling of supporting an important cause—gun violence prevention groups must rely primarily on altruistic incentives, which work well for a relatively small number of especially civic-minded people but are the least effective at mobilizing *en masse*. For this reason, groups advocating for public goods have chronic problems sustaining mass memberships. The twin challenges of enacting social regulation and organizing around public goods are compounded in the case of gun control, where the connection between the specific policy and its effects may not be visible immediately.

So gun regulation advocacy groups start off with some built-in disadvantages that afflict movements for other types of reforms as well. But the gun violence prevention movement has its own unique challenges. For one, its core constituency—people who have suffered from gun violence or live in fear of it—often lack what political scientists call "civic resources." Many survivors and family members are emotionally depleted and may also lack the time, money, and powerful networks that are useful in movement building. Likewise, in the early decades of their existence, gun control groups were ambivalent about organizing at the grassroots level and pursuing the sort of incremental, state-to-state strategies for which movements are well suited. Gun violence prevention groups also struggled to find powerful frameworks to inspire people to join. The modern gun violence prevention movement is beginning to address these shortcomings.

One of the greatest challenges, however, has been that the gun violence prevention movement faces an implacable, well-funded, and occasionally threatening foe. (Pro-gun advocates have been known to show up at gun policy meetings legally carrying loaded weapons and to threaten sexual violence against mothers supporting gun reform. Such tactics have acquired a name, "the hassle factor.") The gun rights movement has millions of supporters delivering a very disciplined message, that gun control is futile at best and un-American at worst, and this message has gained traction among the public and many lawmakers over the last two decades. When activists are literally and figuratively outgunned, it's tempting to get discouraged and move on to other causes where political engagement is more likely to bear fruit. Interestingly, many of the gun violence prevention movement's state and local leaders have been at their jobs for a long time, showing no signs of retreat, but activism among the movement's foot soldiers has been harder to sustain.

As discussed earlier, the movement has grown much stronger in the age of mass shootings. Gun violence prevention groups have more money, more organizations, more activists, more electoral clout, and more political savvy than ever before. The movement is also better organized at the state level, where most gun laws are enacted. Although one should be cautious about drawing conclusions from just a few years' data, analyses by advocates on both sides of the debate show that states have started to enact more laws tightening gun regulations than loosening them.[9] If it continues, this trend would represent a sea change in gun politics.

What Happens After a High-Profile Shooting?

If it happens in England, Australia, or New Zealand, lawmakers enact sweeping gun control laws. In the United States, the response is less rapid and dramatic, yet nevertheless real.

High-profile shootings such as assassinations and massacres in seemingly safe spaces often move a public policy issue onto the public agenda and provide an opportunity to debate and possibly enact legislation. However, the window of opportunity can be narrow. The attention of the public, media, and lawmakers tends to shift quickly, and the regularity of mass shootings can make them seem normal or even inevitable. Aware of these dynamics, gun reformers have started creating new organizations to mobilize and sustain the outrage that follows high-profile tragedies.

In an insight that has stood the test of time, the political scientist Robert Spitzer observed that high-profile shootings often provoke a cycle of outrage, action, and reaction.[10] An especially shocking shooting sparks an outpouring of public emotion, contributions to gun violence prevention groups, and calls on policymakers to tighten the laws. Policymakers respond by considering stricter gun regulations and sometimes enacting them. But pro-gun advocates quickly muster resources and activists to fight these efforts. The challenge for gun regulation advocates is to keep the attention of the media, the public, and policymakers focused for as long as possible. For pro-gun supporters, the goal is to influence the terms of debate or to change the subject entirely. As we discussed in Chapter 8, mass shootings don't change many people's opinions about the wisdom of gun control. But they can intensify the emotional urgency felt by people supporting stronger laws and the threat experienced by those who oppose such regulations.

For gun regulation advocates, continued media coverage is critical. A study of the 1999 Columbine High School shooting found that the national media (specifically, the *New York Times*) followed the story for a month before yielding space to other news events.[11] Media coverage of school shootings unfolds in terms that are favorable to gun regulation advocates, who seek to frame individual incidents as part of broader problems that government has an obligation to address. Over time media stories about school shootings come to focus on the societal implications and future remedies or actions to be taken.[12]

However, just because gun regulation advocates hope that policy change emerges from tragedies, and just because the media gravitate to this story angle, lawmakers don't necessarily oblige. In some cases—say, the assassination of President Kennedy in 1963 or the 2011 shooting of a congresswoman, a federal judge, and 17 others at a Tucson shopping center—high-profile gun violence provokes no policy change. In other cases, high-profile events may contribute to policy change already under consideration or on its way. In rare cases, such shootings prove to be the driving force behind new gun laws, but usually only in circumstances that were already politically hospitable.

At the federal level, when high-profile shootings make a difference in public policy, they do so as catalysts for legislative action already under consideration—providing the proverbial final straw. Take the case of the landmark federal gun control laws enacted in 1968, the Omnibus Crime Control and Safe Streets Act and the Gun Control Act. Key provisions had been under discussion for five years. The assassination of Robert F. Kennedy may have provided the final spur to the House to pass the omnibus bill and to the Johnson administration to push for introduction of the Gun Control Act, a more sweeping bill. But other factors were at work, including rioting and general social disorder, rising fear of crime, broad public support for gun control, and a sympathetic Congress and president. Consider a counterfactual, the aftermath of the near assassination of President Reagan in 1981. At that time, the political conditions were less favorable toward gun reform, and no new federal laws were enacted. The modest federal background check bill bearing the name of Reagan's gravely wounded press secretary, James Brady, did not pass until 12 years later, when Democrats controlled the White House and Congress.

High-profile shootings are more likely to lead directly to policy change at the state level. Typically, these changes are modest, adding incrementally to existing bodies of law. After shootings at a high school in Springfield, Oregon, and a year later in Littleton, Colorado, activists got measures on the popular ballot in those states to require background checks on private sales at gun shows. Both measures passed handily. The Sandy Hook and Marjory Stoneman Douglas shootings provided the impetus to pass stronger gun laws in Connecticut and Florida, respectively, as well as in a handful of other states. These changes reflect public pressure on lawmakers to "do something" in response to tragic events.

That said, mass shootings in gun-friendly states almost never result in tightened restrictions on guns or gun owners. Some high-profile shootings that have provoked no legislative response include those at public schools in Mississippi and Kentucky in 1997 and Arkansas in 1998; at a university in Virginia in 2007; at a military base, high school, and church in Texas between 2009 and 2018; at a church in South Carolina in 2015; and at a synagogue in Pennsylvania in 2018. By and large, states that strengthen their firearms laws after high-profile shootings already have comparatively strong gun laws and weak gun rights lobbies. And it's worth noting that mass shootings may help pro-gun advocates—for example, the 2007 Virginia Tech massacre inspired a successful push to allow firearms on college campuses in some states.

Policy change is one concrete way of assessing the impact of mass shootings. A less easily measured but important consideration is the effect on young people who have grown up under the threat of such events. In a 2018 poll of Americans aged 14 to 29, school shootings were an important issue for nearly 70%—more than any other issue, including health care, access to higher education, jobs, and climate change.[13] Of those surveyed, 45% had taken part in a school shooting drill. Half of all respondents wondered "what kind of world we live in, when so many innocent children die in shootings and our government does little to address it." A separate survey found that 75% of young people (aged 15 to 21), and more than 60% of all Americans, feel stressed about mass shootings. Gun violence was about as stressful as concerns over money.[14]

Students who live through a mass shooting can suffer from depression or post-traumatic stress, particularly if they were physically near the attack, were personally close to a victim, had experienced prior trauma, or were psychologically vulnerable before the shooting.[15] Being able to gain access to supportive people and services ameliorates some of these negative effects.

In short, widely publicized shootings can force the gun issue onto the political agenda and mobilize people and organizations. The importance of presidential leadership is critical to these dynamics. But the effect of any particular shooting on policy change depends on the larger political environment. In states where most voters are sympathetic to strong gun regulations, mass shootings can lead to new laws. In states that are firearm-friendly, these events can prompt lawmakers to allow more guns in more places. And sometimes mass shootings can result in new legislation that offers something to groups on both sides of the gun debate. Unlike legislative changes, the impact that mass shootings have on people's worldview and well-being, particularly over the long term, remains an open question.

Do the Media Favor Gun Control?

Pro-gun advocates and gun-friendly scholars have long complained that the media are allied against firearms owners and in favor of gun control. These critics charge that reporters approach firearms issues with a preconceived storyline—guns are bad—and omit data or arguments at odds with that presumption. Another charge is that reporters tend to write about guns in ways that needlessly frighten the public—for example, by characterizing random upticks in shootings as out-of-control epidemics or by leaving the erroneous impression that machine guns are often used in crime. Finally, these critics provide evidence, some of it open to interpretation, that the media treat the pro-control cause more favorably, in both tone and amount of coverage, than they treat the gun rights cause and gun owners. Whatever organizational advantages the NRA may have, these authors argue, the pro-control groups have an almost monolithically sympathetic media establishment on their side, significantly leveling the political playing field.[16]

While most work on media coverage of gun issues rests on anecdotes or small samples of news reporting, their general conclusion—that the media favor gun control—is consistent with a wider body of research on media norms and incentives. One of the most consistent findings is that the media play up conflict and drama, of which gun crime is an example, to generate ratings. As the saying goes, "If it bleeds, it leads." Thus, one would expect large-scale violence, whether crime waves or mass shootings, to attract more attention than isolated cases of defensive gun use. A long-term study of network news stories on two major gun reforms—the Brady background check law and the assault weapons ban—found that the media's dominant framework centered on a "culture of violence" particularly in inner cities, a theme the study found was also promoted by gun regulation groups.[17] Needless to say, stories about gun misuse do not put firearms in a positive light.

Pro-gun advocates assert that media bias is rooted in the worldviews and political ideology of reporters, whom numerous studies have found to be overwhelmingly Democrats. In reality, any media slant is probably rooted in something much more mundane: the bottom line. The big agenda-setting newspapers in New York and Washington operate in localities with pro-control readerships and relatively weak gun cultures. The network news may skew in the same direction as it tries to attract female viewers, who are both pro-control and coveted by advertisers because they make household buying decisions.

Although some studies have documented a liberal, reformist slant in the traditional mainstream media, and logically that bias should favor gun control, there are reasons not to take the case too far. For example, one of the most-cited, recent studies documenting liberal media bias suggests that, in the area of gun policy, the bias may go the other way. Counting mainstream media mentions of think tanks and interest groups, the study found that the NRA was the 10th most-cited organization generally, with more than five times as many citations as its rival, the organization then known as Handgun Control Inc. (number 46).[18] Clearly, on gun policy the NRA is reporters' go-to organization. Similarly, the study of 1990s national gun control debates mentioned above found no media bias in favor of gun control or gun rights.

A final caveat is in order. Even if the mainstream media demonstrate bias toward gun control, these outlets no longer monopolize the market for information. With the proliferation of niche outlets on the Web, the "narrowcasting" of cable news, and the growth of social media, we are freer than ever to choose our news by seeking out sources suited to our political sensibilities. In such a wide-open media environment, bias by any single media outlet may not matter as much as it once did.

12

IS THERE A WAY FORWARD FOR GUN POLICY?

Every question about guns, gun violence, or gun policy is contentious. Basic facts—the annual number of gun transactions, or even the number of guns in private hands—are not known with any precision. Estimates of the costs and consequences of our nation's gun laws are hotly disputed. Disparate beliefs about whether widespread gun possession is a guarantor of freedom and personal safety, or on the contrary a leading cause of early death and neighborhood decline, fuel acrimonious debates at family gatherings, online, and in the halls of government.

A commentator noted more than four decades ago that Americans were engaged in a great American gun war.[1] This war has shown no signs of abating. Indeed, by some measures the politics of guns has intensified in recent years, raising questions about how we might proceed as a diverse, participatory democracy toward our common goal of reducing firearms violence.

In 2008, when the US Supreme Court found a constitutional right to keep a gun in the home, some commentators thought the ruling might open a new path forward on firearms policy. Fundamental gun rights having been secured, the argument went, the slippery-slope argument was off the table, and America could at last craft careful, consensus-based regulations and other interventions to reduce unnecessary injury and death. Alas, such hopes were not fulfilled. Since the court's landmark ruling, and as of this writing (mid-2019), no significant gun legislation has passed at the national level. A fair number of states have enacted stronger regulations, mainly to plug loopholes in or shore up laws already in place, but in most states the pro-gun lobby continues to have considerable influence.

Indeed, for the last four decades the trend has been toward weaker state and local regulation. The most dramatic change has been to loosen the restrictions on concealed carry. As recently as the 1970s, many states banned private citizens from carrying concealed firearms or restricted the concealed-carry privilege to people who were able to persuade a law-enforcement officer of their trustworthiness and need for a gun. Now concealed carry is either unregulated or legal for anyone with a permit issued to any adult who meets certain minimum requirements. At the same time, state legislatures have been stripping away the restrictions on where guns can be carried. The widespread enactment of state preemption laws (which blocked the cities from regulating the "place and manner" of gun carrying) has been coupled with an easing of state bans on guns in bars, public buildings, universities, parades, polling places, and so forth. The *Heller* decision has, if anything, accelerated this trend.

The widespread deregulation of guns in America has been supported by an ethos of self-reliance together with much-touted (but suspect) research findings that can be summed up by the slogan "An armed society is a polite society." In this view the answer to crime, including mass shootings, is not government restriction on gun possession and carrying; rather, the answer is more guns in more places more of the time. Carrying a gun is not only prudent (given the limited ability of the police to protect us) but also a public service. Indeed, 30 states have adopted stand-your-ground laws that legitimize and offer legal protection for the private use of deadly force against someone perceived as threatening. This movement, and the accompanying rhetoric, is remarkable in part because it is such a departure from the norms that prevailed during the twentieth century and before. Even the nineteenth-century frontier town of Dodge City banned firearms within its limits.

Of course, not everyone is convinced that more guns in more places will ensure greater safety. Most people would endorse the principle that public safety is first and foremost the responsibility of the police and courts. Finding ways to improve police performance would not only reduce violence but also perhaps reduce the felt need for private action. Traditional gun control also has broad support. There is a near-consensus in support of disqualifying people from gun possession who are deemed dangerous due to their criminal or mental health record. Upward of 90% of Americans support universal background checks to prevent disqualified individuals from obtaining a gun. Ten states (including California, New York, and Illinois), encompassing one-third of the US population, were given A– or B+ ratings by the Giffords Law Center, a pro-gun-safety nonprofit.[2] These states have promulgated regulations on gun design, transactions, possession, and use that go well beyond federal laws.

While there has long been a stalemate in Congress, this is far from the case in many statehouses. The Republican Party has generally embraced the gun deregulation agenda, but in some notable cases Republican legislatures have been open to considering new restrictions. After the Marjory Stoneman Douglas school shooting, Florida raised the legal age to buy a gun to 21, imposed a three-day waiting period on firearm purchases, and enacted a red-flag law allowing a judge to order temporary removal of firearms from at-risk individuals. In recent years red states such as Louisiana, Wisconsin, and South Carolina have strengthened their gun laws regarding domestic violence.

So gun policy is very much on the political agenda. While many political leaders are committed to a particular position as an ideological matter, others are concerned about gun violence and genuinely interested in knowing what works in prevention and what might be worth pursuing. Here we offer our judgment about some of the domains where there is a real chance to improve gun policy.

Make Smart Guns Available

For several decades gun violence prevention advocates have urged the development of "personalized" guns, which could be fired by the rightful owner but no one else. For example, a gun can be engineered so that it will fire only when near an electronic key of the sort used to unlock vehicle doors (radiofrequency identification technology). A variety of biometric possibilities have also been engineered. Personalized guns wouldn't reduce violence by reckless or criminal owners, but they would cut down on household diversion to young children who find a loaded handgun in their parents' bedroom, to youths who want to "borrow" a household gun to show off to their friends or worse (as when a 20-year-old took his mother's firearms to murder children and educators at the Sandy Hook school), and to suicidal members of the household for whom a gun poses a deadly temptation. Furthermore, if it were sufficiently difficult to overcome the personalized locking mechanism, smart guns would be of little or no value to thieves, thus cutting off one source of supply to the underground market.

Some gun violence prevention advocates worry that if smart guns become widely available, more people might be comfortable having a gun in the home, thereby actually increasing the overall risk of gun violence. Another worry is that people who already have guns but keep them safely stored might feel at ease keeping a loaded smart gun in a readily accessible place. These forms of "risk compensation" behavior may be a reasonable concern but in our judgment are not likely to negate the gains in safety.

On another front, law-enforcement personnel have been less than enthusiastic about a possible requirement that they carry smart guns. Such a requirement would protect them against the possibility of being shot by their own weapon if an offender grabbed it during a confrontation. But they worry that the smart locking system would malfunction just when they needed to fire the gun to fend off an attack. This concern could presumably be answered through extensive testing.

Smart guns are in production in Europe but not yet sold in the United States. It is hard to see why pro-gun advocates would resist allowing buyers this option—freedom of choice should include the freedom to buy a gun that does not expose household members to unnecessary risks. Gun advocacy groups have opposed the introduction of smart guns into the marketplace because they fear that some state legislatures then would require every gun to be personalized. But given the current power of the pro-gun lobby, such an outcome seems unlikely.

Invest in Policing Gun Violence and Reducing Shootings by the Police

Most gun assaults occur outside the home, meaning that guns involved in robberies and other crimes usually have been carried by the perpetrator in a vehicle or on the person. A traditional goal of urban policing has been to "get the guns off the street," or at least to discourage youths, gang members, and other high-risk people from carrying. In jurisdictions that take guns seriously, most notably New York City, Chicago, and Los Angeles, police made a practice of stopping people whom they had "reasonable suspicion" to believe were engaged in criminal behavior, such as carrying an illegal weapon. This practice may well have deterred the illegal carrying of guns, but it was highly intrusive and placed a heavy burden on police–community relations. To the extent that the selection of "suspects" was influenced by their race, it was unconstitutional as well. A series of successful lawsuits against high-volume "stop, question, and frisk" tactics forced police departments to cut back sharply. For example, the New York Police Department reduced the recorded number of stops from near 700,000 at the peak in 2011 to 12,000 in 2017.[3]

Still, law-enforcement agencies are necessarily on the front lines in reducing gun violence. In addition to (or in place of) targeted patrols against illicit carrying, there are a variety of tactics available for discouraging illicit gun transactions and deterring gun use in violence. The well-known intervention run by the Boston Police Department known as Operation Ceasefire (beginning in 1996) used a focused deterrence strategy, informing gang members in person that gunplay would not be tolerated and that any indication of gun use by a member of a gang would single out that gang for special attention by the police. Variations on this approach to controlling gun crime by gangs have been tested in a number of settings with positive results.[4]

It is also important for courts to cooperate in the view that illicit gun carrying is a serious offense so that they do not routinely dismiss such cases as "victimless." After all, most driving-under-the-influence (DUI) cases are "victimless" in the same sense that there are no immediate victims, but without question reducing DUIs—and illicit carrying—saves lives.

Perhaps most important is that the clearance rate (by arrest and conviction) for criminal shooting cases be sustained at a high level. In fact, there has been a decline in this sort of detective work in many big-city departments.[5] For example, in recent years Chicago has arrested fewer than 20% of offenders who shoot and injure or kill their victim. Both the number of detectives and the clearance rates have drifted downward.[6] Other cities beset by gun violence, including Baltimore, New Orleans, and St. Louis, have similarly dismal records.

Arrest, conviction, and punishment, presumably by imprisonment, reduces gun violence by several mechanisms: deterrence and incapacitation of dangerous offenders and interruption of the cycle of tit-for-tat violence that characterizes a large share of the shootings. Despite the "no snitching" culture, it is possible to solve more shooting cases. But success requires a greater investment on the part of police departments, as well as research on how to improve investigative techniques and police–community relations.[7]

While improved policing is a promising avenue toward gun violence prevention, the police are widely viewed as also part of the problem, and that too warrants a public investment. The *Washington Post*'s tabulation of fatal shootings by law-enforcement officers identifies about 1,000 per year, amounting to 7% of all gun homicides. About one in four of the homicides by officers involves a black victim.[8] Several of these shootings have been recorded on video and appear unwarranted, generating outrage in the African American community and giving rise to the movement known as Black Lives Matter. Victims Michael Brown (Ferguson, Missouri) and Laquan McDonald (Chicago), both shot in 2014, became household names. But it's not just about race—there are simply too many instances all together. Berkeley law professor Franklin Zimring assessed the evidence in his book *When Police Kill*, finding that the bulk of these shootings are justified or likely to be viewed as such by a jury, but that they are still a serious problem that deserves attention.[9] Police departments have widely differing track records with respect to the frequency of shootings, and Zimring believes that better training, clear rules about weapon use, and strong leadership can make a difference.

Rethink the Problem of Mental Illness and Guns

Most people with mental disorders, even serious ones, do not shoot other people. Yet we know that mental illness puts some people at elevated risk for committing violence. How to identify and intervene with those especially at-risk people, while not stigmatizing those with mental illness or unnecessarily infringing on individual freedom, constitutes a vital challenge. Recent mass shootings have brought mental health experts and gun violence prevention advocates together to forge sensible approaches to the larger problem of gun violence prevention.

The role of "mental illness" in serious violence is in part a matter of definition. For example, when a young man takes a gun into a school or place of worship and shoots as many people as he can, most of us would deem his behavior itself sufficient reason to reject the notion that he is psychologically "normal." If he survives (more than half commit suicide or are killed) and is psychologically evaluated, the psychiatrist could surely identify one or more diagnoses in the *Diagnostic and Statistical Manual of Mental Disorders* issued by the American Psychiatric Association. The same could be said for many individuals who commit more routine violent acts. Of course, there are times when gun violence is rational and even the norm—a soldier in wartime or a civilian defending against a deadly assault, for example. But unreasoning anger, impaired self-control, paranoia, substance abuse, and other psychological problems are prevalent in criminal violence.

These prosaic observations are not of much use in thinking about gun violence prevention. In that context, two specific questions arise. One is whether making mental health services more widely available would reduce gun violence. The answer is that it might make a modest contribution, especially with regard to treatment for abuse of alcohol and illicit drugs. Substance abuse is predictive of violence, and intoxication is closely linked to both violence victimization and commission.[10] Those with a dual diagnosis of serious mental illness and substance abuse are at particularly elevated risk.[11] But even if treatment were readily available, it is usually voluntary, and bringing abusers into sustained treatment is a challenge.

The second question is whether certain types of psychological disorder should disqualify a person from obtaining or possessing a firearm. Current federal law disqualifies those who have been involuntarily committed to a mental institution or who in some other context have been ruled mentally incompetent by a judge. There is evidence that this disqualification reduces criminal involvement in the states that make mental health records available to the National Instant Criminal Background Check System (NICS).[12] But these federal provisions miss most people with severe mental illness, including those who may have been voluntarily hospitalized but never by court order. Perhaps more important, much of the violence stemming from psychological problems is not associated with severe mental illness, such as schizophrenia or depression (which are likely to result in hospitalization), but rather the proximate result of circumstantial stressors, intoxication, medical conditions (e.g., dysregulated diabetes), and so forth.[13]

A group of scholars convened by Joshua Horwitz, of the Educational Fund to Stop Gun Violence, reviewed the evidence on these matters and concluded that the focus for gun regulations around the issue of mental illness should be on behavior rather than diagnosis.[14] Noting that the best predictor of future violence is past violence (regardless of diagnosis or the lack thereof), the panel proposed that the list of federal disqualifications for gun possession be expanded to include a conviction for a violent misdemeanor—a disqualification that would be removed in 10 years if the individual had no further convictions. Further, given the close link between violence and substance abuse, the panel proposed a five-year disqualification for those convicted of two DUIs or two misdemeanor drug convictions in the course of five years.

The same group endorsed the creation of legal authority for a judge to issue an extreme risk protection order following an emergency hearing on whether an individual should be deprived of his guns. The basis for such orders is imminent danger to self or others, as evidenced by specific behaviors, with family members or police acting as petitioners. Again, the extreme risk is presumed to be transitory, and the order therefore is temporary. At least 17 states and the District of Columbia have adopted these red-flag laws, and other states are considering doing so.

Connecticut was the first state to adopt such a law, and in recent years it has been used mainly to prevent suicide.[15] Recall that for the majority of Americans who die from gunfire, the wound is self-inflicted. Having thoughts of suicide has considerable overlap with mental illness, particularly clinical depression,[16] and the likelihood that such thoughts will result in death rises considerably when a firearm is handy. Taking steps to keep guns out of the hands of people who are prone to suicide is a task that begins at home and includes teachers, counselors, and others who may be in touch with the at-risk individual.

Formulate and Fund a Productive Research Agenda

The mantra of scholars everywhere is "More research is needed," and the field of gun violence prevention is no exception. This plea has not fallen on deaf ears. Productive research programs are currently underway in social sciences, law, and public health, located in both universities and think tanks. While federal research funding is meager, some states and private foundations have stepped in to fill the void. The first foundation to make a sustained contribution to research in this area was the Chicago-based Joyce Foundation. In 2018, Arnold Ventures announced a $50 million funding program over five years. Starting with the Sandy Hook school massacre in 2012, there has been a surge of research, and new findings are beginning to provide a sound evidence base for policymaking.

What happened to the federal funding? The Centers for Disease Control and Prevention (CDC) initiated a research program on gun violence in the early 1980s and contributed to a growth in relevant public health research through 1996. In that year, Congress, under the influence of the National Rifle Association, adopted the Dickey Amendment, which banned the use of government-funded research to advocate for gun control and cut the CDC budget by $2.6 million—by no coincidence, exactly the budget of the gun violence prevention program.[17] The CDC got the message and stopped funding research directly, although it has continued to be a vital source of support for relevant data sources, including the National Violent Death Reporting System and the "firearms" component of the National Electronic Injury Surveillance System. These data resources, available free to researchers, have done much to facilitate scholarly work on gun violence.

Lost in the debate is the fact that adequate funding does not automatically translate into useful findings. What policymakers want from research is a clear indication of what works and what is worthwhile. In the normal course of events, policies and programs are adopted and analysts can observe gun violence rates before and after. Even if the gun murder rate is lower afterward, we don't know what it would have been if the program had not been introduced. What's missing is a "control group"—people not included in the new program who are otherwise similar to people who were included. Sometimes it's possible to run a true field experiment, with people randomly assigned to a control group and a program ("treatment") group. But these experiments are difficult to run and hence very rare. There are a variety of methods for creating the next best thing, a statistical control group, but experts will not necessarily agree on the details of whatever modeling procedures are utilized. Good research provides guidance but not certitude.

In the spirit of full disclosure about research challenges, we must also admit to the problem known as "external validity." Suppose that open-minded analysts agreed that when Missouri repealed its permit-to-purchase requirement in 2007, the result was a large increase in gun murder—suggesting that the permit system had been effective.[18] The question remains whether repealing a permit-to-purchase requirement in another place and time (say North Carolina, 2020) would also result in a substantial increase in murder. The problem is that the findings from one particular instance may not "export" to another instance where the details of the regulation and the circumstances may be different in relevant ways.

While it is useful, then, to evaluate specific programs and regulations, it is also useful for researchers to investigate the basic mechanisms by which policy affects behavior.[19] These can be understood as the causal building blocks. For example, there is the foundational issue of whether an intervention that is effective in reducing gun use in violence would reduce the murder rate—or simply lead to the substitution of knives and other weapons without reducing deaths. If all that matters in determining whether victims survive the attack is the intent of the assailant, not the type of weapon, then reducing gun use would not reduce murder rates. But if in addition to intent, the unique attributes of a gun matter—the ability to kill quickly, at a distance, with little skill or strength required of the assailant—then the result of separating guns from violent situations would be to sharply reduce the murder rate. This mechanism, the weapon's "instrumentality," can be researched directly and turns out to be important.[20] The popular notion that "guns don't kill people, people kill people" is highly misleading—guns are part of the equation. Research also casts doubt on other mantras: "when guns are outlawed, only outlaws will have guns" (actually, gun availability does affect which weapons violent offenders choose) and "an armed society is a polite society" (widespread gun carrying by civilians is likely increasing crime rates). Research seeks to replace slogans with evidence.

Focus on Social Norms

Government policies can influence behavior but become more effective if they receive social support. Sometimes regulations make unhealthy or unsafe behaviors more problematic, and then social influence does the rest by creating and reinforcing norms that encourage people to make prudent choices. Deaths due to drunk driving have declined because legal penalties are steeper but also because most people no longer think it's okay to "have one for the road." Cigarette taxes and antismoking ordinances have reduced the number of people who light up, but quitting is also a product of individual will reinforced by community approbation.

It is our sense that traditional norms have led hunters and other sportsmen to be very respectful of the harm that guns can do and to embrace best practices in storing, handling, and discharging firearms. A view that respects the dangers posed by a firearm does not deny the pleasures of gun sports and collecting, or even the peace of mind that some gain by having a gun handy for self-defense. What this view does recognize is that guns can end up doing great harm even when in possession of a generally law-abiding adult who might have one too many drinks, be easily provoked to anger, be careless, or lack training in handling a firearm. In dealing with cars, alcohol, medical procedures, and much else, we seek the right balance between risks and benefits—both in government policy and in what we teach our kids and say to our friends. Finding that balanced approach for firearms has not been easy, but it is our hope that there's still a possibility of a reasoned discussion based on the best available information.

That aspiration was the motivation for this book.

NOTES

Chapter 1

1. Authors' calculation from data in the Web-Based Injury Statistics Query and Reporting System (WISQARS), an interactive, online database that provides fatal and nonfatal injury data. WISQARS is maintained by the Centers for Disease Control and Prevention, National Center for Injury Control and Prevention (https://www.cdc.gov/injury/wisqars/facts.html). The fatality data are taken from the National Vital Statistics System, also accessible through WISQARS.
2. Naghavi et al. 2018.
3. WISQARS 2017.
4. Braga and Cook 2018.
5. National Institute on Drug Abuse 2019.
6. Centers for Disease Control and Prevention, "Healthcare-associated infections," https://www.cdc.gov/hai/data/portal/index.html.
7. Davis and Boundy 2019, Table 8.2.
8. Statistics derived from the General Social Survey Data Explorer. Longitudinal data available at https://gssdataexplorer.norc.org/trends/Civil%20Liberties?measure=owngun.
9. Smith and Son 2015.
10. Azrael et al. 2017.
11. Parker et al. 2017.
12. Azrael et al. 2017.
13. Bureau of Alcohol, Tobacco, Firearms and Explosives 2018.
14. Parker et al. 2017.

15. Cook and Ludwig 2003.
16. This ranking is based on the percentage of suicides committed with guns (a well-established proxy for prevalence of gun ownership).
17. WISQARS 2017.
18. Pew Research Center, "Why Own a Gun?" 2013.
19. Cook and Ludwig 1997.
20. Parker et al. 2017.
21. General Social Survey Data Explorer. Longitudinal data available at https://gssdataexplorer.norc.org/trends/Civil%20 Liberties?measure=owngun.
22. Bureau of Alcohol, Tobacco, Firearms and Explosives 2018.
23. Jefferson 1785.
24. The historical information in this paragraph is from DeConde 2001, 49; quote at 49–50.
25. Kennett and Anderson 1975, 136.
26. Stedman and Heberlein 2001.
27. US Department of the Interior 2017.
28. Goo 2013.
29. US Fish and Wildlife Service 2019.
30. US Fish and Wildlife Service 2016.
31. In some cases, the end of the barrel is sawed off to make the gun more easily concealed. Such weapons must be registered with the federal government under the National Firearms Act of 1934.
32. Cook 1993; Bureau of Alcohol, Tobacco, Firearms and Explosives 2018.
33. The 75% figure is calculated from Table 3 in Smith and Cooper 2013; suicide data are from WISQARS 2017.
34. Helmer 1969.
35. WISQARS 2017.
36. Hirsch 2019.

Chapter 2

1. Parker et al. 2017.
2. Tark and Kleck 2004.
3. Hemenway and Solnick 2015.
4. Planty and Truman 2013.
5. Kleck and Gertz 1995.
6. Cook, Ludwig, and Hemenway 1997.
7. Hemenway, Azrael, and Miller 2000.

8. Hemenway, Azrael, and Miller 2000.

9. Hemenway and Azrael 2000.

10. Miller et al. 2013.

11. There were 1,024,788 residential burglaries per year, on average, from 2003 to 2007 (Catalano 2010). Assuming 3% involved self-defense with a gun (Cook and Ludwig 2003), the annual DGU figure in these circumstances would be 30,744.

12. Cook and Ludwig 2003.

13. Data for 2019, available in the Guns to Carry online database (https://www.gunstocarry.com/concealed-carry-statistics/).

14. Florida Department of Agriculture and Consumer Services, "Concealed Weapon or Firearm License Holder Profile," 2019.

15. Carlson 2015.

16. Baum 2010.

17. Carlson 2015, 66–76.

18. Carlson 2015, 66.

19. Baum 2010, 30, 31.

20. Baum 2013, 50; Baum 2010, 33; Carlson 2015, 76–77.

21. Baum 2010, 33.

22. This paragraph summarizes the discussion in Baum 2010; quote at 33.

23. Lott and Mustard 1997.

24. Lott 1998.

25. Wellford, Pepper, and Petrie 2005.

26. Donohue, Aneja, and Weber 2019.

27. Igielnik and Brown 2017.

28. Goo 2013.

29. CNN/ORC poll, October 2015. Finding available through the Roper Center's iPoll database.

30. For all findings presented in this paragraph, see Parker et al. 2017, survey topline.

31. Tarrance Group and Mellman, Lazarus & Lake/U.S. News & World Report, May 16–18, 1994 (1,000 telephone interviews of a national adult sample); Tarrance Group/American Firearms Council, July 21–23, 1996 (1,004 telephone interviews of a national sample of registered voters).

32. Goo 2013. Statistics in this paragraph can be found in the survey topline.

33. Swift 2017.

34. Newport 2015.

35. Parker et al. 2017.
36. Goo 2013.
37. AP/GfK Knowledge Networks poll, July 2016. Finding available through the Roper Center's iPoll database.
38. Pew Research Center, February 13–18, 2013; CNN/Gallup/USA Today, December 1993. Findings available through the Roper Center's iPoll database and on p. 19 of the topline document associated with Pew's "Why Own a Gun?" report (https://www.pewresearch.org/wp-content/uploads/sites/4/legacy-questionnaires/03-12-13-Gun-Ownership-Topline-for-Release.pdf).
39. Polsby and Kates 1997, 1238.
40. *District of Columbia v. Heller* 2008, 27.
41. The Fairleigh Dickinson University's PublicMind Poll reached 863 registered voters by telephone (landline and cell) and had a margin of error of 3.4 percentage points.
42. Kopel, Eisen, and Gallant 2003.
43. Polsby and Kates 1997, 1262.
44. Polsby and Kates 1997, 1237.
45. As Polsby and Kates (1997, 1240) note, gun owners and gun control advocates "are inclined to make very different guesses about how much potential for evil to ascribe to the government of the United States."

Chapter 3

1. These statistics are taken from the Web-Based Injury Statistics Query and Reporting System (WISQARS), an interactive, online database that provides fatal and nonfatal injury data. The fatality data are taken from the National Vital Statistics System. WISQARS is maintained by the Centers for Disease Control and Prevention, National Center for Injury Control and Prevention (https://www.cdc.gov/injury/wisqars/facts.html).
2. Braga and Cook 2018.
3. WISQARS 2017. The data are from the National Electronic Injury Surveillance System—All Injury Program (NEISS-AIP), operated by the US Consumer Product Safety Commission with the Centers for Disease Control and Prevention's National Center for Injury Control and Prevention.
4. Federal Bureau of Investigation 2015, Table 15.
5. WISQARS 2017.

6. Conner et al. 2019; *Washington Post,* "Fatal Force."

7. The FBI's tabulation includes 299 gun homicides as "justified" in 2017; Federal Bureau of Investigation 2017.

8. Cook et al., "Respond," 2017; Cook et al., "Constant Lethality," 2017.

9. WISQARS 2017.

10. WISQARS 2015.

11. Cook 2009.

12. WISQARS 2017.

13. Wolfgang 1958, 83.

14. Zimring 1968.

15. Zimring 1972.

16. Braga and Cook 2018.

17. Cook 1987.

18. Zimring and Hawkins 1997.

19. Cook 2009.

20. Abrams 2012.

21. WISQARS 2017.

22. WISQARS 2017.

23. Harvard T.H. Chan School of Public Health n.d.; Simon et al. 2001.

24. Miller et al. 2013.

25. Miller et al. 2013.

26. WISQARS 2017.

27. WISQARS 2017.

28. Asher and Arthur 2017.

29. Dugan, Nagin, and Rosenfeld 1999; Rosenfeld 2005.

30. Browne, Williams, and Dutton 1999.

31. Campbell et al. 2003.

32. In 2017, the rate of self-inflicted injury for women was 42% higher than for men. WISQARS 2017.

33. Cook and Ludwig 2000.

34. Brådvik 2018.

35. Authors' calculation based on data available through the Gun Violence Archive (https://www.gunviolencearchive.org/).

36. Follman, Aronsen, and Pan 2019.

37. Krouse and Richardson 2015.

38. Associated Press 1927.

39. Mass Shootings in the United States, Wikipedia (https://en.wikipedia.org/wiki/Mass_shootings_in_the_United_States).

40. Bjelopera et al. 2013.
41. Everytown for Gun Safety 2018.
42. Blair and Schweit 2014.
43. Vossekuil et al. 2002, 11–12.
44. Sanger-Katz 2013, quoting University of Virginia Professor John Monahan.
45. WISQARS 2017; Beattie, David, and Roy 2018.
46. Cook and Ludwig, "Public Health vs. Public Policy," 2019.
47. Irvin-Erickson et al. 2017.
48. Zimring 2011.
49. Cook and Ludwig 2000.
50. Cook and Ludwig 2000.
51. War-Related Illness and Injury Study Center, n.d.
52. Fowler et al. 2009.
53. Black males under 18 were shot at a rate of 56.3 per 100,000, most non-fatally. A child exposed to this rate for his or her first 18 years would have a cumulative probability of being shot of 1.0%. WISQARS 2017.
54. Orcutt et al. 2014.
55. Lowe and Galea 2017.
56. Cox and Rich 2018.
57. Fox and Shonkoff 2011, 70.
58. Lynn-Whaley and Sugarmann 2017.
59. Sharkey et al. 2014; Sharkey 2018.

Chapter 4

1. Quoted in Associated Press 2012.
2. Cook, Ludwig, and Braga 2005.
3. Cook and Hawley 1981.
4. Cook, Parker, and Pollack 2015.
5. Cook and Ludwig 2003.
6. Cook and Ludwig 2004.
7. Cook and Ludwig 2002.
8. Cook and Ludwig, "Social Costs," 2019. It is no surprise that not all scholars are on board with this finding. In his book *More Guns, Less Crime*, John Lott (1998) reports an analysis that finds that an increase in gun prevalence is associated with a reduced murder rate. In that study Lott uses a measure of gun prevalence that has not been validated and is of dubious validity (see Cook and Ludwig 2006). His aberrant finding is an example of an

important but unsurprising lesson, that the analytical details, such as just what index of gun prevalence is used, can have a large effect on the results.

9. Bastian 1995; Morgan and Truman 2017.
10. Planty and Truman 2013.
11. US statistic based on authors' calculation from US Centers for Disease Control and Prevention "FastStats: Suicide and Self-Inflicted Injury" (https://www.cdc.gov/nchs/fastats/suicide.htm). Israeli statistic based on authors' calculation from data posted to the University of Sydney's global repository of gun-related information, GunPolicy.org (https://www.gunpolicy.org/firearms/region/israel).
12. Authors' calculations from data posted to GunPolicy.org (https://www.gunpolicy.org/firearms/region/switzerland).
13. Fischer 1989, 771.
14. Hackney 1969, 924.
15. Redfield 2000 [1880], 17.
16. Felson and Pare 2010; Nisbet and Cohen 1996.
17. Authors' calculations based on data in the Web-Based Injury Statistics Query and Reporting System (WISQARS), an interactive, online database that provides fatal and nonfatal injury data. WISQARS is maintained by the Centers for Disease Control and Prevention, National Center for Injury Control and Prevention (https://www.cdc.gov/injury/wisqars/facts.html).
18. Roth 2009.
19. Grinshteyn and Hemenway 2016.
20. Roth 2009, 245–247.
21. Nisbett 1993.
22. Nisbett and Cohen 1996, 42–45.
23. Lee et al. 2007.
24. Anderson 1994.
25. Venn, quoted in Brearley 1932, 36.
26. Mitchell 1929, cited in Brearley 1932, 35.
27. Bushman and Anderson 2015.
28. Bushman and Anderson 2015.
29. Anderson et al. 2017.
30. Ferguson 2015, 194.
31. Plante and Anderson 2017.
32. Ferguson 2015.
33. Ferguson 2015.

34. Huesmann et al. 2003.

35. Anderson et al. 2017.

36. For a review of these studies, see Ferguson 2015.

37. Howitt and Cumberbatch 1975; see discussion in Messner 1986.

38. Pew Research Center, April 4–8, 2017. Finding is available in the Roper Center's iPoll online database.

39. Ferguson 2015.

40. Fisher 2012.

41. Anderson et al. 2010.

42. For a review of these studies, see Plante and Anderson 2017 and Prot et al. 2016.

43. DeLisi et al. 2013.

44. Friedlander et al. 2013.

45. Hopf, Huber, and Weiβ 2008; Graber et al. 2006.

46. Ferguson and Kilburn 2009; Ferguson and Dyck 2012.

47. *Brown v. Entertainment Merchants Association* 564 U.S. 786, 796 (2011).

48. Quoted in Beaujon and Moos 2012.

49. Gorki 1928, quoted in Brearley 1932, 36.

50. For a comprehensive study of the Columbine shooting and its aftermath, see Schildkraut and Muschert 2019.

51. Follman and Andrews 2015.

52. Follman 2015.

53. Fernandez, Turkewitz, and Bidgood 2018.

54. Anonymous source quoted in Follman and Andrews 2015.

55. Langman 2017.

56. Gould 2001.

57. Motto 1970.

58. Sonneck, Etzersdorfer, and Nagel-Kuess 1994.

59. American Foundation for Suicide Prevention et al. n.d.

60. Thompson et al. 2019

61. We are very grateful to Dr. Jeffrey Swanson, of Duke University, for assistance with this section.

62. Saha et al. 2005.

63. For evidence on these laws' effectiveness, see Swanson et al. 2019 and Swanson et al. 2017.

64. For a review of research on the connection between mental illness and violence, see Appelbaum 2013 and Rozel and Mulvey 2017.

65. Joyal et al. 2007. See also Swanson 1994.

66. Mulvey et al. 2006; Pulay et al. 2008; Swanson et al. 1990. For a discussion, see Appelbaum 2013 and Rozel and Mulvey 2017.
67. Rozel and Mulvey 2017.
68. Crump et al. 2013.
69. For a review, see Rozel and Mulvey 2017.
70. Steadman et al. 2015.
71. Silver, Simons, and Craun 2018.
72. Choe, Teplin, and Abram 2008. For a review, see Rozel and Mulvey 2017.
73. Crump et al. 2013.
74. Arsenault-Lapierre, Kim, and Turecki 2004.
75. Appelbaum and Swanson 2010.
76. Swanson et al. 2015.
77. Fitch and Swanson 2019.
78. Swanson et al. 2016.

Chapter 5

1. National Shooting Sports Foundation 2019.
2. Annual data on domestic manufacture, imports, and exports of firearms are from the Bureau of Alcohol, Tobacco, Firearms and Explosives, *Firearms Commerce in the United States: Annual Statistical Update 2018,* and earlier publications in this series.
3. Harkinson 2016.
4. Wintemute 1994.
5. Violence Policy Center 2016.
6. Brauer 2013.
7. Wintemute, Cook, and Wright 2005.
8. US Department of Justice 2013.
9. Garen Wintemute, "Frequency of and Responses to Illegal Activity Related to Commerce in Firearms: Findings from the Firearms Licensee Survey," 2013; Wintemute 2010.
10. Cook 2017.
11. Miller, Hepburn, and Azrael 2017.
12. Cook, Parker, and Pollack 2015.
13. The requirements operate differently in different states. Some states require a background check on all guns at the point of sale, meaning the buyer and seller will usually do the transfer at a retail store, which will run the check. Some states require point-of-sale background checks for handguns only. Yet other states

require the buyer to show a gun-owner permit or license, which in turn would have required a background check to acquire.

14. Cook, Parker, and Pollack 2015.
15. Yablon, "Internet Gun Sales," 2016.
16. Collins et al. 2017; Cook, Parker, and Pollack 2015; Cook, Pollack, and White 2019.
17. Hureau and Braga 2018.
18. Cook et al. 2014; Cook, Pollack, and White 2019.
19. Knight 2013.
20. Hureau and Braga 2018.
21. Bureau of Alcohol, Tobacco, and Firearms 2000.
22. Webster, Crifasi, and Vernick 2014.
23. Bureau of Alcohol, Tobacco, and Firearms 2000; Webster et al. 2006.
24. Cook et al. 2007.
25. Cook, Cukier, and Krause 2009.
26. Corchado 2008.
27. Cook 2018.
28. Langton 2012.
29. Cook 2018.
30. Cook, Parker, and Pollack 2015, Appendix.
31. Cook, Molliconi, and Cole 1995; Webster et al. 2002.
32. Cook et al. 2007.

Chapter 6

1. *McDonald v. City of Chicago*. 561 U.S. 742 (2010) (Stevens, J., dissenting). Quote at 910.
2. *United States v. Miller*. 307 U.S. 174 (1939). Quote at 178.
3. Winkler 2011, 216.
4. *District of Columbia v. Heller*. 554 U.S. 570 (Scalia, J.). Quotes at 628 and 636.
5. *District of Columbia v. Heller*. 554 U.S. 570 (Stevens, J. dissenting). Quotes at 639 and 661.
6. *McDonald v. City of Chicago*. 561 U.S. 742 (2010) (Stevens, J., dissenting). Quotes at 891, 895, 893, and 902.
7. *District of Columbia v. Heller*. 554 U.S. 570 (Scalia, J.). Quotes at 626–627, including footnote 26.
8. *McDonald v. City of Chicago*. 561 U.S. 742 (2010) (Stevens, J., dissenting). Quote at 884.
9. Ruben and Blocher 2018, 1455.

10. *District of Columbia v. Heller*. 554 U.S. 570 (Scalia, J.). Quote at 592.
11. Rosenthal and Winkler 2013, 227.
12. Kessler 2013.
13. Vernick and Hepburn 2003.
14. Kessler 2013.
15. Spitzer 2018, 188.
16. Spitzer 2018, 189.
17. With respect to these groups, the 1968 GCA had barred sales only by federally licensed dealers. The 1986 law barred sales to these groups by all persons.
18. *United States v. Lopez*. 514 U.S. 549 (1995). Quote at 567.
19. Vernick and Hepburn 2003.
20. This estimate is likely low, as eight states either did not or could not supply the information or do not have a licensing scheme.
21. Cassidy 1983, 54, quoted in Goss 2006, 162.
22. Giffords Law Center to Prevent Gun Violence, "Preemption of Local Laws," n.d.
23. Federal Bureau of Investigation 2019.
24. Karberg et al. 2017, Table 1.
25. Luo 2011.
26. Stachelberg, Gerney, and Parsons 2013.
27. Powers 1995.
28. Government Accountability Office 2018.
29. The NRA claims that New York City seized guns from a Staten Island man who had maintained his assault weapons after the ban went into effect. However, according to the NRA's account, the police found the man not through a registry but through his public declaration that he would not comply with the law. See National Rifle Association, "Firearms Registration: New York City's Lesson," January 27, 2000. https://www.nraila.org/articles/20000127/firearms-registration-new-york-city-s.
30. Dingell Introduces Legislation to Address Safety Defects in Firearms 2018.
31. A couple of bills to raise firearm or ammunition taxes were introduced in Congress in the early 1990s but went nowhere.
32. Stolberg 2005.
33. Taylor 2015.
34. Cheng and Hoekstra 2013; Humphries, Gasparrini, and Wiebe 2017; McClellan and Tekin 2017.
35. McClellan and Tekin 2017.

36. Cheng and Hoekstra 2013.
37. Roman 2013.
38. Ackermann et al. 2015.
39. Florida Department of Agriculture and Consumer Services, "Concealed Weapon or Firearm License Applications Distributed," 2019.
40. Timoney 2012.
41. Martin 2013.

Chapter 7
1. Cook and Ludwig 2004.
2. Cook and Ludwig 2006; Cook and Ludwig, "Social Costs," 2019.
3. Azrael, Cook, and Miller 2004; Kleck 2004.
4. Webster and Wintemute 2015; Cook and Donohue 2017.
5. Koper 2004.
6. Chivers et al. 2018.
7. Bureau of Alcohol, Tobacco, Firearms and Explosives, "Firearms Trace Data—2017" (https://www.atf.gov/resource-center/firearms-trace-data-2017).
8. Cook and Ludwig 2006.
9. Leitzel 2003.
10. Reuter and Mouzos 2003.
11. Alpers 2013.
12. Knight 2013.
13. Cook and Braga 2001.
14. Webster, Crifasi, and Vernick 2014.
15. Webster and Wintemute 2015.
16. Raphael and Ludwig 2003.
17. Grunwald and Papachristos 2017.
18. Ludwig and Cook 2000.
19. Government Accountability Office 2012.
20. Campbell et al. 2003.
21. Vigdor and Mercy 2006.
22. Raissian 2016.
23. Cook, Ludwig, and Braga 2005.
24. Wintemute et al. 2001.
25. Luo 2011.
26. Blumstein and Nakamura 2009.
27. Swanson et al. 2013.
28. Yablon 2019.
29. Swanson et al. 2017.

30. Abrams 2012.
31. Kennedy, Piehl, and Braga 1996.
32. Braga, Weisburd, and Turchan 2018.
33. Sherman and Weisburd 1995.
34. Braga, Papachristos, and Hureau 2014.
35. Koper and Mayo-Wilson 2012.
36. Bratton and Murad 2018.
37. He offered the comment via a tweet, January 17, 2013 (https://twitter.com/repthompson/status/291954080048349184).

Chapter 8

1. Spitzer 2018, 17–18.
2. Hofstadter 1970, 4.
3. AP/GfK Knowledge Networks Poll, July 2016. Available through Roper Center iPoll database.
4. Brearley 1932, 75.
5. Celinska 2007.
6. A May 2013 Pew poll found that 48% of Americans prioritized gun rights over gun control, and 11% of them had contacted a public official within the past six months. This period included the first five months after the Sandy Hook school massacre, when new gun control legislation loomed and gun groups were mobilizing their members—and hence provides a good chance to measure the scope of the politically engaged gun owner subculture. A quick calculation suggests that this subculture constitutes 4% to 5% (0.11×0.48) of American adults. However, we take this to be an upper-bound estimate, as people tend to overreport socially desirable practices (such as civic engagement), and such bias is amplified when the relevant sample population is small and the activity uncommon.
7. Kennett and Anderson 1975, 45.
8. Kennett and Anderson 1975, 61.
9. Kennett and Anderson 1975, 116.
10. DeConde 2001, 81.
11. Hosley 1999, 54.
12. Hosley 1999, 60, 63–64.
13. Williamson 1952, 3, cited in Kennett and Anderson 1975, 109.
14. Dykstra 1968, cited in Winkler 2011, 163.
15. Dykstra 1996, 513.
16. Slotkin 1998, 87.

17. Videos of the speech are available on YouTube.
18. Melzer 2009, 127, 133, 135–168.
19. Carlson 2015.
20. Lacombe 2019.
21. Parker et al. 2017.
22. Lacombe 2019.
23. Winkler 2011, 113.
24. Winkler 2011, 114.
25. *State v. Chandler* 5 La. Ann. 489 (1850), at 490.
26. Winkler 2011, 165.
27. Bogus 1992.
28. Cottrol and Diamond 1991.
29. Winkler 2011, 133.
30. Cottrol and Diamond 1995, 1318.
31. Cottrol and Diamond 1991.
32. Kates 1979, 15.
33. We thank Professor Saul Cornell for this observation.
34. Kates 1979, 5.
35. Rankin 1967.
36. Winkler 2011, 239–244.
37. These laws made exceptions for law-enforcement officers, travelers, and people who have been threatened. One state (New Mexico) limited the ban to "settlements." See Warner 1938, 539 n. 26.
38. One exception was Idaho's law, which was held unconstitutional in 1902.
39. Hoffman 1925, 31.
40. Hoffman 1925, 31.
41. Warner 1938, 532.
42. Halbrook 2000, 531.
43. Harcourt 2004, 671.
44. For a fuller history, see Halbrook 2000 and Harcourt 2004.
45. Halbrook 2013, 218.
46. Halbrook (2000) suggests that the registry was "quite useful" (493) to Hitler's regime and "facilitated" repressive measures (502). The same author later goes further, stating that the Nazis "disarmed Berlin's Jews using the Weimar firearm registration records" (Halbrook 2006, 121). However, he provides only inferential, as opposed to direct, evidence for these assertions.
47. Horwitz and Anderson 2009, 152.

Chapter 9

1. Erskine 1972, 456.
2. Gallup Organization 2019.
3. Pew Research Center 2018.
4. Parker et al. 2017.
5. Reinhart 2018.
6. Benenson and Connolly 2013.
7. Newport 2013.
8. Pew Research Center 2019.
9. Silver 2012.
10. Pew Research Center 2017.
11. Parker et al. 2017.
12. Parker 2017.
13. Parker 2017.
14. Authors' analysis based on Pew's American Trends Panel surveys conducted March 13–27 and April 4–18, 2017. Data are available for download at https://www.pewresearch.org/american-trends-panel-datasets/.
15. Barney and Schaffner 2019.
16. Spitzer 2018, 168–170.
17. Lacombe 2019.
18. Spitzer 2018, 170–171.
19. Democratic Party Platform Committee 2016.
20. Kenny, McBurnett, and Bordua 2004.
21. See, for example, Grossback and Hammack 2003 on how these trends intersected in the traditionally Democratic state of West Virginia.
22. Maguire 2017.
23. Center for Responsive Politics, "Gun Rights vs. Gun Control," n.d.

Chapter 10

1. The 4 million figure is based on audited circulation figures for the NRA's four magazines as of December 31, 2018. Members get their choice of magazine when they join. Reporters looking into the NRA's more expansive membership claims have found evidence that they are exaggerated, a practice not unheard of among nonprofit organizations.
2. National Rifle Association Form 990, Part III, 1, 2016. Available at Guidestar.org.

3. For the quote, see the organization's website (gunowners.org).

4. For the quote, see the organization's website (nationalgunrights. org).

5. For the quote, see the Citizens Committee website (ccrkba.org).

6. Reinhart 2018.

7. Cherlin 2012.

8. See, for example, Lacombe 2019; Osnos 2016; Yablon, "How the NRA Stoked," 2016.

9. See Patterson and Singer 2006 for a discussion.

10. Lacombe 2019.

11. Lorelei Kelly (2013) has argued that the NRA's influence has grown with the erosion in Congress's policy expertise, institutional memory, information sharing, and ability to think long term.

12. Spitzer 2018, 132.

13. Epstein 1979, cited in Goss 2006, 75.

14. Drake 2013; Parker et al. 2017, 15.

15. Pew Research Center 2012.

16. Pew Research Center, "Broad Support for Renewed Background Checks," 2013.

17. Schuman and Presser 1981.

18. Pew Research Center, "Broad Support for Renewed Background Checks," 2013.

19. Parker et al. 2017.

20. Schuman and Presser 1981, 46.

21. Pew Research Center, "Broad Support for Renewed Background Checks," 2013.

22. National Rifle Association 2008.

23. Violence Policy Center 2013, 2. As of April 2019, the quotation was no longer on the webpage.

24. Violence Policy Center 2013, 1.

25. Kelly 2013.

26. Barrett 2013.

27. Stone and Hallman 2014.

Chapter 11

1. Goss 2006.

2. Goss 2006, 124.

3. Goss 2006, 18.

4. Authors' calculations based on revenues reported on the organizations' Form 990 informational tax returns for 2004.

5. *Forbes* magazine estimate as of May 2019.
6. For a larger discussion of how the gun control movement has evolved since the late 1990s, see Goss 2019 and Goss 2014.
7. Data compiled by the Center for Responsive Politics and available at www.opensecrets.org.
8. Goss 2006.
9. Astor and Russell 2018.
10. Spitzer 2018.
11. Chyi and McCombs 2004.
12. Muschert and Carr 2006.
13. The SocialSphere survey covered 2,235 US residents, ages 14 to 29, and was conducted September 4–24, 2018. Results are available at https://static1.squarespace.com/static/5b651ae5ee1759e688f559d2/t/5c3516d421c67cb96a41ac44/1546983124689/181210_SocialSphere_US+14-29+Topline_All+Questions.pdf.
14. American Psychological Association 2018.
15. Lowe and Galea 2017; Schultz et al. 2014.
16. For examples of these critiques, see Downs 2002; Kleck 2001; Lott 2003; and Patrick 2002.
17. Callaghan and Schnell 2001.
18. Groseclose and Milyo 2005, 1201–1202.

Chapter 12

1. Bruce-Briggs 1976.
2. Giffords Law Center, "Annual Gun Law Scorecard" (https://lawcenter.giffords.org/scorecard/).
3. Bratton and Murad 2018; Manski and Nagin 2017; Weisburd et al. 2016.
4. Braga, Weisburd, and Turchan 2018.
5. Leovy 2015.
6. Cook and Ludwig, "Public Health vs. Public Policy," 2019.
7. Cook et al. 2019.
8. WISQARS 2017. We note that the Vital Statistics data on police shootings underreport the number of fatal police shootings by almost half, and the statistic on racial composition of victims should hence be taken with a grain of salt. Unfortunately, a complete tabulation such as that provided by the *Washington Post* lacks information on race in a high percentage of cases.
9. Zimring 2017.

10. Cook and Moore 1993.
11. Rozel and Mulvey 2017.
12. Swanson et al. 2013.
13. Swanson et al. 2015.
14. McGinty et al. 2014.
15. Swanson et al. 2017.
16. Ribeiro et al. 2018.
17. Goss 2006.
18. Webster, Crifasi, and Vernick 2014.
19. Ludwig, Kling, and Mullainathan 2011.
20. Zimring 1968; Braga and Cook 2018.

REFERENCES

Chapter 1

Azrael, Deborah, Lisa M. Hepburn, David Hemenway, and Matthew Miller. 2017. "The Stock and Flow of U.S. Firearms: Results from the 2015 National Firearms Survey." *RSF: The Russell Sage Foundation Journal of the Social Sciences* 3(5), 38–57.

Braga, Anthony A., and Philip J. Cook. 2018. "The Association of Firearm Caliber with Likelihood of Death from Gunshot Injury in Criminal Assaults." *JAMA Network Open* 1(3). doi:10.1001/jamanetworkopen.2018.0833

Bureau of Alcohol, Tobacco, Firearms and Explosives. 2018. *Firearms Commerce in the United States: Annual Statistical Update 2018.* Washington, DC: US Department of Justice. https://www.atf.gov/file/130436/download

Centers for Disease Control and Prevention. n.d. "Healthcare-Associated Infections." Bethesda, MD. https://www.cdc.gov/hai/data/portal/index.html

Cook, Philip J. 1993. "Notes on the Availability and Prevalence of Firearms." *American Journal of Preventive Medicine* 9(3, Supp.), 33–38.

Cook, Philip J., and Jens Ludwig. 1997. *Guns in America: Results of a Comprehensive National Survey on Firearms Ownership and Use* Washington, DC: The Police Foundation.

Cook, Philip J., and Jens Ludwig. 2003. "Guns and Burglary." In *Evaluating Gun Policy: Effects on Crime and Violence.* Edited by Jens Ludwig and Philip J. Cook, 74–118. Washington, DC: Brookings Institution Press.

Davis, Stacy C., and Robert G. Boundy. 2019. *Transportation and Energy Data Book*. Edition 37. Oak Ridge, TN: US Department of Energy, Oak Ridge National Laboratory.

DeConde, Alexander. 2001. *Gun Violence in America: The Struggle for Control*. Boston: Northeastern University Press.

Goo, Sara Kehaulani. 2013. "Why Own a Gun? Protection Is Now Top Reason." Washington, DC: Pew Research Center, May 9. https://www.pewresearch.org/fact-tank/2013/05/09/why-own-a-gun-protection-is-now-top-reason/

Helmer, William J. 1969. *The Gun That Made the Twenties Roar*. Highland Park, NJ: Gun Room Press.

Hirsch, Margot. 2019. "Smart Guns Are Smart Business." *The Hill*, March 18. https://thehill.com/blogs/congress-blog/politics/434561-smart-guns-are-smart-business

Jefferson, Thomas. 1785. "Letter to Peter Carr, August 19, 1785." *The Letters of Thomas Jefferson*. http://avalon.law.yale.edu/18th_century/let31.asp

Kennett, Lee, and James Laverne Anderson. 1975. *The Gun in America: The Origins of a National Dilemma*. Westport, CT: Greenwood Press.

Naghavi, Mohsen, et al. 2018. "Global Mortality from Firearms 1990–2016." *Journal of the American Medical Association* 320(8), 792–814.

National Institute on Drug Abuse. 2019. "Overdose Death Rates." https://www.drugabuse.gov/related-topics/trends-statistics/overdose-death-rates

Parker, Kim, Juliana Menasce Horowitz, Ruth Igielnik, J. Baxter Oliphant, and Anna Brown. 2017. "America's Complex Relationship with Guns." Washington, DC: Pew Research Center, June 22. https://www.pewsocialtrends.org/2017/06/22/americas-complex-relationship-with-guns/

Pew Research Center. 2013. "Why Own a Gun? Protection Is Now Top Reason." Washington, DC, March 12. https://www.people-press.org/2013/03/12/why-own-a-gun-protection-is-now-top-reason/ ["Why Own a Gun?"]

Smith, Erica L., and Alexia Cooper. 2013. "Homicide in the U.S. Known to Law Enforcement, 2011." Washington, DC: US Department of Justice, Bureau of Justice Statistics, December. https://www.bjs.gov/content/pub/pdf/hus11.pdf

Smith, Tom W., and Jaesok Son. 2015. *Trends in Gun Ownership in the United States, 1972–2014*. Chicago: NORC at the University of

Chicago. http://www.norc.org/PDFs/GSS%20Reports/GSS_
Trends%20in%20Gun%20Ownership_US_1972-2014.pdf

Stedman, Richard C., and Thomas A. Heberlein. 2001. "Hunting and
Rural Socialization: Contingent Effects of the Rural Setting on
Hunting Participation." *Rural Sociology* 66(4), 599–617.

US Department of the Interior. 2017. "New 5-Year Report Shows 101.6
Million Americans Participated in Hunting, Fishing & Wildlife
Activities." Washington, DC, September 7. https://www.doi.gov/
pressreleases/new-5-year-report-shows-1016-million-americans-
participated-hunting-fishing-wildlife

US Fish and Wildlife Service. 2016. "2016 National Survey of Fishing,
Hunting, and Wild-Life Recreation." Washington, DC: US
Department of the Interior. https://www2.census.gov/programs-
surveys/fhwar/publications/2016/fhw16-nat.pdf

US Fish and Wildlife Service. 2019. "Historical Hunting License
Data." Washington, DC: US Department of the Interior. https://
wsfrprograms.fws.gov/Subpages/LicenseInfo/Hunting.htm

WISQARS. 2015. Web-Based Injury Statistics Query and Reporting
System. Centers for Disease Control and Prevention. https://www.
cdc.gov/injury/wisqars/facts.html

WISQARS. 2017. Web-Based Injury Statistics Query and Reporting
System. Centers for Disease Control and Prevention. https://www.
cdc.gov/injury/wisqars/facts.html

Chapter 2

Baum, Dan. 2010. "Happiness Is a Worn Gun: My Concealed Weapon
and Me." *Harper's*, August.

Baum, Dan. 2013. *Gun Guys: A Road Trip*. New York: Knopf.

Carlson, Jennifer. 2015. *Citizen–Protectors: The Everyday Politics of Guns
in an Age of Decline*. New York: Oxford University Press.

Catalano, Shannon. 2010. "Victimization During Household Burglary."
Washington, DC: US Department of Justice, Bureau of Justice
Statistics. https://www.bjs.gov/content/pub/pdf/vdhb.pdf

Cook, Philip J., and Jens Ludwig. 2003. "Guns and Burglary." In
Evaluating Gun Policy: Effects on Crime and Violence. Edited by Jens
Ludwig and Philip J. Cook, 74–118. Washington, DC: Brookings
Institution Press.

Cook, Philip J., Jens Ludwig, and David Hemenway. 1997. "The Gun
Debate's New Mythical Number: How Many Defensive Uses Per
Year?" *Journal of Policy Analysis and Management* 16(3), 463–469.

District of Columbia v. Heller. 554 U.S. 570 (2008).

Donohue, John J., Abhay Aneja, and Kyle D. Weber. 2019. "Right-to-Carry Laws and Violent Crime: A Comprehensive Assessment Using Panel Data and a State-Level Synthetic Control Analysis." *Journal of Empirical Legal Studies* 16(2), 198–247.

Florida Department of Agriculture and Consumer Services. 2019. "Concealed Weapon or Firearm License Holder Profile." https://www.freshfromflorida.com/content/download/7500/118857/cw_holders.pdf

Goo, Sara Kehaulani. 2013. "Why Own a Gun? Protection Is Now Top Reason." Washington, DC: Pew Research Center, May 9. https://www.pewresearch.org/fact-tank/2013/05/09/why-own-a-gun-protection-is-now-top-reason/

Hemenway, David, and Deborah Azrael. 2000. "Relative Frequency of Offensive and Defensive Gun Use: Results of a National Survey." *Violence and Victims* 15(3), 257–272.

Hemenway, David, Deborah Azrael, and Matthew Miller. 2000. "Gun Use in the United States: Results from Two National Surveys." *Injury Prevention* 6(4), 263–267.

Hemenway, David, and Sara J. Solnick. 2015. "The Epidemiology of Self-Defense Gun Use: Evidence from the National Crime Victimization Surveys 2007–2011." *Preventive Medicine* 79, 22–27.

Igielnik, Ruth, and Anna Brown. 2017. "Key Takeaways on Americans' Views of Guns and Gun Ownership." Washington, DC: Pew Research Center, June 22. https://www.pewresearch.org/fact-tank/2017/06/22/key-takeaways-on-americans-views-of-guns-and-gun-ownership/

Kleck, Gary, and Marc G. Gertz. 1995. "Armed Resistance to Crime: The Prevalence and Nature of Self-Defense with a Gun." *Journal of Criminal Law and Criminology* 86(1), 150–187.

Kopel, David B., Joanne D. Eisen, and Paul Gallant. 2003. "Gun Ownership and Human Rights." *Brown Journal of World Affairs* 9(1), 3–13.

Lott, John R., Jr. 1998. *More Guns, Less Crime: Understanding Crime and Gun Control Laws,* 2nd ed. Chicago: University of Chicago Press.

Lott, John R., Jr., and David B. Mustard. 1997. "Crime, Deterrence, and Right-to-Carry Concealed Handguns." *Journal of Legal Studies* 26(1), 1–68.

Miller, Matthew, Catherine Barber, Richard A. White, and Deborah Azrael. 2013. "Firearms and Suicide in the United States: Is Risk

Independent of Underlying Suicidal Behavior?" *American Journal of Epidemiology* 178(6), 946–955.

Newport, Frank. 2015. "Half in US Continue to Say Gov't Is an Immediate Threat." Gallup Organization, September 21. https://news.gallup.com/poll/185720/half-continue-say-gov-immediate-threat.aspx

Parker, Kim, Juliana Menasce Horowitz, Ruth Igielnik, J. Baxter Oliphant, and Anna Brown. 2017. "America's Complex Relationship with Guns." Washington, DC: Pew Research Center, June 22. https://www.pewsocialtrends.org/2017/06/22/americas-complex-relationship-with-guns/

Planty, Michael, and Jennifer L. Truman. 2013. "Firearm Violence, 1993–2011." US Department of Justice, Bureau of Justice Statistics. May. https://www.bjs.gov/content/pub/pdf/fv9311.pdf

Polsby, Daniel D., and Don B. Kates, Jr. 1997. "Of Holocausts and Gun Control." *Washington University Law Quarterly* 75(3), 1237–1275.

Swift, Art. 2017. "Majority in U.S. Say Federal Government Has Too Much Power." Gallup Organization, October 5. https://news.gallup.com/poll/220199/majority-say-federal-government-power.aspx

Tark, Jongyeon, and Gary Kleck. 2004. "Resisting Crime: The Effects of Victim Action on the Outcomes of Crimes." *Criminology* 42(4), 861–910.

Wellford, Charles F., John V. Pepper, and Carol V. Petrie, eds. 2005. *Firearms and Violence: A Critical Review*. Washington, DC: National Academies Press.

Chapter 3

Abrams, David S. 2012. "Estimating the Deterrent Effect of Incarceration Using Sentencing Enhancements." *American Economic Journal: Applied Economics* 4(4), 32–56.

Asher, Jeff, and Rob Arthur. 2017. "Inside the Algorithm That Tries to Predict Gun Violence in Chicago." *New York Times, The Upshot*, June 13. https://www.nytimes.com/2017/06/13/upshot/what-an-algorithm-reveals-about-life-on-chicagos-high-risk-list.html

Associated Press 1927. "School Dynamiter First Slew Wife." *New York Times*, 3, May 20.

Bjelopera, Jerome P., Erin Bagalman, Sarah W. Caldwell, Kristin M. Finklea, and Gail McCallion. 2013. *Public Mass Shootings in the United States: Selected Implications for Federal Public Health and Safety*

Policy. Washington, DC: Congressional Research Service. https://fas.org/sgp/crs/misc/R43004.pdf

Beattie, Sara, Jean-Denis David, and Joel Roy. 2018. *Homicide in Canada, 2017.* Ottawa: Statistics Canada. https://www150.statcan.gc.ca/n1/pub/85-002-x/2018001/article/54980-eng.htm

Blair, Pete J., and Katherine W. Schweit. 2014. "A Study of Active Shooter Incidents, 2000–2013." Texas State University and US Department of Justice, Federal Bureau of Investigation.

Brådvik, Louise. 2018. "Suicide Risk and Mental Disorders." *International Journal of Environmental Research and Public Health* 15(9), 2028.

Braga, Anthony A., and Philip J. Cook. 2018. "The Association of Firearm Caliber with Likelihood of Death from Gunshot Injury in Criminal Assaults." *JAMA Network Open* 1(3). doi:10.1001/jamanetworkopen.2018.0833

Browne, Angela, Kirk R. Williams, and Donald G. Dutton. 1999. "Homicide Between Intimate Partners: A 20-Year Review." In *Homicide: A Sourcebook of Social Research.* Edited by M. Dwayne Smith and Margaret A. Zahn, 149–164. Thousand Oaks, CA: Sage.

Campbell, Jacquelyn C., Daniel Webster, Jane Koziol-McLain, Carolyn Block, Doris Campbell, Mary Ann Curry, Faye Gary, Nancy Glass, Judith McFarlane, and Carolyn Sachs. 2003. "Risk Factors for Femicide in Abusive Relationships: Results from a Multisite Case Control Study." *American Journal of Public Health* 93(7), 1089–1097.

Conner, Andrew, Deborah Azrael, Vivian H. Lyons, Catherine Barber, and Matthew Miller. 2019. "Validating the National Violent Death Reporting System as a Source of Data on Fatal Shootings of Civilians by Law Enforcement Officers." *American Journal of Public Health* 109, 57–84.

Cook, Philip J. 1987. "Robbery Violence." *Journal of Criminal Law & Criminology* 78(2), 357–376.

Cook, Philip J. 2009. "Robbery." In *Oxford Handbook on Crime and Public Policy.* Edited by Michael Tonry, 102–114. New York: Oxford University Press.

Cook, Philip J., and Jens Ludwig. 2000. *Gun Violence: The Real Costs.* New York: Oxford University Press.

Cook, Philip J., and Jens Ludwig. 2019. "Understanding Gun Violence: Public Health vs. Public Policy." *Journal of Policy Analysis and Management* 38(3), 788–795. ["Public Health vs. Public Policy"]

Cook, Philip J., Ariadne E. Rivera-Aguirre, Magdalena Cerdá, and Garen Wintemute 2017. "Cook et al. Respond." *American Journal of Public Health*, 107(12), e23. https://doi.org/10.2105/AJPH.2017.304101 ["Respond"]

Cook, Philip, Ariadne E. Rivera-Aguirre, M. Magdalena Cerdá, and Garen Wintemute. 2017. "Constant Lethality of Gunshot Injuries from Firearm Assault: United States 2003–2012." *American Journal of Public Health* 107(8), 1324–1328. ["Constant Lethality"]

Cox, John Woodrow, and Steven Rich. 2018. "Scarred by School Shootings." *Washington Post*, March 25. https://www.washingtonpost.com/graphics/2018/local/us-school-shootings-history/?noredirect=on&utm_term=.23e42cedbe68

Dugan, Laura, Daniel S. Nagin, and Richard Rosenfeld. 1999. "Explaining the Decline in Intimate Partner Homicide: The Effects of Changing Domesticity, Women's Status, and Domestic Violence Resources." *Homicide Studies* 3(3), 187–214.

Everytown for Gun Safety. 2018. "Mass Shootings in the United States: 2009–2017." December 8. https://everytownresearch.org/reports/mass-shootings-analysis/

Federal Bureau of Investigation. 2015. *Crime in the United States*. Washington, DC: US Department of Justice. https://ucr.fbi.gov/crime-in-the-u.s/2015/crime-in-the-u.s.-2015/tables/table-15

Federal Bureau of Investigation. 2017. *Crime in the United States*. Expanded Homicide Data Table 15, "Justifiable Homicide." Washington, DC: US Department of Justice. https://ucr.fbi.gov/crime-in-the-u.s/2017/crime-in-the-u.s.-2017/tables/expanded-homicide-data-table-15.xls

Follman, Mark, Gavin Aronsen, and Deanna Pan. 2019. "US Mass Shootings, 1982–2019: Data from *Mother Jones'* Investigation." *Mother Jones*, February 15. https://www.motherjones.com/politics/2012/12/mass-shootings-mother-jones-full-data/

Fowler, Patrick J., Carolyn J. Tompsett, Jordan M. Braciszewski, Angela J. Jacques-Tiura, and Boris B. Baltes. 2009. "Community Violence: A Meta-Analysis on the Effect of Exposure and Mental Health Outcomes of Children and Adolescents." *Development and Psychopathology* 21(1), 227–259.

Fox, Nathan A., and Jack P. Shonkoff. 2011. "How Persistent Fear and Anxiety Can Affect Young Children's Learning, Behavior, and Health." *Early Childhood Matters*, June. Reprinted in *Social and*

Economic Costs of Violence. Edited by Deepali M. Patel and Rachel M. Taylor. Washington, DC: National Academies Press.

Harvard T.H. Chan School of Public Health. n.d. "Means Matter Basics." https://www.hsph.harvard.edu/means-matter/means-matter/

Irvin-Erickson, Yasemin, Mathew Lynch, Annie Gurvis, Edward Mohr, and Bing Bai. 2017. *Gun Violence Affects the Economic Health of Communities*. Washington, DC: Urban Institute.

Krouse, William J., and Daniel J. Richardson. 2015. *Mass Murder with Firearms: Incidents and Victims, 1999–2013*. Washington, DC: Congressional Research Service, July 30. https://fas.org/sgp/crs/misc/R44126.pdf

Lowe, Sarah R., and Sandro Galea. 2017. "The Mental Health Consequences of Mass Shootings." *Trauma, Violence, & Abuse* 18(1), 62–82.

Lynn-Whaley, Jennifer, and Josh Sugarmann. 2017. *The Relationship Between Community Violence and Trauma: How Violence Affects Learning, Health, and Behavior*. Washington, DC: Violence Policy Center.

Mass Shootings in the United States. Wikipedia. https://en.wikipedia.org/wiki/Mass_shootings_in_the_United_States

Miller, Matthew, Catherine Barber, Richard A. White, and Deborah Azrael. 2013. "Firearms and Suicide in the United States: Is Risk Independent of Underlying Suicidal Behavior?" *American Journal of Epidemiology* 178(6), 946–955.

Orcutt, Holly K., George A. Bonanno, Susan M. Hannan, and Lynsey R. Miron. 2014. "Prospective Trajectories of Posttraumatic Stress in College Women Following a Campus Mass Shooting." *Journal of Traumatic Stress* 27(3), 249–256.

Rosenfeld, Richard. 2005. "Patterns in Adult Homicide, 1980–1995." In *The Crime Drop*. Edited by Alfred Blumstein and Joel Wallman, 130–163. New York: Cambridge University Press.

Sanger-Katz, Margot. 2013 "Why Improving Mental Health Would Do Little to End Gun Violence." *National Journal*, January 24. https://www.nationaljournal.com/s/85630/why-improving-mental-health-would-do-little-end-gun-violence

Sharkey, Patrick. 2018. "The Long Reach of Violence." *Annual Review of Criminology* 1, 85–102.

Sharkey, Patrick, Amy Ellen Schwartz, Ingrid Gould Ellen, and Johanna Lacoe. 2014. "High Stakes in the Classroom, High Stakes on the Street: The Effects of Community Violence on Students' Standardized Test Performance." *Sociological Science* 1, 199–220.

Simon, Thomas R., Alan C. Swann, Kenneth E. Powell, Lloyd B. Potter, Marcie-jo Kresnow, and Patrick W. O'Carroll. 2001. "Characteristics of Impulsive Suicide Attempts and Attempters." *Suicide and Life-Threatening Behavior* 32, 49–59.

Vossekuil, Bryan, et al. 2002. *The Final Report and Findings of the Safe School Initiative*. Washington, DC: US Secret Service and US Department of Education, May.

War-Related Illness and Injury Study Center. n.d. "Post-Traumatic Stress Disorder." Washington, DC: US Department of Veterans Affairs. https://www.warrelatedillness.va.gov/education/healthconditions/post-traumatic-stress-disorder.asp

Washington Post. 2018. "Fatal Force." https://www.washingtonpost.com/graphics/2018/national/police-shootings-2018/?utm_term=.ddc1bb75bb26

WISQARS. 2015. Web-Based Injury Statistics Query and Reporting System. Centers for Disease Control and Prevention. https://www.cdc.gov/injury/wisqars/facts.html

WISQARS. 2017. Web-Based Injury Statistics Query and Reporting System. Centers for Disease Control and Prevention. https://www.cdc.gov/injury/wisqars/facts.html

Wolfgang, Marvin E. 1958. *Patterns in Criminal Homicide*. Philadelphia: University of Pennsylvania Press.

Zimring, Franklin E. 1968. "Is Gun Control Likely to Reduce Violent Killings?" *University of Chicago Law Review* 35(4), 721–737.

Zimring, Franklin E. 1972. "The Medium Is the Message: Firearm Caliber as a Determinant of Death from Assault." *Journal of Legal Studies* 1(1), 97–123.

Zimring, Franklin E. 2011. *The City That Became Safe: New York's Lessons for Urban Crime and Its Control*. New York: Oxford University Press.

Zimring, Franklin E., and Gordon Hawkins. 1997. *Crime Is Not the Problem: Lethal Violence in America*. New York: Oxford University Press.

Chapter 4

American Foundation for Suicide Prevention et al. n.d. "Reporting on Suicide: Recommendations for the Media."

Anderson, Craig A., Akiko Shibuya, Nobuko Ihori, Edward L. Swing, Brad J. Bushman, Akira Sakamoto, Hannah R. Rothstein, and

Muniba Saleem. 2010. "Violent Video Game Effects on Aggression, Empathy, and Prosocial Behavior in Eastern and Western Countries: A Meta-Analytic Review." *Psychological Bulletin* 136(2), 151–173.

Anderson, Craig A., Kanae Suzuki, Edward L. Swing, Christopher L. Groves, Douglas A. Gentile, Sara Prot, Chun Pan Lam, Akira Sakamoto, Yukiko Horiuchi, Barbara Krahé, Margareta Jelic, Wei Liuqing, Roxana Toma, Wayne A. Warburton, Xue-Min Zhang, Sachi Tajima, Feng Qing, and Poesis Petrescu. 2017. "Media Violence and Other Aggression Risk Factors in Seven Nations." *Personality and Social Psychology Bulletin* 43(7), 986–998.

Anderson, Elijah. 1994. "The Code of the Streets." *The Atlantic,* May, 80–94.

Appelbaum, Paul S. 2013. "Public Safety, Mental Disorders, and Guns." *JAMA Psychiatry* 70(6), 565–566.

Appelbaum, Paul S., and Jeffrey W. Swanson. 2010. "Gun Laws and Mental Illness: How Sensible Are the Current Restrictions?" *Psychiatric Services* 61(7), 652–654.

Arsenault-Lapierre, Geneviève, Caroline Kim, and Gustavo Turecki. 2004. "Psychiatric Diagnoses in 3275 Suicides: A Meta-Analysis." *BMC Psychiatry* 4(1), 37.

Associated Press. 2012. "Transcript: Statement by National Rifle Association's Wayne LaPierre, Dec. 21, 2012." https://www.masslive.com/news/2012/12/transcript_statement_by_nation.html

Bastian, Lisa. 1995. "Criminal Victimization 1993." Washington, DC: US Department of Justice, Bureau of Justice Statistics, May. https://bjs.gov/content/pub/pdf/Cv93.pdf

Beaujon, Andrew, and Julie Moos. 2012. "Factcheck: NRA Blames Media for Gun Violence." Poynter Institute, December 21. https://www.poynter.org/reporting-editing/2012/factcheck-nra-blames-media-for-gun-violence/

Brearley, Harrington Cooper. 1932. *Homicide in the United States.* Chapel Hill: University of North Carolina Press.

Brown v. Entertainment Merchants Association 564 U.S. 786 (2011).

Bushman, Brad J., and Craig A. Anderson. 2015. "Understanding Causality in the Effects of Media Violence." *American Behavioral Scientist* 59(14), 1807–1821.

Centers for Disease Control and Prevention. n.d. "FastStats: Suicide and Self-Inflicted Injury." Bethesda, MD. https://www.cdc.gov/nchs/fastats/suicide.htm

Choe, Jeanne Y., Linda A. Teplin, and Karen M. Abram. 2008. "Perpetration of Violence, Violent Victimization, and Severe Mental Illness: Balancing Public Health Concerns." *Psychiatric Services* 59(2), 153–164.

Cook, Philip J., and Karen Hawley. 1981. "North Carolina's Pistol Permit Law: An Evaluation." *Popular Government*, Spring, 1–6.

Cook, Philip J., and Jens Ludwig. 2002. "The Costs of Gun Violence Against Children." *Future of Children* 12(2), 87–99.

Cook, Philip J., and Jens Ludwig. 2003. "Guns and Burglary." In *Evaluating Gun Policy: Effects on Crime and Violence*. Edited by Jens Ludwig and Philip J. Cook, 74–118. Washington, DC: Brookings Institution Press.

Cook, Philip J., and Jens Ludwig. 2004. "Does Gun Prevalence Affect Teen Gun Carrying After All?" *Criminology* 42(1), 27–54.

Cook, Philip J., and Jens Ludwig. 2006. "Aiming for Evidence-Based Gun Policy." *Journal of Policy Analysis and Management* 25(3), 691–736.

Cook, Philip J., and Jens Ludwig. 2019. "The Social Costs of Gun Ownership: A Reply to Hayo, Neumeier and Westphal." *Empirical Economics* 56(1), 13–22. ["Social Costs"]

Cook, Philip J., Jens Ludwig, and Anthony Braga. 2005. "Criminal Records of Homicide Offenders." *Journal of the American Medical Association* 294(5), 598–601.

Cook, Philip J., Susan T. Parker, and Harold A. Pollack. 2015. "Sources of Guns to Dangerous People: What We Learn by Asking Them." *Preventive Medicine* 79, 28–36.

Crump, Casey, Kristina Sundquist, Marilyn A. Winkleby, and Jan Sundquist. 2013. "Mental Disorders and Vulnerability to Homicidal Death: Swedish Nationwide Cohort Study." *British Medical Journal* 346, f557.

DeLisi, Matt, Michael G. Vaughn, Douglas A. Gentile, Craig A. Anderson, and Jeffrey J. Shook. 2013. "Violent Video Games, Delinquency, and Youth Violence: New Evidence." *Youth Violence and Juvenile Justice* 11(2), 132–142.

Felson, Richard B., and Paul-Philippe Pare. 2010. "Firearms and Fisticuffs: Region, Race, and Adversary Effects on Homicide and Assault." *Social Science Research* 39(2), 272–284.

Ferguson, Christopher J. 2015. "Does Movie or Video Game Violence
     Predict Societal Violence? It Depends on What You Look at and
     When." *Journal of Communication* 65(1), 193–212.

Ferguson, Christopher J., and Dominic Dyck. 2012. "Paradigm Change
     in Aggression Research: The Time Has Come to Retire the General
     Aggression Model." *Aggression and Violent Behavior* 17(3), 220–228.

Ferguson, Christopher J., and John Kilburn. 2009. "The Public Health
     Risks of Media Violence: A Meta-Analytic Review." *Journal of
     Pediatrics* 154(5), 759–763.

Fernandez, Manny, Julie Turkewitz, and Jess Bidgood 2018. "For
     'Columbiners,' School Shootings Have a Deadly Allure." *New York
     Times*, May 30. https://www.nytimes.com/2018/05/30/us/school-
     shootings-columbine.html

Fischer, David H. 1989. *Albion's Seed: Four British Folkways in America.*
     New York: Oxford University Press.

Fisher, Mark. 2012. "Ten-Country Comparison Suggests There's Little
     or No Link Between Video Games and Gun Murders." *Washington
     Post*, December 17. https://www.washingtonpost.com/news/
     worldviews/wp/2012/12/17/ten-country-comparison-suggests-
     theres-little-or-no-link-between-video-games-and-gun-murders/
     ?utm_term=.43a3d0c59fa4

Fitch, W. Lawrence, and Jeffrey W. Swanson. 2019. "Civil Commitment
     and the Mental Health Care Continuum: Historical Trends and
     Principles for Law and Practice." Rockville, MD: US Department
     of Health and Human Services, Substance Abuse and Mental
     Health Services Administration, Office of the Chief Medical Officer.
     https://www.samhsa.gov/sites/default/files/civil-commitment-
     continuum-of-care.pdf

Follman, Mark. 2015. "Inside the Race to Stop the Next
     Mass Shooter." *Mother Jones*, November/December.
     https://www.motherjones.com/politics/2015/10/
     mass-shootings-threat-assessment-shooter-fbi-columbine/

Follman, Mark, and Becca Andrews. 2015. "How Columbine
     Spawned Dozens of Copycats." *Mother Jones*, October
     5. https://www.motherjones.com/politics/2015/10/
     columbine-effect-mass-shootings-copycat-data/

Friedlander, Laura J., Jennifer A. Connolly, Debra J. Pepler, and Wendy
     M. Craig. 2013. "Extensiveness and Persistence of Aggressive
     Media Exposure as Longitudinal Risk Factors for Teen Dating
     Violence." *Psychology of Violence* 3(4), 310–322.

Gorki, Maxim. 1928. "About Murderers." *Dial* 85, September, 201–210.

Gould, Madelyn S. 2001. "Suicide and the Media." *Annals of the New York Academy of Sciences* 932(1), 200–224.

Grinshteyn, Erin, and David Hemenway. 2016. "Violent Death Rates: The US Compared with Other High-Income OECD Countries, 2010." *American Journal of Medicine* 129(3), 266–273.

Graber, Julia A., Tracy Nichols, Sarah D. Lynne, Jeanne Brooks-Gunn, and Gilbert J. Botvin. 2006. "A Longitudinal Examination of Family, Friend, and Media Influences on Competent Versus Problem Behaviors Among Urban Minority Youth." *Applied Developmental Science* 10(2), 75–85.

Hackney, Sheldon. 1969. "Southern Violence." *American Historical Review* 74(3), 906–925.

Hopf, Werner H., Günter L. Huber, and Rudolf H. Weiß. 2008. "Media Violence and Youth Violence: A 2-Year Longitudinal Study." *Journal of Media Psychology* 20(3), 79–96.

Howitt, Dennis, and Guy Cumberbatch. 1975. *Mass Media, Violence and Society.* New York: Wiley.

Huesmann, L. Rowell, Jessica Moise-Titus, Cheryl-Lynn Podolski, and Leonard D. Eron. 2003. "Longitudinal Relations Between Children's Exposure to TV Violence and Their Aggressive and Violent Behavior in Young Adulthood: 1977–1992." *Developmental Psychology* 39(2), 201–221.

Joyal, Christian C., Jean-Luc Dubreucq, Catherine Gendron, and Frederic Millaud. 2007. "Major Mental Disorders and Violence: A Critical Update." *Current Psychiatry Reviews* 3(1), 33–50.

Langman, Peter. 2017. "Role Models, Contagions, and Copycats: An Exploration of the Influence of Prior Killers on Subsequent Attacks." www.schoolshooters.info

Lee, Matthew R., William B. Bankston, Timothy C. Hayes, and Shaun A. Thomas. 2007. "Revisiting the Southern Culture of Violence." *Sociological Quarterly* 48(2), 253–275.

Lott, John R., Jr. 1998. *More Guns, Less Crime: Understanding Crime and Gun Control Laws,* 2nd ed. Chicago: University of Chicago Press.

Messner, Steven F. 1986. "Television Violence and Violent Crime: An Aggregate Analysis." *Social Problems* 33(3), 218–235.

Mitchell, Alice Miller. 1929. *Children and Movies.* Chicago: University of Chicago Press.

Morgan, Rachel E., and Jennifer L. Truman. 2017. "Criminal Victimization, 2017." US Department of Justice, Bureau of Justice

Statistics. December. https://www.bjs.gov/content/pub/pdf/cv17.pdf

Motto, Jerome A. 1970. "Newspaper Influence on Suicide: A Controlled Study." *Archives of General Psychiatry* 23(2), 143–148.

Mulvey, Edward P., Candice Odgers, Jennifer Skeem, William Gardner, Carol Schubert, and Charles Lidz. 2006. "Substance Use and Community Violence: A Test of the Relation at the Daily Level." *Journal of Consulting and Clinical Psychology* 74(4), 743–754.

Nisbett, Richard E. 1993. "Violence and U.S. Regional Culture." *American Psychologist* 48(4), 441–449.

Nisbett, Richard E., and Dov Cohen. 1996. *Culture of Honor: The Psychology of Violence in the South*. Boulder, CO: Westview.

Plante, Courtney, and Craig A. Anderson. 2017. "Media, Violence, Aggression, and Anti-Social Behavior: Is the Link Causal?" In *The Wiley Handbook of Violence and Aggression*. Edited by Peter Sturmey, 435–446. Malden, MA: John L. Wiley & Sons.

Planty, Michael, and Jennifer L. Truman. 2013. "Firearm Violence, 1993–2011." US Department of Justice, Bureau of Justice Statistics. May. https://www.bjs.gov/content/pub/pdf/fv9311.pdf

Prot, Sara, Craig A. Anderson, Muniba Saleem, Christopher L. Groves, and Johnie J. Allen. 2016. "Understanding Media Violence Effects." In *The Social Psychology of Good and Evil*, 2nd ed. Edited by Arthur G. Miller, 119–139. New York: Guilford Press.

Pulay, Attila J., et al. 2008. "Violent Behavior and DSM-IV Psychiatric Disorders: Results from the National Epidemiologic Survey on Alcohol and Related Conditions." *Journal of Clinical Psychiatry* 69(1), 12–22.

Redfield, H. V. 2000 [1880]. *Homicide, North and South*. Columbus: Ohio State University Press.

Roth, Randolph. 2009. *American Homicide*. Cambridge: Belknap Press of Harvard University Press.

Rozel, John S., and Edward P. Mulvey. 2017. "The Link Between Mental Illness and Firearm Violence: Implications for Social Policy and Clinical Practice." *Annual Review of Clinical Psychology* 13, 445–469.

Saha, Sukanta, David Chant, Joy Welham, and John McGrath. 2005. "A Systematic Review of the Prevalence of Schizophrenia." *PLOS Medicine* 2(5), e141. doi:10.1371/journal.pmed.0020141

Schildkraut, Jaclyn, and Glenn W. Muschert. 2019. *Columbine, 20 Years Later and Beyond: Lessons from Tragedy*. Santa Barbara, CA: ABC-CLIO/Praeger.

Silver, James, Andre Simons, and Sarah Craun. 2018. "A Study of
   the Pre-Attack Behaviors of Active Shooters in the United States
   Between 2000 and 2013." US Department of Justice, Federal Bureau
   of Investigation, June. https://www.fbi.gov/file-repository/pre-
   attack-behaviors-of-active-shooters-in-us-2000-2013.pdf/view
Sonneck, Gernot, Elmar Etzersdorfer, and Sibylle Nagel-Kuess. 1994.
   "Imitative Suicide on the Viennese Subway." *Social Science and
   Medicine* 38(3), 453–457.
Steadman, Henry J., John Monahan, Debra A. Pinals, Roumen
   Vesselinov, and Pamela Clark Robbins. 2015. "Gun Violence and
   Victimization of Strangers by Persons with a Mental Illness: Data
   from the MacArthur Violence Risk Assessment Study." *Psychiatric
   Services* 66(11), 1238–1241.
Swanson, Jeffrey W. 1994. "Mental Disorder, Substance Abuse, and
   Community Violence: An Epidemiological Approach." In *Violence
   and Mental Disorder: Developments in Risk Assessment.* Edited by John
   Monahan and Henry J. Steadman, 101–136. Chicago: University of
   Chicago Press.
Swanson, Jeffrey W., Michele M. Easter, Kelly Alanis-Hirsch, Charles
   M. Belden, Michael A. Norko, Allison G. Robertson, Linda
   K. Frisman, Hsui-Ju Lin, Marvin S. Swartz, and George F. Parker.
   2019. "Indiana's Experience with a Risk-Based Gun Seizure
   Law: Criminal Justice and Suicide Outcomes." *Journal of the
   American Academy of Psychiatry and Law* 47(2), 188–197.
Swanson, Jeffrey W., Michele M. Easter, Allison G. Robertson, Marvin
   S. Swartz, Kelly Alanis-Hirsch, Daniel Moseley, Charles Dion, and
   John Petrila. 2016. "Gun Violence, Mental Illness, and Laws That
   Prohibit Gun Possession: Evidence from Two Florida Counties."
   Health Affairs 35(6), 1067–1075.
Swanson, Jeffrey W., Charles E. Holzer, Vijay K. Ganju, and Robert
   Tsutomu Jono. 1990. "Violence and Psychiatric Disorder in the
   Community: Evidence from the Epidemiologic Catchment Area
   Surveys." *Hospital and Community Psychiatry* 41(7), 761–770.
Swanson, Jeffrey W., Michael A. Norko, Hsiu-Ju Lin, Kelly Alanis-
   Hirsch, Linda K. Frisman, Madelon V. Baranoski, Michele M. Easter,
   Allison G. Robertson, Marvin S. Swartz, and Richard J. Bonnie.
   2017. "Implementation and Effectiveness of Connecticut's Risk-
   Based Gun Removal Law: Does It Prevent Suicides?" *Law &
   Contemporary Problems* 80, 179–208.

Swanson, Jeffrey W., Nancy A. Sampson, Maria V. Petukhova, Alan M. Zaslavsky, Paul S. Appelbaum, Marvin S. Swartz, and Ronald C. Kessler. 2015. "Guns, Impulsive Angry Behavior, and Mental Disorders: Results from the National Comorbidity Survey Replication (NCS-R)." *Behavioral Sciences and the Law* 33(2–3), 199–212.

Thompson, Rebecca R., Nickolas M. Jones, E. Alison Holman, and Roxane Cohen Silver. 2019. "Media Exposure to Mass Violence Events Can Fuel a Cycle of Distress." *Science Advances* 5, eaav3502.

Venn, F. E. 1924. "Murder." *Independent* 113, November 8, 361–362.

WISQARS. 2015. Web-Based Injury Statistics Query and Reporting System. Centers for Disease Control and Prevention. https://www.cdc.gov/injury/wisqars/facts.html

WISQARS. 2017. Web-Based Injury Statistics Query and Reporting System. Centers for Disease Control and Prevention. https://www.cdc.gov/injury/wisqars/facts.html

Chapter 5

Brauer, Jurgen. 2013. "Demand and Supply of Commercial Firearms in the United States." *Economics of Peace and Security Journal* 8(1), 23–27.

Bureau of Alcohol, Tobacco and Firearms. 2000. *Following the Gun: Enforcing Federal Laws Against Firearms Traffickers.* Washington, DC: US Department of the Treasury.

Bureau of Alcohol, Tobacco, Firearms and Explosives. 2018. *Firearms Commerce in the United States: Annual Statistical Update 2018.* Washington, DC: US Department of Justice. https://www.atf.gov/file/130436/download

Collins, Megan E., Susan T. Parker, Thomas I. Scott, and Charles E. Wellford. 2017. "A Comparative Analysis of Crime Guns." *RSF: The Russell Sage Foundation Journal of the Social Sciences* 3(5), 96–127.

Cook, Philip J. 2017. "At Last, a Good Estimate of the Size of the Private Sale Loophole for Firearms." *Annals of Internal Medicine* 166(4), 301–302.

Cook, Philip J. 2018. "Gun Theft and Crime." *Journal of Urban Health* 95(3), 305–312.

Cook, Philip J., Wendy Cukier, and Keith Krause. 2009. "The Illicit Firearms Trade in North America." *Criminology and Criminal Justice* 9(3), 265–286.

Cook, Philip J., Richard J. Harris, Jens Ludwig, and Anthony A. Braga. 2014. "Some Sources of Crime Guns in Chicago: Dirty Dealers, Straw Purchasers, and Traffickers." *Journal of Criminal Law & Criminology* 104(4), 717–760.

Cook, Philip J., Jens Ludwig, Sudhir Venkatesh, and Anthony A. Braga. 2007. "Underground Gun Markets." *Economic Journal* 117(524), 588–618.

Cook, Philip J., Stephanie Molliconi, and Thomas B. Cole. 1995. "Regulating Gun Markets." *Journal of Criminal Law & Criminology* 86(1), 59–92.

Cook, Philip J., Susan T. Parker, and Harold A. Pollack. 2015. "Sources of Guns to Dangerous People: What We Learn by Asking Them." *Preventive Medicine* 79, 28–36.

Cook, Philip J., Harold A. Pollack, and Kailey White. 2019. "The Last Link: From Gun Acquisition to Criminal Use." *Journal of Urban Health.* doi:10.1007/s11524-019-00358-0

Corchado, Alfredo. 2008. "Outgoing U.S. Ambassador to Mexico Lashes Out on Drug War." *Dallas Morning News*, November 27.

Harkinson, Josh. 2016. "Fully Loaded." *Mother Jones*, June 14. https://www.motherjones.com/politics/2016/06/fully-loaded-ten-biggest-gun-manufacturers-america/

Hureau, David M., and Anthony A. Braga. 2018. "The Trade in Tools: The Market for Illicit Guns in High-Risk Networks." *Criminology* 56(3), 510–545.

Langton, Lynn. 2012. "Firearms Stolen During Household Burglaries and Other Property Crimes, 2005–2010." Washington, DC: US Department of Justice, Bureau of Justice Statistics. November. https://www.bjs.gov/content/pub/pdf/fshbopc0510.pdf

Miller, Matthew, Lisa Hepburn, and Deborah Azrael. 2017. "Firearm Acquisition Without Background Checks: Results of a National Survey." *Annals of Internal Medicine* 166(4), 233–239.

National Shooting Sports Foundation. 2019. *Firearms and Ammunition Industry Economic Impact Report 2019*. Newtown, CT: NSSF. https://d3aya7xwz8momx.cloudfront.net/wp-content/uploads/2019/02/2019-Economic-Impact.pdf

US Department of Justice. 2013. "Review of ATF's Federal Firearms Licensee Inspection Program." Washington, DC: US Department of Justice, Office of the Inspector General, April.

Violence Policy Center. 2016. *An Analysis of the Decline in Gun Dealers: 1994 to 2016*. Washington, DC.

Webster, Daniel W., Maria T. Bulzacchelli, April M. Zeoli, and Jon
S. Vernick. 2006. "Effects of Undercover Police Stings of Gun
Dealers on the Supply of New Guns to Criminals." *Injury Prevention*
12(4), 225–230.

Webster, Daniel W., Cassandra K. Crifasi, and Jon S. Vernick.
2014. "Effects of the Repeal of Missouri's Handgun Purchaser
Licensing Law on Homicides." *Journal of Urban Health* 91(2),
293–302.

Webster, Daniel W., Lorraine H. Freed, Shannon Frattaroli, and
Moderna H. Wilson. 2002. "How Delinquent Youths Acquire
Guns: Initial Versus Most Recent Gun Acquisitions." *Journal of
Urban Health* 79(1), 60–69.

Wintemute, Garen. 1994. *Ring of Fire: The Handgun Makers of Southern
California.* Sacramento, CA: Violence Prevention Research Program.

Wintemute, Garen. 2010. "Firearm Retailers' Willingness to Participate
in an Illegal Gun Purchase." *Journal of Urban Health* 87(5), 865–878.

Wintemute, Garen. 2013. "Frequency of and Responses to Illegal
Activity Related to Commerce in Firearms: Findings from the
Firearms Licensee Survey." *Injury Prevention* 19(6), 412–420.

Wintemute, Garen J., Philip J. Cook, and Mona A. Wright. 2005.
"Risk Factors Among Handgun Retailers for Frequent and
Disproportionate Sales of Guns Used in Violent and Firearm-
Related Crimes." *Injury Prevention* 11(6), 357–363.

Yablon, Alex. 2016. "Internet Gun Sales and Background Checks,
Explained." *The Trace*, January 7. https://www.thetrace.org/2016/
01/internet-gun-sales-background-checks/ ["Internet Gun Sales"]

Chapter 6

Ackermann, Nicole, Melody S. Goodman, Keon Gilbert, Cassandra
Arroyo-Johnson, and Marcello Pagano. 2015. "Race, Law, and
Health: Examination of 'Stand Your Ground' and Defendant
Convictions in Florida." *Social Science & Medicine* 142, 194–201.

Cassidy, Warren. 1983. "Morton Grove: The Next Step." *The American
Rifleman*, April, 54.

Cheng, Cheng, and Mark Hoekstra. 2013. "Does Strengthening Self-
Defense Law Deter Crime or Escalate Violence? Evidence from
Expansions to Castle Doctrine." *Journal of Human Resources* 48(3),
821–854.

"Dingell Introduces Legislation to Address Safety Defects
in Firearms." 2018. Press Release, April 18. https://

debbiedingell.house.gov/media-center/press-releases/
dingell-introduces-legislation-address-safety-defects-firearms

District of Columbia v. Heller. 554 U.S. 570 (2008).

Federal Bureau of Investigation. 2019. "NICS Firearm Background
Checks: Month/Year." Washington, DC: US Department of Justice.
https://www.fbi.gov/file-repository/nics_firearm_checks_-_
month_year.pdf/view

Florida Department of Agriculture and Consumer Services. 2019.
"Concealed Weapon or Firearm License Applications Distributed."
https://www.freshfromflorida.com/content/download/7501/
118863/CW_app_dist.pdf

Giffords Law Center to Prevent Gun Violence. n.d. "Preemption of
Local Laws." https://lawcenter.giffords.org/gun-laws/policy-
areas/other-laws-policies/preemption-of-local-laws/

Goss, Kristin A. 2006. *Disarmed: The Missing Movement for Gun Control in
America.* Princeton, NJ: Princeton University Press.

Government Accountability Office. 2018. *Few Individuals Denied Firearms
Purchases Are Prosecuted and ATF Should Assess Use of Warning
Notices in Lieu of Prosecutions.* Washington, DC. https://www.gao.
gov/products/GAO-18-440

Humphries, David K., Antonio Gasparrini, and Douglas J. Wiebe. 2017.
"Evaluating the Impact of Florida's 'Stand Your Ground' Self-
Defense Law on Homicide and Suicide by Firearm: An Interrupted
Time Series Study." *JAMA Internal Medicine* 177(1), 44–50.

Karberg, Jennifer C., Ronald J. Frandsen, Joseph M. Durso, Trent
D. Buskirk, and Allina D. Lee. 2017. *Background Checks for Firearm
Transfers, 2015—Statistical Tables.* Washington, DC: US Department
of Justice, Bureau of Justice Statistics.

Kessler, Glenn. 2013. "The NRA's Fuzzy, Decades-Old Claim of
'20,000' Gun Laws." *Washington Post*, February 5. https://www.
washingtonpost.com/blogs/fact-checker/post/the-nras-fuzzy-
decades-old-claim-of-20000-gun-laws/2013/02/04/4a7892c0-6f23-
11e2-ac36-3d8d9dcaa2e2_blog.html?utm_term=.683f44add414

Luo, Michael. 2011. "Felons Finding It Easy to Regain Gun Rights."
New York Times, November 13.

Martin, Susan Taylor. 2013. "Florida 'Stand Your Ground' Law Yields
Some Shocking Outcomes Depending on How Law is Applied."
Tampa Bay Times, February 17. http://www.tampabay.com/news/
publicsafety/crime/florida-stand-your-ground-law-yields-some-
shocking-outcomes-depending-on/1233133

McClellan, Chandler, and Erdal Tekin. 2017. "Stand Your Ground Laws, Homicides, and Injuries." *Journal of Human Resources* 52(3), 621–653.

McDonald v. City of Chicago. 561 U.S. 742 (2010).

Powers, William. F. 1995. "Dressed to Kill." *Washington Post*, May 4.

Roman, John K. 2013. *Race, Justifiable Homicide, and Stand Your Ground Laws: Analysis of FBI Supplementary Homicide Report Data*. Washington, DC: Urban Institute.

Rosenthal, Lawrence E., and Adam Winkler. 2013. "The Scope of Regulatory Authority Under the Second Amendment." In *Reducing Gun Violence in America*. Edited by Daniel W. Webster and Jon S. Vernick, 225–236. Baltimore, MD: Johns Hopkins University Press.

Ruben, Eric, and Joseph Blocher. 2018. "From Theory to Doctrine: An Empirical Analysis of the Right to Keep and Bear Arms After *Heller*." *Duke Law Journal* 67(7), 1433–1509.

Spitzer, Robert J. 2018. *The Politics of Gun Control*, 7th ed. New York: Routledge.

Stachelberg, Winnie, Arkadi Gerney, and Chelsea Parsons. 2013. *Blindfolded, and with One Hand Tied Behind the Back*. Washington, DC: Center for American Progress.

Stolberg, Sheryl Gay. 2005. "Congress Passes New Legal Shield for Gun Industry." *New York Times*, October 21.

Taylor, Rebecca A. 2015. "Stand Your Ground." Excerpted from *Civil Rights Litigation: Representing Plaintiffs Today*. Chicago: ABA Book Publishing. https://www.americanbar.org/groups/gpsolo/publications/gpsolo_ereport/2015/february_2015/stand_your_ground/

Timoney, John F. 2012. "Florida's Disastrous Self-Defense Law." *New York Times*, March 23. https://www.nytimes.com/2012/03/24/opinion/floridas-disastrous-self-defense-law.html

United States v. Lopez. 514 U.S. 549 (1995).

United States v. Miller. 307 U.S. 174 (1939).

Vernick, Jon S., and Lisa M. Hepburn. 2003. "State and Federal Gun Laws: Trends for 1970–99." In *Evaluating Gun Policy: Effects on Crime and Violence*. Edited by Jens Ludwig and Philip J. Cook, 345–402. Washington, DC: Brookings Institution Press.

Winkler, Adam. 2011. *Gunfight: The Battle over the Right to Bear Arms in America*. New York: Norton.

Chapter 7

Abrams, David S. 2012. "Estimating the Deterrent Effect of Incarceration Using Sentencing Enhancements." *American Economic Journal: Applied Economics* 4(4), 32–56.

Alpers, Philip. 2013. "The Big Melt: How One Democracy Changed After Scrapping a Third of Its Firearms." In *Reducing Gun Violence in America*. Edited by Daniel W. Webster and Jon S. Vernick, 205–211. Baltimore, MD: Johns Hopkins University Press.

Azrael, Deborah, Philip J. Cook, and Matthew Miller. 2004. "State and Local Prevalence of Firearms Ownership: Measurement, Structure, and Trends." *Journal of Quantitative Criminology* 20(1), 43–62.

Blumstein, Alfred, and Kiminori Nakamura. 2009. "Redemption in the Presence of Widespread Criminal Background Checks." *Criminology* 47(2), 327–359.

Braga, Anthony A., Andrew V. Papachristos, and David M. Hureau. 2014. "The Effects of Hot Spots Policing on Crime: An Updated Systematic Review and Meta-Analysis." *Justice Quarterly* 31(4), 633–663.

Braga, Anthony A., David Weisburd, and Brandon Turchan. 2018. "Focused Deterrence Strategies and Crime Control: An Updated Systematic Review and Meta-Analysis of the Empirical Evidence" *Criminology & Public Policy* 17(1), 205–250.

Bratton, William J., and Jon Murad. 2018. "Precision Policing: A Strategy for the Challenges of 21st Century Law Enforcement." In *Urban Policy 2018*, Chapter 2. New York: Manhattan Institute. https://www.manhattan-institute.org/html/urban-policy-2018-precision-policing-strategy-21st-century-law-enforcement-11508.html

Bureau of Alcohol, Tobacco, Firearms and Explosives. 2017. "Firearms Trace Data—2017." Washington, DC: US Department of Justice. https://www.atf.gov/resource-center/firearms-trace-data-2017

Campbell, Jacquelyn C., Daniel Webster, Jane Koziol-McLain, Carolyn Block, Doris Campbell, Mary Ann Curry, Faye Gary, Nancy Glass, Judith McFarlane, and Carolyn Sachs. 2003. "Risk Factors for Femicide in Abusive Relationships: Results from a Multisite Case Control Study." *American Journal of Public Health* 93(7), 1089–1097.

Chivers, CJ, Larry Buchanan, Denise Lu, and Karen Yourish. 2018. "With AR-15s, Mass Shooters Attack with the Rifle Firepower Typically Used by Infantry Troops." *New York Times*, April 28. https://www.nytimes.com/interactive/2018/02/28/us/ar-15-rifle-mass-shootings.html

Cook, Philip J., and Anthony A. Braga. 2001. "Comprehensive Firearms Tracing: Strategic and Investigative Uses of New Data on Firearms Markets." *Arizona Law Review* 43(2), 277–309.

Cook, Philip J., and John J. Donohue. 2017. "Saving Lives by Regulating Guns: Evidence for Policy." *Science* 358(6368), 1259–1261.

Cook, Philip J., and Jens Ludwig. 2004. "Does Gun Prevalence Affect Teen Gun Carrying After All?" *Criminology* 42(1), 27–54.

Cook, Philip J., and Jens Ludwig. 2006. "Aiming for Evidence-Based Gun Policy." *Journal of Policy Analysis and Management* 25(3), 691–736.

Cook, Philip J., and Jens Ludwig. 2019. "The Social Costs of Gun Ownership: A Reply to Hayo, Neumeier and Westphal." *Empirical Economics* 56(1), 13–22. ["Social Costs"]

Cook, Philip J., Jens Ludwig, and Anthony Braga. 2005. "Criminal Records of Homicide Offenders." *Journal of the American Medical Association* 294(5), 598–601.

Government Accountability Office. 2012. *Gun Control—Sharing Promising Practices and Assessing Incentives Could Better Position Justice to Assist States in Providing Records for Background Checks.* Washington, DC. http://www.gao.gov/products/GAO-12-684

Grunwald, Ben, and Andrew V. Papachristos. 2017. "Project Safe Neighborhoods in Chicago: Looking Back a Decade Later." *Journal of Criminal Law & Criminology* 107(1), 131–160.

Kennedy, David M., Anne M. Piehl, and Anthony A. Braga. 1996. "Youth Violence in Boston: Gun Markets, Serious Youth Offenders, and a Use-Reduction Strategy." *Law & Contemporary Problems* 59(1), 147–196.

Kleck, Gary. 2004. "Measure of Gun Ownership for Macro-Level Crime and Violence Research." *Journal of Research in Crime and Delinquency* 41(1), 3–36.

Knight, Brian. 2013. "State Gun Policy and Cross-State Externalities: Evidence from ATF Trace Data." *American Economic Journal: Economic Policy* 5(4), 200–229.

Koper, Christopher S. 2004. *Updated Assessment of the Federal Assault Weapons Ban: Impacts on Gun Markets and Gun Violence 1994–2003.* Washington, DC: National Institute of Justice, US Department of Justice.

Koper, Christopher S, and Evan Mayo-Wilson. 2012. "Police Strategies to Reduce Illegal Possession and Carrying of Firearms: Effects on Gun Crime." *Campbell Systematic Reviews*, 11.

Leitzel, Jim. 2003. "Comment." In *Evaluating Gun Policy: Effects on Crime and Violence*. Edited by Jens Ludwig and Philip J. Cook, 145–156. Washington, DC: Brookings Institution.

Ludwig, Jens, and Philip J. Cook. 2000. "Homicide and Suicide Rates Associated with Implementation of the Brady Handgun Violence Prevention Act." *Journal of the American Medical Association* 284(5), 585–591.

Luo, Michael. 2011. "Felons Finding It Easy to Regain Gun Rights." *New York Times*, November 13.

Raissian, Kerri M. 2016. "Hold Your Fire: Did the 1996 Federal Gun Control Act Expansion Reduce Domestic Homicides?" *Journal of Policy Analysis and Management* 35(1), 67–93.

Raphael, Stephen, and Jens Ludwig. 2003. "Prison Sentence Enhancements: The Case of Project Exile." In *Evaluating Gun Policy: Effects on Crime and Violence*. Edited by Jens Ludwig and Philip J. Cook, 251–276. Washington, DC: Brookings Institution Press.

Reuter, Peter, and Jenny Mouzos. 2003. "Australia: A Massive Buyback of Low-Risk Guns." In *Evaluating Gun Policy: Effects on Crime and Violence*. Edited by Jens Ludwig and Philip J. Cook, 121–141. Washington, DC: Brookings Institution Press.

Sherman, Lawrence W., and David L. Weisburd. 1995. "General Deterrent Effects of Police Patrol in Crime 'Hot Spots': A Randomized Controlled Trial." *Justice Quarterly* 12(4), 626–648.

Swanson, Jeffrey W., Michael A. Norko, Hsiu-Ju Lin, Kelly Alanis-Hirsch, Linda K. Frisman, Madelon V. Baranoski, Michele M. Easter, Allison G. Robertson, Marvin S. Swartz, and Richard J. Bonnie. 2017. "Implementation and Effectiveness of Connecticut's Risk-Based Gun Removal Law: Does It Prevent Suicides?" *Law & Contemporary Problems* 80, 179–208.

Swanson, Jeffrey W., Allison Gilbert Robertson, Linda K. Frisman, Michael A. Norko, Hsiu-Ju Lin, Marvin S. Swartz, and Philip J. Cook. 2013. "Preventing Gun Violence Involving People with Serious Mental Illness." In *Reducing Gun Violence in America*. Edited by Daniel W. Webster and Jon S. Vernick, 33–52. Baltimore, MD: Johns Hopkins University Press.

Vigdor, Elizabeth R., and James A. Mercy. 2006. "Do Laws Restricting Access to Firearms by Domestic Violence Offenders Prevent Intimate Partner Homicide?" *Evaluation Review* 30(3), 313–346.

Webster, Daniel W., Cassandra K. Crifasi, and Jon S. Vernick. 2014. "Effects of the Repeal of Missouri's Handgun Purchaser Licensing Law on Homicides." *Journal of Urban Health* 91(2), 293–302.

Webster, Daniel W., and Garen J. Wintemute. 2015. "Effects of Policies Designed to Keep Firearms from High-Risk Individuals." *Annual Review of Public Health* 36, 21–37.

Wintemute, Garen J., Mona A. Wright, Christiana M. Drake, and James J. Beaumont. 2001. "Subsequent Criminal Activity Among Violent Misdemeanants Who Seek to Purchase Handguns." *Journal of the American Medical Association* 285(8), 1019–1026.

Yablon, Alex. 2019. "Use of Red Flag Laws Varies Widely Among Local Police." *The Trace*, April 23. https://www.thetrace.org/2019/04/use-of-red-flag-laws-varies-widely-among-local-police/

Chapter 8

Bogus, Carl T. 1992. "Race, Riots, and Guns." *Southern California Law Review* 66, 1365–1388.

Brearley, Harrington Cooper. 1932. *Homicide in the United States*. Chapel Hill: University of North Carolina Press.

Carlson, Jennifer. 2015. *Citizen–Protectors: The Everyday Politics of Guns in an Age of Decline*. New York: Oxford University Press.

Celinska, Katarzyna. 2007. "Individualism and Collectivism in America: The Case of Gun Ownership and Attitudes toward Gun Control." *Sociological Perspectives* 50(2), 229–247.

Cottrol, Robert J., and Raymond T. Diamond. 1991. "The Second Amendment: Second Toward an Afro-Americanist Reconsideration." *Georgetown Law Journal* 80, 309–362.

Cottrol, Robert J., and Raymond T. Diamond. 1995. " 'Never Intended to Be Applied to the White Population': Firearms Regulation and Racial Disparity—The Redeemed South's Legacy to a National Jurisprudence." *Chicago-Kent Law Review* 70, 1307–1335.

DeConde, Alexander. 2001. *Gun Violence in America: The Struggle for Control*. Boston: Northeastern University Press.

Dykstra, Robert R. 1968. *The Cattle Towns*. New York: Knopf.

Dykstra, Robert R. 1996. "Overdosing on Dodge City." *Western Historical Quarterly* 27(4), 505–514.

Halbrook, Stephen P. 2000. "Nazi Firearms Law and the Disarming of the German Jews." *Arizona Journal of International & Comparative Law* 17, 483–532.

Halbrook, Stephen P. 2006. "Nazism, the Second Amendment, and the NRA: A Reply to Professor Harcourt." *Texas Review of Law & Politics* 11(1), 113–131.

Halbrook, Stephen P. 2013. *Gun Control in the Third Reich.* Oakland, CA: The Independent Institute.

Harcourt, Bernard E. 2004–5. "On Gun Registration, the NRA, Adolf Hitler, and Nazi Gun Laws: Exploding the Gun Culture Wars (a Call to Historians)." *Fordham Law Review* 73, 653–680.

Hoffman, Frederick L. 1925. *The Homicide Problem, a Paper by Frederick L. Hoffman.* Newark, NJ: Prudential Press.

Hofstadter, Richard. 1970. "America as a Gun Culture." *American Heritage*, October, 4–11, 82–85.

Horwitz, Joshua, and Casey Anderson. 2009. *Guns, Democracy, and the Insurrectionist Idea.* Ann Arbor: University of Michigan Press.

Hosley, William. 1999. "Guns, Gun Culture and the Peddling of Dreams." In *Guns in America: A Historical Reader.* Edited by Jan E. Dizard, Robert Merrill Muth, and Steve Andrews, Jr., 47–85. New York: New York University Press.

Kates, Don B., ed. 1979. *Restricting Handguns: The Liberal Skeptics Speak Out.* Croton-on-Hudson, NY: North River Press.

Kennett, Lee, and James LaVerne Anderson. 1975. *The Gun in America.* Westport, CT: Greenwood Press.

Lacombe, Matthew J. 2019. *Gunning for the Masses: How the NRA Has Shaped Its Supporters' Behavior, Advanced Its Political Agenda, and Thwarted the Will of the Majority.* Ph.D. Diss., Northwestern University.

Melzer, Scott. 2009. *Gun Crusaders: The NRA's Culture War.* New York: New York University Press.

Parker, Kim, Juliana Menasce Horowitz, Ruth Igielnik, J. Baxter Oliphant, and Anna Brown. 2017. "America's Complex Relationship with Guns." Washington, DC: Pew Research Center, June 22. https://www.pewsocialtrends.org/2017/06/22/americas-complex-relationship-with-guns/

Rankin, Jerry. 1967. "Heavily Armed Negro Group Walks into Assembly Chamber." *Los Angeles Times*, May 3.

Slotkin, Richard. 1998. *Gunfighter Nation: The Myth of the Frontier in Twentieth-Century America.* Norman: University of Oklahoma Press.

Spitzer, Robert J. 2018. *The Politics of Gun Control*, 7th ed. New York: Routledge.

State v. Chandler 5 La. Ann. 489 (1850).

Warner, Sam B. 1938. "The Uniform Pistol Act." *Journal of the American Institute of Criminal Law and Criminology* 29(4), 529–554.

Williamson, Harold F. 1952. *Winchester, the Gun That Won the West*. Washington, DC: Combat Forces Press.

Winkler, Adam. 2011. *Gunfight: The Battle over the Right to Bear Arms in America*. New York: Norton.

Chapter 9

Barney, David J., and Brian F. Schaffner. 2019. "Reexamining the Effect of Mass Shootings on Public Support for Gun Control." *British Journal of Political Science*, 1–11. doi:10.1017/S0007123418000352

Benenson, Joel, and Katie Connolly. 2013. "Don't Know Much About Gun Laws." *New York Times*, April 6.

Center for Responsive Politics. n.d. "Gun Rights vs. Gun Control." https://www.opensecrets.org/news/issues/guns

Democratic Party Platform Committee. *2016 Democratic Party Platform*. 2016. https://democrats.org/wp-content/uploads/2018/10/2016_DNC_Platform.pdf

Erskine, Hazel. 1972. "The Polls: Gun Control." *Public Opinion Quarterly* 36(3), 455–469.

Gallup Organization. 2019. "Guns." https://news.gallup.com/poll/1645/guns.aspx

Grossback, Lawrence, and Allan Hammock. 2003. "Overcoming One-Party Dominance: How Contextual Politics and West Virginia Helped Put George Bush in the White House." *Politics and Policy* 31(3), 406–431.

Kenny, Christopher, Michael McBurnett, and David Bordua. 2004. "The Impact of Political Interests in the 1994 and 1996 Congressional Elections: The Role of the National Rifle Association." *British Journal of Political Science* 34(2), 331–344.

Lacombe, Matthew J. 2019. *Gunning for the Masses: How the NRA Has Shaped Its Supporters' Behavior, Advanced Its Political Agenda, and Thwarted the Will of the Majority*. Ph.D. Diss., Northwestern University.

Maguire, Robert. 2017. "Audit Shows NRA Spending Surged $100 Million Amidst Pro-Trump Push in 2016." Washington, DC: Center for Responsive Politics, November 15. https://www.opensecrets.org/news/2017/11/audit-shows-nra-spending-surged-100-million-amidst-pro-trump-push-in-2016/

Newport, Frank. 2013. "Americans Wanted Gun Background Checks to Pass Senate." Gallup Organization, October 13. https://news.gallup.com/poll/162083/americans-wanted-gun-background-checks-pass-senate.aspx

Parker, Kim. 2017. "Among Gun Owners, NRA Members Have a Unique Set of Views and Experiences." Pew Research Center, July 5. https://www.pewresearch.org/fact-tank/2017/07/05/among-gun-owners-nra-members-have-a-unique-set-of-views-and-experiences/

Parker, Kim, Juliana Menasce Horowitz, Ruth Igielnik, J. Baxter Oliphant, and Anna Brown. 2017. "America's Complex Relationship with Guns." Washington, DC: Pew Research Center, June 22. https://www.pewsocialtrends.org/2017/06/22/americas-complex-relationship-with-guns/

Pew Research Center. 2017. "Public Views About Guns." Washington, DC, June 22. https://www.people-press.org/2017/06/22/public-views-about-guns/#total

Pew Research Center. 2018. "Gun Policy Remains Divisive, But Several Proposals Still Draw Bipartisan Support." Washington, DC, October 18. https://www.people-press.org/2018/10/18/gun-policy-remains-divisive-but-several-proposals-still-draw-bipartisan-support/

Reinhart, R.J. 2018. "Six in 10 Americans Support Stricter Gun Laws." Gallup Organization, October 17. https://news.gallup.com/poll/243797/six-americans-support-stricter-gun-laws.aspx

Silver, Nate. 2012. "Party Identity in a Gun Cabinet." FiveThirtyEight. *New York Times*, December 18.

Spitzer, Robert J. 2018. *The Politics of Gun Control*, 7th ed. New York: Routledge.

Chapter 10

Barrett, Paul M. 2013. "Why Gun Makers Fear the NRA." *Bloomberg Businessweek*, March 14. https://www.bloomberg.com/news/articles/2013-03-14/why-gun-makers-fear-the-nra

Cherlin, Reid. 2012. " 'We Do Absolutely Anything They Ask': How the NRA's Grading System Keeps Congress on Lockdown." *GQ*, July 24. https://www.gq.com/story/nra-grades-and-congress

Drake, Bruce. 2013. "Gun Policy More of a 'Make or Break' Voting Issue for Gun Rights Defenders." Pew Research Center, May 31.

Washington, DC. https://www.pewresearch.org/fact-tank/2013/
05/31/gun-policy-more-of-a-make-or-break-voting-issue-for-gun-
rights-defenders/

Epstein, Aaron. 1979. "How Pentagon Boosted NRA." *Philadelphia
Inquirer*, May 14.

Goss, Kristin A. 2006. *Disarmed: The Missing Movement for Gun Control in
America*. Princeton, NJ: Princeton University Press.

Kelly, Lorelei. 2013. "How Groups Like the NRA Captured Congress—
And How to Take It Back." *The Atlantic*, March 7. https://www.
theatlantic.com/politics/archive/2013/03/how-groups-like-the-
nra-captured-congress-and-how-to-take-it-back/273623/

Kelly, Mark. 2013. "NRA Leadership Should Refocus Its Priorities."
Houston Chronicle, May 1. https://www.chron.com/default/
article/NRA-leadership-should-refocus-its-priorities-4480769.php

Lacombe, Matthew J. 2019. *Gunning for the Masses: How the NRA
Has Shaped Its Supporters' Behavior, Advanced Its Political Agenda,
and Thwarted the Will of the Majority*. Ph.D. Diss., Northwestern
University.

National Rifle Association. 2008. "Senate Passes NICS Improvement
Act, House Concurs." January 8. https://www.nraila.org/articles/
20080108/hr-2640

National Rifle Association. 2016. Form 990. www.guidestar.org.

Osnos, Evan. 2016. "Making a Killing." *The New Yorker*, June 27.

Parker, Kim, Juliana Menasce Horowitz, Ruth Igielnik, J. Baxter
Oliphant, and Anna Brown. 2017. "America's Complex
Relationship with Guns." Washington, DC: Pew Research Center,
June 22. https://www.pewsocialtrends.org/2017/06/22/
americas-complex-relationship-with-guns/

Patterson, Kelly D., and Matthew M. Singer. 2006. "Targeting
Success: The Enduring Power of the NRA." In *Interest Group
Politics*. Edited by Allan J. Cigler and Burdett A. Loomis, 37–64.
Washington, DC: CQ Press.

Pew Research Center. 2012. "After Newtown, Modest Change
in Opinion About Gun Control." Washington, DC,
December 20. https://www.people-press.org/2012/12/20/
after-newtown-modest-change-in-opinion-about-gun-control/

Pew Research Center. 2013. "Broad Support for Renewed Background
Checks, Skepticism About Its Chances." Washington, DC,
May 23. https://www.people-press.org/2013/05/23/

broad-support-for-renewed-background-checks-bill-skepticism-
about-its-chances/ ["Broad Support for Renewed Background
Checks"]

Reinhart, R. J. 2018. "Record U.S. Partisan Divide on Views of the
N.R.A." Gallup Organization, June 28. https://news.gallup.com/
poll/236315/record-partisan-divide-views-nra.aspx

Schuman, Howard, and Stanley Presser. 1981. "The Attitude–Action
Connection and the Issue of Gun Control." *Annals of the American
Academy of Political and Social Science* 455, 40–47.

Spitzer, Robert J. 2018. *The Politics of Gun Control*, 7th ed.
New York: Routledge.

Stone, Peter, and Ben Hallman. 2014. "NRA Gun Control Crusade
Reflects Firearms Industry Financial Ties." *HuffPost*, January 23.
https://www.huffpost.com/entry/nra-gun-control-firearms-
industry-ties_n_2434142

Violence Policy Center. 2013. *Blood Money II: How Gun Industry Dollars
Fund the NRA.* Washington, DC, September.

Yablon, Alex. 2016. "How the NRA Stoked the Populist Rage That Gave
America President Trump." *The Trace*, November 11. https://www.
thetrace.org/2016/11/nra-endorsements-donald-trump-populist-
rage/ ["How the NRA Stoked"]

Chapter 11

American Psychological Association. 2018. "Stress in
America: Generation Z." October.

Astor, Maggie, and Karl Russell. 2018. "After Parkland, a New Surge in
State Gun Control Laws." *New York Times*, December 14. https://
www.nytimes.com/interactive/2018/12/14/us/politics/gun-
control-laws.html

Callaghan, Karen, and Frauke Schnell. 2001. "Assessing the Democratic
Debate: How the News Media Frame Elite Policy Discourse."
Political Communication 18(2), 183–212.

Chyi, Hsiang Iris, and Maxwell McCombs. 2004. "Media Salience
and the Process of Framing: Coverage of the Columbine School
Shootings." *Journalism and Mass Communication Quarterly*
81(1), 22–35.

Downs, Douglas. 2002. "Representing Gun Owners: Frame
Identification as Social Responsibility in News Media Discourse."
Written Communication 19(1), 44–75.

Goss, Kristin A. 2006. *Disarmed: The Missing Movement for Gun Control in America*. Princeton, NJ: Princeton University Press.

Goss, Kristin A. 2014. "Two Years After Sandy Hook, the Gun Control Movement Has New Energy." *Washington Post*, December 16. https://www.washingtonpost.com/news/monkey-cage/wp/2014/12/16/two-years-after-sandy-hook-the-gun-control-movement-has-new-energy/?utm_term=.7c70d08dbf82

Goss, Kristin A. 2019. "Whatever Happened to the 'Missing Movement'? Gun Control Politics over Two Decades of Change." In *Gun Studies: Interdisciplinary Approaches to Politics, Policy, and Practice*. Edited by Jennifer Carlson, Kristin A. Goss, and Harel Shapira, 13–50. New York: Routledge.

Groseclose, Tim, and Jeffrey Milyo. 2005. "A Measure of Media Bias." *Quarterly Journal of Economics* 120(4), 1191–1237.

Kleck, Gary. 2001. "Modes of News Media Distortion." In *Armed: New Perspectives on Gun Control*. Edited by Gary Kleck and Don B. Kates, 173–212. Amherst, NY: Prometheus Books.

Lott, John R., Jr. 2003. *The Bias Against Guns: Why Almost Everything You've Heard About Gun Control Is Wrong*. New York: Regnery.

Lowe, Sarah R., and Sandro Galea. 2017. "The Mental Health Consequences of Mass Shootings." *Trauma, Violence, & Abuse* 18(1), 62–82.

Muschert, Glenn W., and Dawn Carr. 2006. "Media Salience and Frame Changing Across Events: Coverage of Nine School Shootings, 1997–2001." *Journalism and Mass Communication Quarterly* 83(4), 747–766.

Patrick, Brian Anse. 2002. *The National Rifle Association and the Media: The Motivating Force of Negative Coverage*. New York: Peter Lang.

Schultz, James M., Siri Thoresen, Brian W. Flynn, Glenn W. Muschert, Jon A. Shaw, Zelde Espinel, Frank G. Walter, Joshua B. Gaither, Yanira Garcia-Barcena, Kaitlin O'Keefe, and Alyssa M. Cohen. 2014. "Multiple Vantage Points on the Mental Health Effects of Mass Shootings." *Current Psychiatry Reports* 16, 469. https://doi.org/10.1007/s11920-014-0469-5

Spitzer, Robert J. 2018. *The Politics of Gun Control*, 7th ed. New York: Routledge.

Chapter 12

Braga, Anthony A., and Philip J. Cook. 2018. "The Association of Firearm Caliber with Likelihood of Death from Gunshot Injury

in Criminal Assaults." *JAMA Network Open* 1(3). doi:10.1001/
jamanetworkopen.2018.0833

Braga, Anthony A., David Weisburd, and Brandon Turchan. 2018.
"Focused Deterrence Strategies and Crime Control: An Updated
Systematic Review and Meta-Analysis of the Empirical Evidence"
Criminology & Public Policy 17(1), 205–250.

Bratton, William J., and Jon Murad. 2018. "Precision Policing: A
Strategy for the Challenges of 21st Century Law Enforcement."
In *Urban Policy 2018*, Chapter 2. New York: Manhattan Institute.
https://www.manhattan-institute.org/html/urban-policy-2018-
precision-policing-strategy-21st-century-law-enforcement-11508.
html

Bruce-Briggs, B. 1976. "The Great American Gun War." *The Public
Interest* 45(Fall), 37–62.

Cook, Philip J., Anthony A. Braga, Brandon Turchan, and Lisa Barao.
2019. "Why Do Gun Murders Have a Higher Clearance Rate than
Gunshot Assaults?" *Criminology & Public Policy* 18(3), 525–551.

Cook, Philip J., and Jens Ludwig. 2019. "Understanding Gun
Violence: Public Health vs. Public Policy." *Journal of Policy Analysis
and Management* 38(3), 788–795. ["Public Health vs. Public Policy"]

Cook, Philip J., and Mark J. Moore. 1993. "Economic Perspectives on
Reducing Alcohol-Related Violence." In *Alcohol and Interpersonal
Violence: Fostering Multidisciplinary Perspectives*. Edited by Susan
Martin, 193–212. Bethesda, MD: National Institutes of Health,
National Institute on Alcohol Abuse and Alcoholism.

Goss, Kristin A. 2006. *Disarmed: The Missing Movement for Gun Control in
America*. Princeton, NJ: Princeton University Press.

Leovy, Jill. 2015. *Ghettoside: A True Story of Murder in America*.
New York: Spiegel & Grau/Random House.

Ludwig, Jens, Jeffrey R. Kling, and Sendhil Mullainathan. 2011.
"Mechanism Experiments and Policy Evaluations." *Journal of
Economic Perspectives* 25(3), 17–38.

Manski, Charles F., and Daniel S. Nagin. 2017. "Assessing Benefits,
Costs, and Disparate Racial Impacts of Confrontational Proactive
Policing." *Proceedings of the National Academy of Sciences*, 114(35),
9308–9313.

McGinty, Emma E., Shannon Frattaroli, Paul S. Appelbaum, Richard
J. Bonnie, Anna Grilley, Joshua Horwitz, Jeffrey W. Swanson, and
Daniel W. Webster. 2014. "Using Research Evidence to Reframe
the Policy Debate Around Mental Illness and Guns: Process and

Recommendations." *American Journal of Public Health* 104(11), e22–e26.

Ribeiro, Jessica D., Xieyining Huang, Kathryn R. Fox, and Joseph C. Franklin. 2018. "Depression and Hopelessness as Risk Factors for Suicide Ideation, Attempts and Death: Meta-Analysis of Longitudinal Studies." *British Journal of Psychiatry* 212(5), 279–286.

Rozel, John S., and Edward P. Mulvey. 2017. "The Link Between Mental Illness and Firearm Violence: Implications for Social Policy and Clinical Practice." *Annual Review of Clinical Psychology* 13, 445–469.

Swanson, Jeffrey W., Michael A. Norko, Hsiu-Ju Lin, Kelly Alanis-Hirsch, Linda K. Frisman, Madelon V. Baranoski, Michele M. Easter, Allison G. Robertson, Marvin S. Swartz, and Richard J. Bonnie. 2017. "Implementation and Effectiveness of Connecticut's Risk-Based Gun Removal Law: Does It Prevent Suicides?" *Law & Contemporary Problems* 80, 179–208.

Swanson, Jeffrey W., Allison Gilbert Robertson, Linda K. Frisman, Michael A. Norko, Hsiu-Ju Lin, Marvin S. Swartz, and Philip J. Cook. 2013. "Preventing Gun Violence Involving People with Serious Mental Illness." In *Reducing Gun Violence in America*. Edited by Daniel W. Webster and Jon S. Vernick, 33–52. Baltimore, MD: Johns Hopkins University Press.

Swanson, Jeffrey W., Nancy A. Sampson, Maria V. Petukhova, Alan M. Zaslavsky, Paul S. Appelbaum, Marvin S. Swartz, and Ronald C. Kessler. 2015. "Guns, Impulsive Angry Behavior, and Mental Disorders: Results from the National Comorbidity Survey Replication (NCS-R)." *Behavioral Sciences and the Law* 33(2–3), 199–212.

Webster, Daniel W., Cassandra K. Crifasi, and Jon S. Vernick. 2014. "Effects of the Repeal of Missouri's Handgun Purchaser Licensing Law on Homicides." *Journal of Urban Health* 91(2), 293–302.

Weisburd, David, Alese Wooditch, Sarit Weisburd, and Sue-Ming Yang. 2016. "Do Stop, Question and Frisk Tactics Deter Crime?" *Criminology & Public Policy* 15(1), 31–56.

WISQARS. 2017. Web-Based Injury Statistics Query and Reporting System. Centers for Disease Control and Prevention. https://www.cdc.gov/injury/wisqars/facts.html

Zimring, Franklin E. 1968. "Is Gun Control Likely to Reduce Violent Killings?" *University of Chicago Law Review* 35(4), 721–737.

Zimring, Franklin E. 2017. *When Police Kill*. Cambridge, MA: Harvard University Press.

INDEX

9 780190 073459